ACHIEVING BODHICHITTA

Achieving Bodhichitta

Instructions of Two Great Lineages Combined into a Unique System of Eleven Categories

---

Commentary

by

Sermey Khensur Lobsang Tharchin

Oral Commentary Series

Mahayana Sutra and Tantra Press

HOWELL, NEW JERSEY
1999

Mahayana Sutra and Tantra Press
112 West Second Street
Howell, New Jersey 07731

Library of Congress Cataloging-in-Publication Data

Tharchin, Sermey Geshe Lobsang, 1921-

  Achieving bodhichitta : the instructions of
two great lineages combined into a unique system of
eleven categories / commentary by Sermey Khensur
Lobsang Tharchin.

  p. cm.
Includes bibliographical references and index.
ISBN 0-918753-14-7
1. Bodhichitta (Buddhism)
2. Spiritual life—Buddhism.
I. Title.

BQ5398.5.T526   1998
294.3 '422—dc21   98-11331
                                          CIP

Cover photo of Avalokiteshvara, Buddha of Compassion.
Back cover photo of Khensur Rinpoche courtesy of Barbara Taylor.

CONTENTS

Foreword

The instructions in this text are the means of generating the precious bodhichitta in one's mind according to the system established by the great Jamgön Lama[1] Tsongkapa. They are a way of training the mind by combining the *Sevenfold Cause and Effect Instruction* and the instruction known as *Equalizing and Exchanging Self and Others* into an eleven-step process that begins with immeasurable equanimity and culminates with achieving bodhichitta. I have presented this instruction exactly as I heard it many times from the mouths of Lamas who are authentic holders of this lineage. Whatever errors appear here are my own and I request patient understanding from those among you who are scholars. As the great Acharya Vasubandhu wrote in the *Treasury of Higher Knowledge* (*Abhidharmakosha*):

> Whatever errors are found here are my fault.
> In the supreme system of Dharma,
> The only reliable ones are the Buddhas. (Ch. 8, v. 40)

—Sermey Khensur Lobsang Tharchin

---

[1]Jamgön Lama is an epithet of Je Tsongkapa. *Jamgön*, or "Gentle Lord," is a reference to Mañjushri, implying that Je Tsongkapa's essence is one with the deity Mañjushri, who embodies all Buddhas' wisdom.

Acknowledgments

I would like to thank Peter Baker of Milarepa Center in Vermont, who originally requested the teachings presented in this volume; Wilson Hurley for transcribing the Vermont and Washington, D.C. teachings, along with Barbara Taylor, who transcribed portions of the Vermont lectures; Steve Bruzgulis for transcription of supplementary materials from a 1992 retreat; Wilson and Sharon Hurley for their generous donation toward the printing of this book; Lolly Gewissler for assistance in creating the index; Venerable Ani Thupten Chönyid for research, editorial assistance, and proofreading the final draft; and Artemus B. Engle, Maria Montenegro, and Vincent Montenegro for collaboratively bringing this volume to completion.

I would like to dedicate the virtue of these teachings to those who worked on this volume.

Editors' Note

In preparing this book, we have chosen to use phoneticized Tibetan and Sanskrit terms, that is, a close approximation of the way Tibetan and Sanskrit terms sound in English, within the body of the text, with only key Tibetan terms transliterated in the footnotes. Sanskrit terms, in most instances the titles of Indian Buddhist works and the names of their authors, are phoneticized in both the text and the footnotes. The bibliography, however, includes all listings of both Indian Buddhist and Tibetan works in transliteration under the author's name.

.

INTRODUCTION

In 1981 several members of Milarepa Center in Barnet, Vermont requested instruction from Sermey Khensur Rinpoche Lobsang Tharchin on the practice of Lojong, or Mind Training. This book is a compilation of oral teachings that he began in Vermont in 1981, and completed at the Mahayana Sutra and Tantra Center in Washington, D.C., in 1987. In order to elaborate Rinpoche's points in certain sections, we have drawn upon material from Rinpoche's teachings on bodhichitta given during a 1992 retreat in Howell, New Jersey. Although a Question-and-Answer session generally followed each of the Vermont and Washington teachings, the editors have reinserted this material at the end of the related teachings in order to retain clarity and flow.

Khen Rinpoche began the class by leading a recitation of the *Heart Sutra*. He said that by doing this, harmful spirits are driven away, allowing us to be free from their influence during class. He added that just thinking about *shunyata* is the most powerful protection and the most effective way to eliminate inner, outer, and secret obstacles.

Next, the following verse for taking refuge and generating bodhichitta was recited:

> I go for refuge until I achieve enlightenment to the
>   Buddha, Dharma, and the Supreme Assembly.
> Through the merit collected from giving and the other
>   perfections,
> May I achieve Buddhahood for the benefit of all beings.

Khen Rinpoche explained that all Buddhist practice, teaching, and knowledge are based on taking refuge. He stressed that without taking refuge, any practice you do, whether it's recitation or meditation and so on, cannot turn into virtue, and without taking refuge you cannot be a Buddhist. Therefore, at the beginning of any practice, reciting the prayer for taking refuge and generating bodhichitta while thinking

about its meaning has great significance. Eight special results of taking refuge are mentioned in the commentaries,[2]
but briefly, all Buddhist knowledge is based on this practice.

Khen Rinpoche went on to explain that among Buddhist
practices and teachings, the Mahayana is the highest stage.
We should think, "I am going to develop bodhichitta—the
mind that wishes to achieve complete Buddhahood in order
to benefit myself and others. By achieving Buddhahood I
benefit myself, but the purpose of achieving Buddhahood is
only to be able to help all beings—to free them from samsara's suffering." Taking refuge is the basis of all Buddhist
practice in general, and bodhichitta in particular is the basis
of all Mahayana practice.

Finally, students offered the mandala of the universe as
part of the request to the Lama to teach Dharma. About this
offering, Rinpoche noted that Buddha Shakyamuni declared
that no one should teach Dharma without first being asked
to do so by disciples. To teach without first being asked
would be like selling something on the street, "Wanna
buy...get your such-and-such here!" It is improper to teach
Dharma without being asked; disciples have to request the
Buddha and Lamas for teaching. The mandala offering
forms part of this request. After the mandala offering was
completed, Rinpoche began the following instruction on
Lojong.

---

[2]These results are enumerated as follows: 1) we become a Buddhist, 2) refuge
serves as the foundation for all other Buddhist vows, 3) we remove negative
karma accumulated in the past, 4) we collect extensive merit, 5) we avoid
human and nonhuman harm, 6) we avoid falling into lower states, 7) we
easily achieve all temporary and ultimate goals, and 8) we will quickly
achieve Buddhahood.

LOJONG, OR MIND TRAINING

*L*OJONG MEANS MIND TRAINING; "Mind" can refer to a general mind or a specific mind. "General mind" is your ordinary, regular mind that you have to tame and turn into a spiritual or virtuous mind. In particular, you have to turn it into a Mahayana mind, which means you have to awaken bodhichitta—the mind that wants very much to achieve enlightenment for the benefit of all beings. This is the mind that you have to develop, increase, and strengthen. Lojong, or Mind Training, covers this whole field of practice.

Lojong is a well-known and special term in the Mahayana Buddhist field. Lojong practice consists of two main parts: the first is called *dakshen nyamje,* or Equalizing and Exchanging Self and Others; the second is *tonglen,* or Giving and Taking. *Dakshen nyamje* is actually a compound noun that refers to two stages of practice. The first, *dakshen nyampa,* means to practice thinking of oneself and all beings as the same in the sense of equally wanting happiness and not wanting suffering. The second, *dakshen jewa,* means to exchange position with others, or to shift the mind's focus from concern for oneself to concern for other beings.

To succeed at developing that kind of mind, you have to practice the second main part of Mind Training, known as *tonglen* or Giving and Taking. *Tong* means giving and *len* means taking.

What are you *giving*? You are giving your body, all your wealth, ability, and virtue by mentally transforming these into the things that beings want or need. By doing this, you practice charity toward others. What are you *taking*? All the suffering and problems of the beings of each of the six realms. You do this by imagining that you bring those sufferings to you and dissolve them into your self-cherishing mind, or *dak che dzin*. Great scholars came to refer to the combination of these two practices—Equalizing and Exchanging Self and Others along with Giving and Taking—as Lojong.

The Lojong Lineage Tradition

Lojong instructions came from Buddha and were passed by him to Mañjushri, from Mañjushri to Shantideva, and then through a number of Indian pandits down to Suvarnadvipa Guru, or as we call him in Tibetan, Lama Serlingpa. They were then passed to the great Lama Atisha, who received the complete set of instructions, including the two major elements of *dakshen nyamje* and *tonglen*, from the Lineage Lamas. It was Lama Atisha who brought the complete set of instructions together with the unbroken stream of blessings to Tibet. Lama Atisha then passed them to his main disciple, the great Lama Dromtön Gyalwey Jung-ne, who passed them on to Potowa Rinchen Sel, who in turn passed them to Sharawa Yönten Drak, and he to Chekawa Yeshe Dorje. Chekawa eventually wrote a special root text, which is divided into seven sections or seven great points, the well-known *Seven Point Mind Training*, or as it is called in Tibetan, *Lojong Dön Dunma*. The Lojong instructions, along with the complete, faultless, pure blessing continuum have been passed down through our Lineage Lamas to the present day.

The Importance of Right Motivation

There is an aphorism in the *Seven Point Mind Training* that states, "Two activities: one for the beginning and one for the end." This means that all scholars, sages, yogis, and yoginis should begin every activity by correcting their motivation and finish it by dedicating the merit or virtue generated by it.

What is right motivation? We have to correct our motivation at the beginning because the virtuous activities we do are only as good as our motivation. If our motivation is focused on the Hinayana way of practicing, all the resulting virtues will yield only Hinayana nirvana. But if we have a Mahayana motivation, all our virtue will bring the result of complete Buddhahood, which is the fruit of the Mahayana path. Just as business people always want to make a profit and never want to take a loss, yogis, yoginis, sages, and scholars want the Dharma field's profit, which is great virtue, great knowledge, and great understanding. To profit this way, we must have a great motivation, which means we must develop bodhichitta, or the mind that wants more than anything else to attain Buddhahood in order to benefit all sentient beings.

The main subject of this teaching is how to awaken bodhichitta, how to develop it, and how to achieve its result. Therefore, it is very important to learn about the benefits or good results of bodhichitta.

Je Tsongkapa declared that bodhichitta is like a great highway. If you want to go to New York and you take the main highway, you will definitely reach there. Similarly, bodhichitta is like the great highway that leads to the field where Buddhas live, or Buddhahood. If you want to reach Buddhahood, you definitely have to take the highway of bodhichitta.

Bodhichitta is not something that was invented by a few scholars or Lamas. All previous Buddhas have gone this way, present Buddhas are going this way, and all future Buddhas will have to go this way. There are no two highways to Buddhahood; there is only one and that is bodhichitta. If you achieve bodhichitta you have set out on the Buddhas' highway. Bodhichitta is the very basis of all Bodhisattvas' and Buddhas' activities.

A Bodhisattva's daily activities or daily practices are the six perfections[3] and the four ways of gathering disciples.[4]

---

[3]The six perfections or *paramitas* are: giving, morality, patience, effort, concentration, and wisdom.

[4]The four ways of gathering disciples are: giving to disciples; pleasing speech, which refers to teaching Dharma; beneficial conduct, which refers to

Together, these are sometimes called the "ten perfections." All Buddhas' and Bodhisattvas' activities are included in these ten practices. Because these activities are based on bodhichitta, no Buddha or Bodhisattva or we ourselves could possibly do them without that mind. Therefore, bodhichitta is very important for being able to practice Bodhisattva activities.

If you prostrate, make offerings to the Buddha, Dharma, and Sangha, meditate, recite, or do visualizations motivated only by renunciation, your virtues will only turn into causes for achieving nirvana, but not complete Buddhahood. If your mental attitude of renunciation turns into bodhichitta, that bodhichitta is like the mercury that Arya Nagarjuna used to turn iron into gold.

Everybody has heard of Arya Nagarjuna, the great scholar, sage, and Bodhisattva. By applying the skill and power he developed through holy instruction, he used mercury to turn iron into gold and used that gold to buy food for Nalanda Monastery. By doing this he was able to feed twenty thousand monks every day for twelve years. Bodhichitta is like that mercury; if you achieve it, all of your virtues turn into the gold of Mahayana virtues, which lead you not just to temporary goals like actual gold, but to the ultimate goal, which is complete Buddhahood.

Bodhichitta is so precious. If you have it, all Buddhas think of you as their child, calling you, "my son" or "my daughter," which is extraordinary. Likewise, Bodhisattvas think of you as their brothers and sisters. This brings you very close to them, like becoming a part of the family of Buddhas and Bodhisattvas. You can then receive their power and blessings very quickly. If you have bodhichitta, you have what is necessary for them to be able to help and teach you easily.

---

causing followers to train gradually on the path of the holy Dharma; and sameness of purpose, which means to practice Dharma in the same way that we instruct others to practice.

The Power of Bodhichitta

Although people in this country don't really believe in bad spirits, demons, or ghosts, they actually do exist and there are many of them. What makes a demon a demon is its bad mental attitude. Demons are extremely cruel; their main activity is to constantly harm other beings, particularly those who want to practice Dharma and meditation. They try to influence such people not to succeed, not to gain knowledge, and so forth. But if you have actual bodhichitta, no matter how hard they try, they cannot harm you at all because of the power of that holy mind. In fact, bodhichitta's power can change their attitude and status. Eventually, you can turn those demons into good spirits with noble minds, and instead of harming you, they will help you. All of this comes from the power of bodhichitta. Therefore, bodhichitta has great meaning and importance for us.

So far we have discussed the benefits of acting positively toward Buddhas and Bodhisattvas. Because of such beings' unique nature, which is that they have bodhichitta, you can even benefit if you act negatively toward them. As the great Shantideva declared,

> I prostrate to the bodies of those
> In whom the holy jewel of
> Highest mind is born;
> I take refuge in those sources of great joy
> Who lead to bliss
> Even those who harm them.[5]

I prostrate to the person who has bodhichitta. Why does Shantideva say, "I prostrate to the bodies of those in whom the holy jewel of highest mind is born"? Because prostrating to a Bodhisattva creates a relationship with him or her and with other Bodhisattvas as well. Establishing a good relationship, or even a bad relationship with them will still yield a good result.

---

[5]*Engaging in Bodhisattva Activities* (*Bodhicharyavatara*), ch. 1, v. 36.

In general, thinking harmful thoughts, saying harmful words, or doing harmful activities are negative deeds that yield only bad results; there is no way to get a good result from those kinds of activities. But there is one exception. If you do something bad, such as speaking harshly to a Bodhisattva, on the one hand you collect a lot of negative karma, but on the other hand you make a connection with that Bodhisattva through that deed, making it easy for him or her to help you. That Bodhisattva gets a good opportunity to help you because you have created a relationship with him or her—even if it's a bad relationship. At some point when you are experiencing serious sufferings due to the relationship that you established in that way, the Bodhisattva will appear to you. Your sufferings came as a result of the bad deeds that you collected in relation to Bodhisattvas. Therefore, they can help you because of that relationship.

For example, in Tibet about two miles east of Lhasa city there was a great monastery called Gungtang, where there lived a high Lama who was also a real Bodhisattva. In that region there also lived a family of farmers. The mother of this family was a very short-tempered woman who never gave the slightest thought to collecting virtue but was constantly thinking only of this life. As a result, she was always collecting bad deeds. Realizing her condition, this great Lama tried many times to help her, to lead her to develop a virtuous mind and to do virtuous activities. He tried many times but failed. No matter what he did, he just couldn't succeed. So then he thought, "Well, I can't manage to cultivate a good relationship with this short-tempered farm woman, so now I'll at least try creating a *bad* connection with her so that in the future I will definitely be able to help her." Thinking this he set out to find her. That particular day she was working in the field, so the Lama went there and tried to do something she wouldn't like. He tried all kinds of things, but unfortunately, she didn't get angry. Usually she got angry very easily, but that day she didn't get angry at all. So he failed to make either a positive or negative connection with her.

Bodhichitta is so holy and so important. With it, if we can establish a good relationship, needless to say, we can get a good result. But even if we create a bad relationship, it will still help in the long run, at some great and important time. You should be aware of how important bodhichitta is and have the same attitude that you'd have while window-shopping in New York and seeing all kinds of lovely things: "Wow, I want it, I want it.... How beautiful! I want it, I really want it!" You have to want bodhichitta with all your heart, thinking, "Bodhichitta is so beautiful, so important, so holy!" Even though you may want that holy mental attitude, you cannot buy it with money. You have to try to achieve it through practice.

The Ten Benefits of Achieving Bodhichitta

Among the benefits of bodhichitta, the scriptures describe ten in particular, the first of which is that *bodhichitta is the only entrance to the Mahayana path*. Buddha taught in the Mahayana Sutra vehicle and the Mahayana Tantra vehicle that bodhichitta is the only entrance to the Mahayana path. If you want to achieve ultimate happiness you have to achieve Buddhahood. If you want to achieve Buddhahood, you have to enter the Mahayana path. In order to gain entry to the Mahayana path, you have to gain bodhichitta. From the moment you generate bodhichitta, you are a Mahayana person.

The second benefit is that if you achieve bodhichitta *you will come to be known as a Bodhisattva by all the Buddhas and Bodhisattvas*. They will call you a Buddha's son or a Buddha's daughter, just as a father calls his child "my son" or "my daughter."

The third benefit is that *you will surpass the Listener and Solitary Realizer disciples by your spiritual lineage*. In the Buddhist field there are three vehicles: the Listeners' vehicle, the Solitary Realizers' vehicle, and the Mahayana or Great vehicle. If you are the prince or princess of a royal lineage, all ordinary subjects have to respect you. Even if you don't know how to eat or drink politely, they must still show you respect because of your lineage. Similarly, the dignity of the sages and great Arhats of the Listeners' and Solitary Realizers' vehicles cannot compare with that of a person who has just entered the Mahayana path by achieving bodhichitta for the first time.

Not only humans can generate bodhichitta, but birds and other animals and even hell beings can generate it. For example, Buddha Shakyamuni generated bodhichitta for the first time when he was a hell being. If beings have enough good seeds in their mind from hearing Dharma, thinking about it, and practicing it in their previous lives, even a minor circumstance can cause them to easily achieve bodhichitta.

A Jataka tale is a story about the Buddha's previous lives. There is one such tale about a little bird that generated bodhichitta during a huge forest fire in India. Because of that fire, many creatures were being burned to death. The bird, overwhelmed by great compassion, generated bodhichitta and flew to a nearby lake where he dipped his wings into the water. Returning to the forest, he flapped his wings furiously over the fire. By the power of this holy and virtuous attitude, it is said that those few drops of water caused the entire forest fire to be extinguished.

The fourth benefit is that *you will become the highest object worthy of honor.* If you give a cookie or some fruit to an animal with a good motivation, you can collect virtue. But you will collect much more virtue if you give that cookie to an ordinary being or to a beggar, because a human being is capable of doing more beneficial activities than an animal. Similarly, you will gain still greater virtue with someone who is sick, a monk, your parents, or a Dharma teacher. But if you give a cookie to a Bodhisattva, the virtue is measureless. A Bodhisattva is the highest field of merit. The cookie is the same but the field in relation to whom you are giving the offering is completely different. Therefore, you become the most worthy object of receiving offerings by generating bodhichitta.

The fifth benefit is that *you can easily accumulate great merit*. There are two accumulations that we need to gather to attain Buddhahood: the accumulation of merit and the accumulation of wisdom. Because of achieving bodhichitta we can gain great amounts of virtue. Usually we have to make great effort to collect virtue. But Bodhisattvas can easily collect a huge amount of virtue even through small activities. The only way to achieve Buddhahood is by accumulating virtue and abandoning bad deeds. There is no other way. So if you want to collect a huge amount of virtue easily, you have to try to achieve bodhichitta.

The sixth benefit is that *you will quickly remove bad karma and mental obstacles*. If you generate bodhichitta you can remove your bad deeds and obstacles very quickly.

The seventh is that after achieving bodhichitta *you will easily achieve all the goals you wish*.

The eighth benefit is that *you cannot be harmed by demons or other obstacles*, because that bodhichitta protects you.

The ninth benefit is that *you will quickly complete all the paths*. There are five main paths that the Bodhisattva has to realize: the Path of Accumulation, the Path of Preparation, the Path of Seeing, the Path of Meditation, and the Path of No More Learning. The first path itself has nine levels and the Path of Accumulation has four main divisions and so on. The point is that there are many, many levels to advance on. When you reach the Path of Seeing, in which you perceive emptiness directly, you become a Mahayana Arya, at which point you become actual Sangha as opposed to Sangha in name only. You also achieve the real Dharma Jewel. After achieving that level, you have to practice the ten Bodhisattva *bhumis* or stages. As you advance through them, you have to gain many levels of knowledge and eliminate many kinds of obstacles. When you finish this entire process you achieve perfect enlightenment. If you achieve bodhichitta, you can advance through all these levels and paths easily and quickly.

The tenth benefit is that *you become a field that produces every happiness for sentient beings*. All real happiness and goodness come from Bodhisattvas and their activities. If you achieve bodhichitta you become the main source of all sentient beings' happiness. These are the ten benefits that you have to study about and learn one by one.

The Two Instructions for Achieving Bodhichitta

There are two main sets of instructions for achieving bodhichitta. The first is the *Sevenfold Cause and Effect Instruction*,[6] a series of topics which, when meditated on one after the other, should result in achieving bodhichitta. You have to learn each of the seven steps of the Sevenfold Instruction. This teaching system came from Buddha, was passed down to Maitreya, to Asanga, to Lama Serlingpa, to Lama Atisha, to Je Tsongkapa, and then through our Lineage Lamas down to the present.

The second set of instructions is called *Equality and Exchange of Self and Others*, or *dakshen nyamje*, which I mentioned already. *Dakshen nyamje* and *tonglen* are the two main elements of the Lojong tradition. You should become very familiar with these terms.

By practicing either of these two sets of instructions—the Sevenfold Instruction or Equalizing and Exchanging Self and Others—you can achieve bodhichitta.

Equalizing and Exchanging Self and Others, along with Giving and Taking are included in the *Seven Point Mind Training* tradition. These instructions came from Buddha, passed to Mañjushri, to Shantideva, and later to Lama Serlingpa, Lord Atisha, Je Tsongkapa, and down to our present Lineage Lamas.

Je Tsongkapa combined these two great rivers of instruction to make one powerful and efficient river. He joined the steps of the Sevenfold Instruction with the points of *dakshen nyamje*. The resulting eleven-step practice is Je Tsongkapa's unique system; it is a faster and more powerful method of achieving bodhichitta.

---

[6]*rgyu 'bras man ngag bdun;* not to be confused with Lama Chekawa's *Seven Point Mind Training* text mentioned earlier.

Before you can do this combined practice you have to learn the points of each of these two sets of instructions separately. First you have to learn what the seven steps of the Sevenfold Instruction are, and then you have to learn about the two major parts of Equalizing and Exchanging Self and Others. After learning these, you have to join the two systems and practice all their steps as part of one system.

༄༅། །རྒྱུ་འབྲས་མན་ངག་བདུན། །

PART I

SEVENFOLD
CAUSE AND EFFECT
INSTRUCTION

EQUANIMITY

བཏང་སྙོམས།

BEFORE WE CAN GO to the first numbered step of the Sevenfold Cause and Effect Instruction, which is "Recognizing That All Beings Have Been My Mother," we must first prepare our mind by cultivating equanimity toward all beings.

Right now, when we think of our home, our own mother, our father, or our brothers and sisters, we feel close to them and want to be with them. And when we think of other places, there may be people that we dislike or hate, and we see them as our enemies. We don't like them and they don't like us. We want to stay away from them. We have to examine why these two thoughts come up in our mind. Are these proper mental attitudes or not? If we have those two kinds of wrong thoughts—strong attraction to those we like and hatred toward those we dislike—we have to try very carefully to remove them. There is a big difference between those two kinds of thoughts. We have to be able to say, "I realized by studying and reading Buddha's teachings that all beings have been my mother or a close relative many times. Therefore, my tendency to discriminate between people is wrong, and has to be removed."

In order to do that, we have to practice equanimity (*tang nyom*). In Buddhism, the term *equanimity* has several different meanings. But in this context it refers to developing an attitude that is free from hatred toward some and attachment or desire toward others. This practice is called *immeasurable equanimity*, because all beings are the object of our practice and all beings are immeasurable in number.

There are several ways to do this practice. In our lineage there are two main methods. In the first, we begin by taking

a neutral person or someone whom we neither like nor dislike, as the meditation object. Then we strengthen our equanimity toward that object. Later, we practice having that attitude toward someone we see as an enemy, and then finally
toward a close relative or friend. The second main method,
and the one preferred by this particular lineage system, in-
structs us to do one visualization that includes a close friend,
a worst enemy, and a neutral person or someone whose
background we do not know.

As you focus on each, you will definitely gain three very
different thoughts. Just seeing your friend pleases you and
makes you happy. Just seeing your enemy upsets you and
causes you to feel hatred. When visualizing the neutral person you won't care about him or her one way or the other.
You have to recognize very clearly how these three attitudes
arise in your mind.

When visualizing your enemy, you should ask yourself
why you feel hatred toward that person. You will discover
that it's because at some point that person did something
bad to you, something that you didn't like, not only once but
many times. "That's why I hate him." Why do you feel desire toward your friend? By "desire" I mean that you like
him and because of that you don't want to lose him—you
feel you need him to stay with you closely. Why? Because he
helped you in the past, he gave you something, he helped
you at some important time when you needed it. Toward a
neutral person you will feel indifferent. "I don't know him
so I don't care." The main reaction that you have toward a
neutral person is one of ignorance, which in this case is the
ignorance of not knowing that he or she has been your
mother in the past. Even though you never saw the person
before or don't know him, according to Buddha's speech he
was still your mother—your closest relative—in a previous
life. At that time, she protected your life with great concern.
Therefore, not caring about such people is due to ignorance.

Although it is true that a friend might have helped you,
in the past that person has hurt you as well. That person
may even have beaten and killed you at some point in the
past. And while you can think of several reasons for hating

your present enemies, that is wrong too, because in previous lives they have helped and protected you many times. Though it is true that the time is different, whether someone helped you in the past or this year doesn't change the fact that they have helped you. Likewise, last year's beating and this year's beating are the same kind of activity. Therefore, it is completely wrong to have desire toward some, hatred toward others, and indifference toward still others over small things.

We can rely on both the Buddha's speech and on logic to determine that all sentient beings have been our parents. Thinking of beings as permanent, that is, as absolute and unchanging friends, enemies, or strangers is wrong.

You can also examine this from the perspective of the object, that is, from the side of the friend, enemy, or neutral person. It's wrong to feel close to some, distant from others, and ignore the rest, since from their side they are all the same in wanting to be happy and not wanting to suffer. Tell yourself, "I am trying to gain bodhichitta. Since all of those beings are in the same situation, it's wrong for me to distinguish between them by considering some as friends, some as enemies, and some as strangers."

Je Tsongkapa stated in the *Great Stages of the Path* (*Lamrim Chenmo*) that equanimity is the starting point and that even if it takes many months just to master equanimity, it is essential to do so. Kyabje Pabongka Rinpoche and Kyabje Trijang Rinpoche stated this as well. If you paint a wall, first you have to prepare it by making it smooth, then you can easily paint it. Similarly, to realize that all beings have been your mother, you must first practice to gain equanimity in relation to each and every being. If your equanimity is very good, it will be much easier for you to be able to realize that all beings have been your mother.

When you meditate on equanimity, your mind should stay within the field of equanimity. The agent in this case is your meditating mind, the action is thinking about equanimity, and the object is the three types of person I mentioned already: friend, enemy, and neutral person. The desire, hatred, and ignorance that arise respectively when you focus on them are mental derivatives (*sem jung*). Mental derivatives are associated with the main mental consciousness. Mind consciousness is like the king and mental derivatives are like the king's subjects. Mental consciousness focuses on and grasps its object's general nature, while the mental derivatives focus on some particular quality of the object. It is the nature of the mental derivatives that by their own power they perceive the three objects (friend, enemy, and neutral person) differently. When you are practicing, you have to keep in mind how your main mind consciousness and mental derivatives work together. If you lose sight of that, your meditation will not be good. With practice, your mind will change in the way that your mental derivatives apprehend those objects.

Je Tsongkapa explained that temporary friend, temporary enemy, and temporary neutral person do in fact exist. But there is no such thing as *permanent* or unchangeable enemy, friend, or neutral person. Therefore, you have to make the distinction. If your mind is focusing on them in order to realize how you are grasping them as permanent, then that is not wrong, that is right.

What are you rejecting in relation to those three objects during meditation on equanimity? You have to try to reject the way you are thinking of those objects. Desire, hatred, and ignorance arise in your mind because you perceive "friend," "enemy," and "neutral person" as unchanging. "Unchanging" is the kind of thought you have to reject. There is no reason that desire should arise in relation to those people, and there is no reason that hatred or ignorance should arise in relation to them. They may be an enemy for the time being, but not an absolute, unchanging enemy. They might be a friend for the time being, but not permanently.

He is not my unchanging enemy. He is changeable. At some point he might become my best friend. On the other hand, he is not my permanent friend; he is also changeable, and could very well become my worst enemy. Therefore, why am I still allowing hatred and desire to arise in my mind? Actually, friend and enemy are the same. Not only in this life, but in previous lives they were my closest family members and my worst enemies. In order to practice loving-kindness and compassion toward all beings you have to be able to focus on them with equal concern, which is why practicing equanimity is so important. Therefore, you cannot gain proper and perfect loving-kindness, compassion, and much less bodhichitta, without perfect equanimity.

Desire, hatred, and ignorance are mental derivatives that cause your mind to be biased. Actually, main mind is neutral. Fortunately, we can separate our minds from those mental derivatives, which takes practice and understanding. By understanding the definitions of those mental derivatives—their functions, qualities, and results—we can practice their respective antidotes. Desire's antidote is being satisfied with what you have. Compassion and loving-kindness are the antidotes to hatred, and wisdom is the antidote to ignorance. By practicing them we can definitely move our mind in the right direction.

When practicing equanimity, you are focusing your mind on beings equally. Once you improve the way in which you apprehend these objects—in this case your own friend, your enemy, and someone who is a stranger to you—and can focus on them with the same degree of equanimity, you can then change your meditation object from these to all sentient beings. Kyabje Pabongka Rinpoche said that you have to practice equanimity for months or even years until you achieve the proper level of realization. While you can collect a lot of virtue by practicing equanimity for just a few meditation sessions, such practice won't yield any great result. To expect that the practice that leads to full enlightenment could be done by meditating for just a few sessions is mistaken. Meditating on a topic for just a few periods won't bring any real spiritual progress at all.

STEP ONE:
RECOGNIZING THAT ALL BEINGS HAVE BEEN MY MOTHER

ᘯᖦ:ᗺᙀ

THE FIRST NUMBERED PRACTICE in the Sevenfold Cause and Effect Instruction is realizing that all beings have been our mother. This is a very important point but difficult to realize with strong conviction because our mind has associated with ordinary thoughts and ordinary samsaric ways for so many lifetimes throughout many eons. Our mind is simply not used to thinking this way. On top of that, we are directly aware only of this life. We cannot see our past or future lives because our mind is not developed enough to perceive them. For these reasons, it is difficult for us to really believe in the existence of our own previous and future lives.

Here we have to apply the reasons formulated by the seventh-century Indian Buddhist logician Dharmakirti in his great logic system. The system of Buddhist logic provides unbelievably sharp, powerful, and useful reasons for understanding important spiritual principles. Dharmakirti said that the reason "if it cannot be seen, it does not exist"[7] is not valid to prove that something doesn't exist. For example, does nirvana exist? Do Arhats exist? Do hells exist? Do hungry ghosts exist? These are some of the subjects that can be debated. For example, if you say, "No, hells do not exist, nirvana does not exist," and I ask, "Why not?" you might say, "Because I cannot see them." By this you are saying that the only things that exist are things you can see. But it is not necessary to see something in order for it to exist. Therefore, you cannot say that your previous lives and your future

---

[7]*Commentary on Valid Cognition (Pramanavarttika)*, ch. 2, v. 85.

lives don't exist because you cannot perceive them. Your inability to perceive them is not a valid reason to disprove their existence. More than that, it's actually a mistaken reason.

How can you use logic to realize that your previous and future lives do exist? It is much easier to have correct or valid cognition in relation to external objects than to have it in relation to subtler objects such as past and future lives. If I say, "This flower is very beautiful. Where did it come from?" you will say, "That flower came from its seed." You cannot see that seed directly at this moment because its result—the flower—has come about and the cause that produced it—its seed—has already disappeared. That is natural. In this example you can see an outer object's quality, nature, or function. You can realize what came before it and understand that it arose from its seed; you can determine all of that. But it is much more difficult to realize your previous and future lives than it is to understand that a flower comes from its seed.

How can you gain correct cognition in relation to your previous and future lives? One way that we develop correct cognition is through hearing a Buddha's speech. When Buddha Shakyamuni taught in India, he declared that among beings there isn't a single one who hasn't been your mother, father, friend, or other relative at least a hundred times. "One hundred times" is used here to refer to "many"; some Sutras say "countless times." This means that any given being has been your mother, your father, your friend, your relative, your brother, sister, or child at least a hundred times. If Buddha said this, is it true or not? Whether a Buddha's speech is true or not must also be determined by using logic.

Buddha eliminated every obstacle by practicing its antidote for many eons, and also refined and perfected all good qualities. During that entire time, he put an end to telling any kind of lie. He did this in order to achieve Buddhahood. So why, after achieving Buddhahood, would he lie to us? There is no reason. Therefore, we can believe what he said.

In addition to using scriptural authority[8] to gain the correct cognition that all beings have been your mother, you can also use another method, which is the reasoning system found in Dharmakirti's logic text, the *Commentary on Valid Cognition*:

When you take birth,
Your breath, sense faculties, and mind
Do not arise only from the body,
To which they are unrelated in kind.[9]

Dharmakirti stated that when you were conceived in your mother's womb you acquired a new life, a new body. Because of that, you got breath, sense faculties, and mind. Your body is something you got from your mother and father. At the moment of conception you had a mind; but where did that mind come from? Did your parents give it to you? Did they give you your mind at the same time that they gave you your body? You have to think about this.

If you think, "Yes, definitely, when they gave me my body they gave me my mind also," consider the fact that many bright parents have very dull kids. Why wouldn't they give their kids a very bright mind? If they had the power to, of course they would give their child a bright mind, but they can't do that because the mind comes another way.

You get your body from your parents at the moment of conception. You get your mind at that very same moment. Dharmakirti's system tells us that the mind existing at that moment has to come from its own corresponding cause. We know how a flower comes from its seed; that seed came from a previous seed, and that seed came from a previous seed's seed, and so on. A seed cannot suddenly come into

---

[8]Buddhist logic recognizes scriptural authority as a valid means of inference.
[9]*Commentary on Valid Cognition*, ch. 2, v. 36. This is the first verse in the text that addresses the argument to prove the existence of past and future lives. The line "To which they are unrelated in kind" means that if breath, sense faculties, and mind arose "only from the body," they would arise from a dissimilar cause. Thus, Dharmakirti's premise is that mind in particular must arise from a similar cause, that is, a previous mind.

existence by itself, that is, without a cause. Because of that, self-existent phenomena, or things that exist independently or without causes, cannot exist. Everything is related to its causes. That child's body at conception came from parts of the parents' bodies. The mind, which is also an entity, must have its own causes.

Among phenomena there are things that have form and things that don't have form. Formless things cannot turn into form and form cannot turn into formless things. Stones and trees cannot turn into mind nor can mind turn into stones and trees. You have to think about this.

Although our mind has no form, it is still an entity—it exists. Every entity comes from its own unique causes. The unique cause of mind is mind. So, the mind at the moment of conception must come from something mental. That mental cause must have existed prior to conception. To whom does that mind that existed prior to conception belong? As a mind, it must belong to someone. Therefore, it must be the mind that came from your previous life. That previous life is also an entity that has its own unique causes; it too came from a previous life, and so on. In this way you can prove the existence of your previous lives.

Buddhist texts say that all Buddhas have the same level of knowledge and achievement. They have no obstructions; nothing can hinder their ability to perceive all things. Buddhas can perceive all things directly. But no Buddha ever said to anyone, "This is your very first lifetime. You didn't exist before this." All Buddhas have said that your previous lives are beginningless.

After you've learned these points through having heard a Buddha's speech and through logical reasoning, you should not forget them. You have to use this knowledge you've gained from listening to develop correct cognition when you meditate. You have to improve your knowledge by meditating, making it more firm and stable so that it becomes correct cognition. To do that, you yourself must practice contemplating these good reasons during meditation.

EDITORS' NOTE: *At this point in the teaching Khensur Rinpoche began to explain how to meditate properly on the instruction. Rinpoche covered the* five *defects (kyön nga)—
which he refers to as the five enemies of meditation—and the
eight* antidotes (du je gye) *to those five faults. He also gave
instruction on what constitutes a proper meditation object, the
importance of meditating for short periods in the beginning
while trying to remain focused on the meditation object or
topic with a clear and undistracted mind. Later he explained
the elements of correct meditation posture; gave more detailed
instruction about the defects of* mental sinking (jing wa) *and*
mental scattering (gö pa) *as well as methods of overcoming
them; taught how to calm the mind with a breathing meditation; and described how perfect meditation must include the
three crucial elements of* steadiness (ne cha), clarity (sel
cha), *and a clarity that possesses intensity (sel che ngar).
Because most of these explanations are often taught within the
larger context of how to develop* shamatha (shi-ne) *or* quiescence, *we have combined them with additional instructions
given at other times by Khensur Rinpoche to form a more
complete account of that topic. This expanded discussion can
be found in the Appendix.*

If your previous lives are beginningless, your mothers
are also countless. You must have had as many mothers as
you've had lives, and if you've had countless previous lives,
you've also had countless mothers.[10] As Buddha said, all
beings have been your mother. Here, you have to actually
realize this and understand that a mother is a lifetime's closest, most important, and kindest relative. Because of this, realizing that all beings have been your mother is the first step

---

[10]Buddhism describes four kinds of birth: from a womb, from an egg, from
warmth and moisture, and spontaneous. Although only womb and egg
births require a mother, this distinction does not alter the basic premise of the
argument.

of the Sevenfold Instruction. If that knowledge is good and firm in your mind, you will be able to realize the remaining six steps of the instruction easily.

Some people gain knowledge very quickly when they practice, while others make very slow progress. Why is this? Along with your main meditation practice, you have to do other activities to collect as much virtue as you can. The power of the virtue you collect helps you to gain knowledge and to succeed in your practice. If you lack virtue, even if you practice hard, it will take a long time to achieve the goals and it will be very difficult. Therefore, in the future, if something like that happens and you are not progressing quickly, you must remember this and try to collect virtue. By collecting virtue and practicing well, you will eventually gain the realization that all beings have been your mother in previous lives. You must have that strong conviction before you move on to the next topic.

How do you know whether you've gained this knowledge? When you see your mother you don't need any introduction; you know without a doubt that she's your mother. There is a very close feeling of love between a mother and her child. Also, look at any small child and you can see that it is completely dependent on its mother. An infant cannot survive for a single day, for an hour, or even a minute without her.

The measure of success after practicing this stage is to have the same degree of recognition when you see something like a bug or other small creature. Your daily practice will have influenced your mind so that you will think, "This creature was born as an insect this time—a lower realm's life—but when it was my mother and I was her son or daughter, I had to depend on her for everything." When this recognition arises naturally toward any being you encounter, you have achieved the first stage of the Sevenfold Cause and Effect Instruction.

ಬಿ

QUESTION: *You talked about how children of the same parents can have different traits. Do you include genes in that process? In the genetic material that forms a new embryo, one chain of genes comes from the father and another chain comes from the mother. Isn't it the genes that form the new embryo and determine what traits it will have?*

KHEN RINPOCHE: When you are conceived in your mother's womb, you acquire a new life. This new life's existence is made up of five heaps. Among your five heaps, your parents give you the form heap, which is your physical body. The remaining four heaps are mostly composed of mental entities, which come from your previous life's mental continuum.

Buddhist commentaries explain that the material for the bones of a new being come from the father's seed, while the blood, flesh, and skin come from the mother's unique substance. Tantric teachings further describe a system of nerves, winds, and drops, but that is not a subject I should discuss here. All these explanations show how the various elements that make up a being's complete body are acquired from its parents.

The mind and body are different. Although the body comes from our parents, the mind does not, and this distinction is important to prove the existence of past and future lives. The mind comes from a source other than the physical body, that is, from a previous mind that had to belong to a previous life.

As far as different traits are concerned, I will give you an easy example. Even if I were going to die tomorrow, I still believe it would be worthwhile for me to study as much as I can today. This is an important Buddhist attitude. Buddhism teaches that there are two kinds of wisdom, innate wisdom and wisdom gained through study and effort.

Innate wisdom comes from activities that you did in previous lives, like studying to remove ignorance and to plant seeds of knowledge in your mind. Because of that, in your next life you can have a mind that is naturally bright. That is why some people can learn everything very fast and perfectly, while others cannot learn nicely even though they try very hard. It is the result of karmic seeds. Some people are rich in good seeds; others are not. Therefore, even if I were going to die tomorrow, it would still be worthwhile to study as much as possible today. This is an important point that relates to the subject of former lives and future lives.

This life's physical body is also a resultant stage, not a causal one. What is the cause of this result? The drawing representing the Wheel of Life[11] includes twelve stages in its outer rim. The second limb, called "immature karma," is often depicted as a potter making pots or as an artist drawing a picture. These images represent the karma we did in our previous lives. This is immature karma whose power has not yet ripened. It is like grain that has been harvested from a field and is being kept in a storehouse.

The tenth limb of the Wheel of Life, called "mature karma," also represents karma, but karma of a different stage. If you take grain from your storehouse and plant it in a field that receives sunlight, and you then fertilize and water that field, the seed you planted will produce a sprout. Therefore, the tenth stage in the Wheel of Life is like a seed that is ready to produce a sprout.

If you plant some seeds, the primary cause of the resulting plants are those seeds. The secondary causes are such things as water, good soil, sunlight, warmth, and so on. Similarly, your previous karma is the main cause of your new life's physical body. The secondary causes are the unique substances that you get from your parents. This is why children who come from the same parents can have completely different characteristics, including their appear-

---

[11]For a lengthier discussion on the limbs of the Wheel of Life, please refer to *King Udrayana and the Wheel of Life*, trans. by Sermey Geshe Lobsang Tharchin, et al. See bibliography.

ance, intelligence, ability, and so on. The main cause of those children is their own past karma. You should understand this system. Buddha taught that the result of your deeds is exactly like those deeds themselves. He said:

> Whatever kind of deed is done
> The result it brings will be similar.

STEP TWO:
RECALLING THE KINDNESS OF ALL MOTHER BEINGS

ཉིན་ཉག།

REALIZING THAT ALL BEINGS have been your mother is the first numbered step in this instruction after preparing the mind with immeasurable equanimity. This is like a basic knowledge that allows you to realize the remaining practices more easily. Once you realize the first step, move on to the second step, which is to meditate on all beings' great kindness. Start by considering this life's mother and all the things she has done for you.

From the moment she conceives a child, a good mother takes care not to smoke, drink alcohol, or eat certain foods. The main reason she does this is to protect her baby. After giving birth, the mother must serve her baby every minute of every day in order to protect and nurture that baby's life. It is very difficult just to raise a small plant, to say nothing of raising children. Raising a child takes much longer, is far more difficult, more expensive, and much more risky. Absolutely everything we need is provided for by our mother— by both our parents—but most of all by our mother.

Several years ago, an airplane crashed into a bridge over a river in Washington, D.C. At that time, one man saved a woman's life. The president gave him an award for his heroism, which is very good, but actually that man only saved that lady's life once. Our mothers have saved our lives countless times. So why don't we think of that as a great kindness toward us?

One way a mother shows her kindness is by serving, feeding, and raising her children. She makes sure that all the child's needs are met. She does whatever has to be done. In that way we are able to grow up and develop a strong body. About the only thing we can take to school on our own is our body—our parents have to arrange for everything else, clothes or school uniforms, school supplies like paper and pencils—everything. All of these come from our parents' great kindness.

Later on when we can stand on our own two feet and do everything for ourselves, we tend to forget our parents' and especially our mother's incredible kindness. But if we think about it and study, we won't easily forget. Therefore, we have to develop and make firm in our minds the thought of our mother's great kindness. When that thought becomes very strong, we then have to realize our father's great kindness toward us; that is, we take this life's father as an object of meditation and think about how he benefited us when he too was our mother in a previous life. Then we move on to contemplate the kindness of all other beings. All beings have done the same thing in the same way for us. All beings did what they could for us, so we cannot distinguish between them thinking that some were very kind and others were not. Every single being has been our mother hundreds or thousands of times, and some of them even countless times. Therefore, they are all alike in that they have shown us immeasurable kindness. We have to think that way.

If you filled your house with pure gold dust, there might still be some grains of dirt or sand mixed in. Similarly, sometimes you hear about a mother killing her infant by putting it in a grocery bag and throwing it into a garbage can. Those are unusual cases. Such people do not have a real mother's quality.

A Special Form of Recalling the Kindness of Beings

Our Lineage Lamas have a special instruction about meditating on the kindness of sentient beings. When beings were our mother, they were incredibly kind. But even when they weren't or aren't our mother, they are still kind in measureless ways. If you don't think about this, you might very well go around thinking, "Everything I have done, I have done on my own. Nobody did anything for me." We are here listening to and teaching Dharma. We can sit here comfortably. How did this come to be? Who arranged for all this? Nothing was arranged by us alone, other beings arranged everything nicely for us to be able to sit here. Therefore, beings have shown us great kindness.

The situation is the same everywhere you go. If you want to go food shopping you have to go to the grocery store. You can easily get what you want and even check the price and go to another store and compare. Who arranged the quality and the price of the goods? Usually we have no idea who arranged those things. It's because of everybody's efforts that we can live comfortably. For example, we didn't have any gas for the stove last night. We had a man come to fill it and now we can use the stove, even though we had to pay money. And where does that money come from? It's not self-existent. We don't have a factory to print money. If we tried to print money, the police would catch up with us. Who made that money? Who gave us the value of that money? Absolutely everything relies upon other things. That's how you can understand about other beings' incredible kindness.

When someone gets sick and has to go to the hospital, the hospital itself is well kept, the beds are clean, the service is good, the doctors and nurses attend to you. While those people aren't our parents, they're still unbelievably kind. We don't know them. If you have money you have to pay, but if you don't have money, the government or some local organization will help you. All of these come from other beings' effort and kindness. Thinking this is a more powerful and effective way to recall the great kindness of all beings. This is our Lineage Lamas' specific instruction, remembering the great kindness of mothers in general and of all beings in particular, whether or not they are our mother. When you meditate, you can think about this a lot and by doing that you can make great spiritual progress. If you have enough wisdom you will be able to find many good reasons that will help you to prove this point in your own mind.

I have explained all of the main points as they appear in Kyabje Pabongka Rinpoche's work, *Liberation in Our Hands*.[12] This book is a transcript of a twenty-four-day teaching given by Kyabje Pabongka Rinpoche, which was written down by his disciple Kyabje Trijang Rinpoche. When I was nineteen years old, I attended another Lamrim teaching given by Kyabje Pabongka Rinpoche that lasted more than three months. In that teaching Kyabje Rinpoche used eight commentaries[13] including Je Tsongkapa's *Great Stages of the Path*, all of which are based on Lama Atisha's root text called *Lamp of the Path to Buddhahood*. Each day the teachings started at nine in the morning, with a short break for lunch, and continued until six o'clock in the evening. If I were to try to teach you in that much detail, we would not be able to finish. The main point is to meditate and think about all beings' great kindness.

---

[12]See bibliography.

[13]Je Tsongkapa's three works on the Stages of the Path (*Lamrim*): *The Great Stages of the Path to Enlightenment* (*Byang chub lam gyi rim pa chen mo*), *The Shorter Stages of the Path* (*Lam rim chung ngu*), and *The Brief Stages of the Path* (*Lam rim bsdus don*); the Third Dalai Lama Sönam Gyatso's *Essence of Refined Gold* (*Byang chub lam gyi rim pa'i khrid gser gyi yang zhun*); the Fifth Dalai Lama Ngawang Lobsang Gyatso's *Mañjughosha's Oral Instruction* ('*Jam dpal zhal lung*); the First Panchen Lama Lobsang Chökyi Gyaltsen's *Easy Path* (*bDe lam*); the Second Panchen Lama Lobsang Yeshe's *Quick Path* (*Myur lam*); and Dakpo Ngawang Drakpa's *Quintessence of Excellent Speech* (*Legs gsungs nying khu*).

STEP THREE:
REPAYING THE KINDNESS OF ALL MOTHER BEINGS

རྗེན་གཟོ།

To REALIZE THAT ALL beings have been our mothers and to remember that they have been extremely kind is not enough. When you grow up and get stronger, of course your parents' health wanes and their abilities decrease; this is only natural. Therefore, it is very important to think, "Now that I have grown stronger, finished school, have many skills, wisdom, and knowledge, I have to serve my parents, I have to help them in return."

Here, the specific point is that all mother beings are in samsara, and have been experiencing samsara's suffering from beginningless time. In the future also they will have to experience nearly endless suffering as illustrated in the Wheel of Life until they reach nirvana.

Toward the center of drawings of the Wheel of Life there are five, or more often, six sections between the rim and the hub. Those six sections represent the six realms—the three lower realms (hell realms, hungry ghost realm, and animal realm) and the two or three higher realms (human realm, demigod realm, and the god realm or human realm with the god and demigod realms counted together). These six realms are the types of existence in which the twelve links of the Wheel of Life occur and are repeated again and again, which means that no matter where you are born in samsara, whether as a god, demigod, human, animal, hungry ghost, or hell being, the essential condition is the same. Sometimes you'll go up, sometimes down, but the condition of circling endlessly in samsara's suffering is the same for all ordinary beings. There is no real freedom at all in samsara.

In relation to this, the holy Shantideva said,

Crazed by the mental afflictions, blinded by
  ignorance,
And stumbling with each and every step
Down a path lined with many steep cliffs,
I and others are always in a pitiful state.
All beings suffer in this way.[14]

People go crazy. A crazy person's mind is unstable and
constantly changing; many different thoughts come to mind.
Because of that, crazy people cannot control their mind.
Similarly, samsaric beings are like a crazy person because of
the huge number of mental afflictions they have. Their
mental afflictions make them seem crazy. Having mental afflictions is real craziness, much worse than what we usually
think of as craziness.

There are many different kinds of mental afflictions that
can be very powerful. For example, when you are in your
normal state you can see that the ground is brown or gray
and the grass is green. You can see the natural colors of such
objects; you can see people's faces, their colors and shapes.
But when you get angry, things seem to change and everything looks red. The color of outer things doesn't change but
your anger makes it seem so; you become like a crazy person
because at that moment you cannot control your mind. Your
mind's power has been seized by your anger. Everything
appears as your enemy. When you're angry, there is no way
you can have love in your mind at all.

---

[14]From a series of concluding verses in Shantideva's *Compendium of Training*
(*Shikshasamuchaya*).

ཉྫ

QUESTION: What if anger arises toward someone you love? What should you do then?

KHEN RINPOCHE: Bite them! Just joking. Telling a joke during class can be very important; it wakes everybody up. When Kyabje Pabongka Rinpoche taught, sometimes people would fall asleep. When he saw this, he would tell a joke, making everybody laugh. Those who were sleeping would wake up and ask, "What happened?" Then they would pay attention again.

You have to study about anger and the bad results of anger. The results of anger are always bad. Generally, it is considered improper to get angry. In particular, anger brings bad results to both ourselves and to others. Therefore, if you know about Dharma and are a person of noble character, you will think about anger's bad results and try to stop yourself from getting angry. Various root texts on Mind Training explain that the best way to practice is to stop anger before it comes. The Tibetan expression for this is *bur jom*, which means not giving anger the chance to arise.

If you do become angry, you should immediately think of its bad results. All of anger's results are bad and very powerful. From a worldly perspective, becoming angry immediately destroys your happiness and peace of mind and disturbs others as well. When you are angry there can be no peace where you happen to be. Thinking this, you have to subdue and tame your anger.

Some Westerners think it is a positive thing to let your anger explode. If you let it explode, maybe it will disappear for the time being, but then something will make your anger arise very soon if you always give in to it. Then you will have to explode all the time—boom, Boom, BOOM—like fireworks. Therefore, the sage's way is not to give anger the opportunity to arise. Or, if you start to get angry, you have to try to stop it. How? Good practitioners know the bad results of anger. By being very familiar with the results of anger, you can definitely stop it from arising in your mind.

Anger's results are extremely serious and unpleasant. Lord Shantideva said in his *Engaging in Bodhisattva Activities*:

> There is no evil like hatred;
> There is no austerity like patience.[15]

If someone asked Buddha or a sage, "Among all the bad deeds, which one is the worst?" they would answer, "Anger is the worst bad deed." If they were also asked what the greatest virtue is, they would of course answer that it is to practice anger's opposite, which is patience. This was not only said by Shantideva but also by Buddha, who mentioned it many times in the Sutras. Chandrakirti wrote something similar as well in his text *Entering the Middle Way*.[16]

> QUESTION: *What if someone intentionally tries to make you angry when you are trying to be patient? This seems like you are just putting off your anger. You feel as though this person is taking advantage of you because you're being patient. What should you do in that situation?*

KHEN RINPOCHE: I've been asked questions like this many times. I will give a scholar's answer. If you want to experience beneficial results and not harmful ones, then you must practice patience no matter what situation you find yourself in. The root text of *Entering the Middle Way* explains that if you didn't establish a bad karmic relationship with another person, then even if he gets angry and tries to harm you, he won't succeed. You can't experience a bad result because you don't have the bad karma that is its cause. But if you have collected bad causes, it is almost inevitable that you will have to experience bad results. Therefore, Buddha said that when bad experiences do come, you have to accept your karma. You should think, "Yes, of course. I can't complain or

---

[15]*Engaging in Bodhisattva Activities*, ch. 6, v. 2.
[16]*Madhyamakavatara.*

blame other people for this result, because I collected the bad karma that is its cause. It is actually my own fault." That is the scholar's way of thinking. But if you say something like this to an ordinary person, they will think you are a coward or foolish. That is a different viewpoint altogether.

QUESTION: *Suppose you have previously created bad karma for yourself by becoming uncontrollably angry. Then when a result comes around and you are more wise, if you absorb the anger or nullify it by practicing patience, have you ended that bad karma? Is it then completely finished?*

KHEN RINPOCHE: It depends on your attitude and the power of your practice. If your motivation, attitude, and practice are powerful enough, you can remove bad karma completely. Even if you don't remove it completely, you can definitely reduce its strength. Dharma teaches that you have to do two kinds of activities: collecting virtue (*tsok sak*) and purifying yourself of bad deeds (*drip jang*).

You can collect virtue in many different ways, for example by reciting prayers, making prostrations, and practicing any of the six perfections: giving, morality, patience, effort, concentration, and wisdom. To remove your bad deeds you must do a kind of purification practice that includes what are known as the four strengths. If you practice these strengths, it is easy to remove your bad deeds; if you don't, it is very difficult to remove them.

The first strength is to have strong faith in the Buddha, Dharma, and Sangha and have great concern for all beings. This is because all our bad deeds are collected by acting against either the Three Jewels or sentient beings. Therefore, to purify ourselves we have to rely on these two objects. This is the first strength.

The second strength is regret. You have to think, "I made a big mistake by doing that. I shouldn't have done it." You have to practice purification with that kind of regret.

Just admitting your bad deeds, however, is not enough to purify yourself. You must also counteract them by doing any of several possible activities. For example, you can meditate on emptiness, do rituals that include reciting holy mantras like Vajrasattva's hundred syllable mantra, read holy scriptures, or make prostrations to the Buddha, Dharma, and Sangha. Activities that are done to make up for negative deeds represent the third strength, or the strength of practicing an antidote.

The fourth and last strength is to practice restraint. The expression, "I don't want to make the same mistake again," nicely conveys the meaning of restraint.

ཉྫ

Anger is only one mental affliction. In one of the Sutras Buddha taught that there are more than four hundred different mental afflictions. Other Sutras describe eighty-four thousand different kinds of mental afflictions. So there are many different powerful mental afflictions that can arise in our mind.

All mother beings in samsara are like crazy people because of their mental afflictions. Crazy people who have good hearing and good eyesight can still go wherever they want and still protect their bodies and life; they won't go and jump off a cliff. But if a blind person goes crazy, the problem doubles. If he cannot control his mind or see, he could easily fall into some dangerous place. Similarly, all mother beings who are circling in samsara have been made crazy by the mental afflictions and are blinded by ignorance. They don't have the wisdom that distinguishes right from wrong, or what they should or shouldn't do.

A crazy person who is also blind is always in danger of harm. Likewise, not only are mother beings stuck in samsara, they are also constantly collecting bad deeds by body, speech, and mind. If you collect bad deeds, what are you likely to experience as a result? Of course, you will have to experience the hells or one of the other lower realms— definitely. Collecting bad deeds is like a blind crazy person stumbling toward the edge of a cliff and plunging straight to his death.

This basic situation is the same for all beings in samsara. Humans, along with all other beings, go through life this way. The kind of life may vary, but the main suffering condition is the same. So you should think, "Although all mother beings are alike in this way, I am very lucky, not because I have a strong body, but because I have strong faith in Dharma." Likewise, instead of taking pride in your worldly talents, think of having spiritual wisdom and knowledge of Dharma. If you try this time, you can do everything. "I can help all beings; I *must* help them. I am the best off this time. I can find a Dharma teacher. If I study, I can learn the meanings. If I practice, I can reach the goals. Because of that, I must do something in return for their great kindness."

Just giving food or shelter only benefits temporarily—it won't really help in an ultimate way. The best help you can give is to place beings in a state of unchanging happiness, that is, Buddhahood. You have to think, "I must lead them to Buddhahood." But right now you can guess what your own level is. You know the extent of your knowledge. "Right now, my ability and level are limited, so I must achieve Buddhahood first. When I do, I will be able to lead other beings and help them in an ultimate way. I will place them in Buddhahood. Then I will be able to give them an unchanging, steady goodness in return for their great kindness to me."

> While not recognizing them as kin through the
>   passing of birth and death,
> We can see that beings are like one who has
>   fallen into a whirlpool;
> Therefore, nothing could be more ungrateful
>   than to abandon all those
> Who are trapped in the ocean of samsara,
>   seeking to free ourselves alone.[17]

If you examine the situation of beings during your meditation you will realize that all mother beings experience

---

[17]Chandragomi's *Letter to a Disciple* (*Shishyalekha*), v. 95.

endless suffering in the ocean of samsara—both general suffering and each realm's specific sufferings. It is as though they have all fallen into a river's swirling rapids. But you are in a different place. When you meditate, you can see their condition. Ignoring their situation and trying to free only yourself from samsara's sufferings is what we call *marab* in Tibetan. *Marab* means shameless. A shameless person doesn't care what others think, has no respect whatsoever for other beings, and never pays attention to their situations or circumstances. Don't be like that; try to be a good and noble person.

By this time you should have become a noble person because you have finished practicing the first and second steps and are now practicing the third, in which you recognize that you must help beings. It is appropriate that they look to us for help by thinking, "Who can help us? Who can guide us? Who can save us?" just as a mother thinks, "Now my son is very strong and capable; he can definitely save me; I don't have to worry." Because you are a noble person, you have to recognize this and resolve to start doing whatever you can immediately.

ཨༀ

QUESTION: *The third step in the Sevenfold Cause and Effect Instruction is that we should repay the kindness of all mother sentient beings. The reason you gave was that it would be shameless not to do so. Are there any other reasons and could you say more about this point?*

KHEN RINPOCHE: There are many, many reasons, but the reason I gave covers almost all situations. You can think about this reason in relation to all sentient beings or only in relation to this life's mother. If your mother was blind and became crazy and was walking toward the edge of an abyss, that would be extremely dangerous for her. If you were there and you could see and hear everything, and you had the ability to help her but you didn't, who else would? If you were there with her, your mother would naturally think, "He will help me. My son will help me." Therefore, if you didn't help her, that would be completely shameful.

That "abyss" can be interpreted in many ways. It can be the abyss of falling from the higher realms to the lower realms. It can also mean falling from the possibility of achieving nirvana's status into samsara or falling from the Mahayana path to samsara. It can also represent many levels within the Mahayana path.

You have to reach all these levels of the path and have all the abilities and knowledge associated with them. In other words, eventually you have to achieve Buddhahood. When you reach that supreme state, you can automatically help those who are at a lower level than you. You will know what is proper to do, what is the right time to do it, and so on.

Why is it necessary to achieve Buddhahood in order to help sentient beings? It is very difficult to succeed at helping others. There are obstacles between you and the sentient beings you want to help. Also, unless you achieve Buddhahood, you will not have enough ability and power to help. Your connection with sentient beings may not be strong enough. These are all factors that make it very difficult for you to succeed at helping others.

When you achieve Buddhahood, you have omniscience. Buddha's omniscience can directly perceive all phenomena without any obstruction or lack of clarity. That omniscience can see everything—other beings' wishes, their levels of understanding, how much virtue they have, their relationship and connection with you, and the proper time to help them.

Just seeing these things is not enough. In addition, a Buddha has achieved ultimate compassion, which urges him and won't let him ignore others for even a single moment. When the right time comes, a Buddha acts immediately.

Even omniscience and compassion are not enough. A Buddha also has complete power and skill. He can project emanations of himself in whatever form is needed. If Buddha appeared in front of us in his natural form, we would not see him. Therefore, he has to emanate himself in a form that is suitable for us, that we can see, hear, and talk with. Therefore, if we achieve Buddhahood, we can have all these qualities. Then we can do all the activities that will repay sentient beings for the kindness they have shown us in the past.

ཨེད་རོང་གི་བྱམས་པ།

BUT HOW CAN YOU help them? To begin with, you should not distinguish among beings, feeling close to some, avoiding others, and ignoring the rest. You have to know how to think about beings and focus on all of them with equanimity as I mentioned before. If ten hungry people come to your door begging for food and you don't know any of them, you would go get food and give to each of them equally. They are all hungry, they all want food, so you would give food to all of them. But if you gave food to some and not to others, that would be foolish and very improper. Therefore, you have to give to them equally. Similarly, you have to love all beings equally. Loving-kindness is the fourth stage.

The loving-kindness taught as the fourth step in this Sevenfold Instruction is called the loving-kindness that sees beings as very, very dear.[18] This is distinguished from the general meaning of loving-kindness, which is the wish that beings gain happiness.[19]

The loving-kindness that sees beings as precious is like the love a mother has for her only child. Whenever she sees that child, she is spontaneously filled with this kind of loving-kindness. That child appears to her as the nearest and dearest of objects. She likes to see him; she loves to hear him; she wants to help him and is glad to provide whatever he might need.

There is a Tibetan proverb that says, "When it comes to kids, mine are best; when it comes to crops, my neighbors'

---

[18]*yid 'ong gi byams pa.*
[19]*bde ba dang phrad 'dod.*

are best." When children are playing together, a mother who's watching won't even notice the others; but her heart practically leaps out to her own child. Words alone can't express this kind of attitude. Some of the points and essential knowledges of the Lamrim teachings are indescribable. You have to experience them for yourself. You can learn and feel what they are by gaining experience through practicing and checking.

One day, an old lady came to visit the great scholar and sage Geshe Potowa and asked him to teach her about loving-kindness. That woman had a son whose name was Tölekor. "Loving-kindness is very easy," Geshe Potowa told her. "How do you feel about your son Tölekor? The way you feel about him is loving-kindness." That is the loving-kindness that ordinary people feel. Among ordinary people that is the best and strongest loving-kindness, even though it cannot compare with the loving-kindness of a Bodhisattva by one percent.

So when you are practicing loving-kindness, you have to generate the kind of feeling a mother has for her own child. First you cultivate this loving-kindness toward a friend, then toward a neutral person, and finally toward an enemy. When you can develop the same kind of love toward all three, then you have to practice having this feeling toward all sentient beings. Eventually, when you develop the same loving-kindness for all sentient beings that a mother has for her own child, then you have achieved the proper level of loving-kindness.

It is very important to understand the difference between desire and loving-kindness. Loving-kindness is an object to be practiced; it is one of the causes for attaining Buddhahood. Desire, on the other hand, is an object to be abandoned because it is a cause of samsara. They're very different, but if you don't study, you won't be able to distinguish between them.

The Eight Benefits of Loving-Kindness

Practicing loving-kindness toward beings is a great virtue and has powerful benefit. How much virtue is there in practicing loving-kindness? Nagarjuna says in his *Precious Garland*:

> Giving three hundred plates of food
> Three times each day does not equal
> One part of the merit accumulated
> In just an instant of loving-kindness.

> Even if you don't achieve liberation, you will
> Receive the eight benefits of loving-kindness:

> (1) Gods and humans will befriend you, and
> (2) They will also protect you.
> (3) You will find joy and
> (4) Much happiness;
> (5) Poisons and
> (6) Weapons will not harm you;
> (7) You will achieve your goals effortlessly; and
> (8) You will be reborn in Brahma's realm.[20]

Let me give an example that relates to this verse. In Tibet shepherds had to carry their lunch bags with them when they went far into the fields and mountains to let their herds of yaks, *dris*,[21] sheep, and other animals graze. That lunch bag was very important to them because their homes were so far away. It would be difficult for them if they lost it. Knowing its importance, would it be a great virtue if a shepherd practiced charity by giving his lunch to another being? Of course. Even though he himself is hungry, he gives away his own lunch to another hungry being. If the shepherd did this not just once but a hundred times, he would collect a hundred times that amount of virtue. But, if you practice loving-kindness for just an instant—the amount of time it

---

[20]*Precious Garland* (*Ratnavali*), ch. 3, vv. 76–78.

[21]A *dri* is the female counterpart of the yak.

takes to snap your fingers—that virtue would be a hundred thousand times greater.

There was once a sage who was meditating on loving-kindness for all beings. Nearby there were some bad spirits and hungry ghosts who were trying to harm him because of his virtuous attitude. But by the power of his practice, they couldn't harm him. At one point, the spirits were talking among themselves right behind him. Another spirit came along and asked the others, "What are you doing?" They responded, "We've been waiting for days to harm him, but we haven't had a chance." Then the one spirit demanded, "What are you doing that for? He's always thinking about our own happiness and well-being—and still you try to harm him! That's no good!" The spirits discussed the situation with each other like that. This is a real story, not fiction. It actually happened this way. Gods, demigods, and demons can change their mental attitudes and activities toward you. They can become better, feel closer to you, and later they will even protect you. This is not only true for spirits, but for humans as well.

If you love others, of course you will not fight with them, or say harsh words; you won't harm or plan to harm them in any way. Because of this, even people who think badly of you or who harm you, will definitely change and may even become your close friends.

Some people are always unhappy. If you feel upset and unhappy, practicing loving-kindness can make you happy and calm. Not only will it make you happy, but it will bring you many other kinds of happiness as well.

Practicing loving-kindness can protect you from poisonous food, weapons, and sickness. Your mind will become noble, good, and clear, and you will succeed at whatever you do. These are among the eight good results of practicing loving-kindness.

Dharma teaches the easiest and most efficient way to collect virtue. When you've heard these crucial points, you should not forget them; try to practice them. For example, you can take notes in a class, but you can also lose them. A notebook is just a notebook. The best notebook is putting the instructions into practice. If you put them into practice, they can't get lost or burned. And later you can add to your knowledge.

STEP FIVE:
GREAT COMPASSION FOR ALL BEINGS

ষ্ণীন্হ্ট্রেক্ল্ক্ষ্ট্যা

THE MAIN CAUSE FOR gaining great compassion is to have loving-kindness for all beings with the same intensity and strength that a mother has for her child. Many people who have heard about both loving-kindness and compassion have difficulty distinguishing between them, but there is a big difference between them, like the difference between beginning and completion. Mainly, the object of love is whatever good things beings might be lacking. Loving-kindness is the mental attitude that wants beings to have everything they wish for: "They should have everything they need; how nice it would be if they could have that. They should have happiness, they should have every good thing." Compassion's object is what beings already have but don't want, that is, suffering and problems. "They shouldn't have that suffering. How nice it would be if they were free of every kind of suffering."

Therefore, compassion relates to beings in terms of what they have but don't want—suffering. Loving-kindness, on the other hand, relates to beings in terms of what they do not have but wish for—happiness. Compassion is looking upon mother beings with the attitude, "If only mother beings were free from suffering! How nice it would be if they didn't suffer!" It is wishing or willing that they be completely free of suffering. Through constant practice that compassion will at some point remain in your mind naturally. But you have to understand what "naturally" means.

If a good mother has a child who gets sick, she will worry and do everything she can to help that child—call the doctor, take him or her to the hospital, buy medicine—whatever is necessary. That attitude is completely natural for her. Nobody has to tell her, "Why don't you *do* something? Don't you have any compassion for your sick child?" Compassion arises automatically in her mind. Similarly, when we think about, see, hear, or become aware of the sufferings of all other beings and compassion arises in us to that extent and with that intensity, we have finished the fifth stage, which is compassion.

ฺ๛

QUESTION: *I didn't understand the difference between loving-kindness and compassion. Could you explain it again?*

KHEN RINPOCHE: The aim of loving-kindness is that beings have happiness and its causes. When you are practicing loving-kindness toward beings, you should think, "How nice it would be if all beings had happiness and the causes of happiness." When you hear this kind of instruction in a Dharma class, don't lose your understanding of it. You have to keep it, and then think about, study, and practice it more and more. In the future, you can hear more instructions as well. By improving your knowledge this way, you can eventually gain a more complete understanding of this subject.

The aim of compassion is that beings be free of suffering and its causes. Sentient beings are suffering all the time. Not only that, they will have to continue suffering because they have so many causes of suffering in their mind. Therefore, you are practicing compassion when you think, "I wish to free all beings of suffering and the causes of suffering."

QUESTION: *Between loving-kindness and compassion, is either one more fundamental or more important than the other?*

KHEN RINPOCHE: You have to practice the stages of each instruction in the proper order. In the Sevenfold Instruction, loving-kindness is practiced first, followed by compassion. In this system of practice, you can't gain compassion properly without first developing the loving-kindness that sees beings as precious. The loving-kindness that emphasizes the wish that beings have happiness and its causes is practiced in the system of instruction taught by Shantideva, which I will explain later. In that system, loving-kindness is practiced after compassion.[22]

> QUESTION: *When you have a lot of suffering and problems, it seems that your loving-kindness decreases and you just want to think about yourself. Is there a way to turn your suffering and problems into compassion or loving-kindness?*

KHEN RINPOCHE: There is a lot of instruction about this point. The third section of Lama Chekawa's *Seven Point Mind Training* is called "The Method of Turning Bad Experiences into Causes for Enlightenment." This instruction shows how practitioners can change problems into good causes that help them develop their compassion and loving-kindness, and especially their bodhichitta.[23]

---

[22]See pp. 96 and 102–103.
[23]This forms the Third Point of the *Seven Point Mind Training*, see p. 105 below.

STEP SIX:
EXTRAORDINARY COMPASSION FOR ALL BEINGS

ལྷག་བསམ་རྣམ་དག

THE QUALITY OF COMPASSION at the fifth
stage is a wish: "I wish all beings were free; they should be
free from their sufferings!" Just wishing that all beings be
free of suffering is not enough. The sixth stage is extraordinary compassion. More than just wishing, it is the attitude in
which you decide, "I myself will take responsibility to free
them from suffering. I must take responsibility." Hinayana
Aryas and Arhats have compassion, but not this particular
superior intention. This kind of intention is unique to the
Mahayana field. Extraordinary compassion is the direct
cause that immediately precedes bodhichitta. How quickly
you gain bodhichitta depends on the strength of this extraordinary compassion. If you make a special effort to dou-
ble or triple your extraordinary compassion, you will
achieve bodhichitta more quickly and it will be that much
stronger. If you do that, it might be the smallest thing, like
cleaning or gazing at a holy image, that could trigger the
arising of actual bodhichitta. There are many stories that describe this kind of experience.

The first line of the *Seven Point Mind Training* says, "I
prostrate to Great Compassion." While "Great Compassion"
is often used as another name for Avalokiteshvara, the deity
whose essence is all the Buddhas' compassion, in this case
Great Compassion refers instead to the compassion of Bodhisattvas who have just achieved that extraordinary compassion for the very first time. That extraordinary compassion is
so holy and so important. Because of that, there are many
places in the Sutras where Buddha declares that rather than
prostrating to the Buddhas he prostrates to that compassion.

His disciples asked him why he said that and he responded that all Buddhas are produced by that compassion.

When the great Chandrakirti composed *Entering the Middle Way*, he too prostrated to great compassion at the very beginning. Extraordinary compassion is not just a wish, but actually taking responsibility to free all beings from samsara's sufferings.

In Buddhist logic we distinguish between different types of causes. For example, when a potter makes a pot, the clay is the main cause,[24] and the potter's skill, wheel, and tools are its secondary causes. Similarly, extraordinary compassion is the main cause that comes just before bodhichitta. All six of these stages—extraordinary compassion and the other five before it—are causes of bodhichitta. There are six causes and one result in this Sevenfold Cause and Effect Instruction.

---

[24]Main cause, or *nyer len gyi rgyu*, in Buddhist philosophy is similar to the Aristotelian material cause, that is, the thing out of which an object arises. For example, the seed is the material cause of the sprout.

STEP SEVEN:
THE RESULT: BODHICHITTA

_____

བྱང་སེམས།

THE SEVENTH STAGE AND result is bodhichitta itself. You now have a basic understanding of the many processes that have to be completed in order to achieve actual bodhichitta. What exactly is this bodhichitta that is so important and difficult to practice?

The essence of bodhichitta is mind consciousness. Bodhichitta has two main features, one is that it focuses on achieving Buddhahood, while the other is that it focuses on all sentient beings for the purpose of helping and leading them out of samsara's suffering. There is a famous expression that describes bodhichitta as giving rise to the mind that is made up of two wishes.[25] The ultimate goal of both wishes is the same: to place beings in Buddhahood. But right now we don't have the power to do that. We need to develop extra ability and knowledge, which is why we need to achieve Buddhahood ourselves first, so that we can fulfill the wish of benefiting all beings in an ultimate way.

Another characteristic of bodhichitta is that if you gain it you become a Bodhisattva. The term "Bodhisattva" refers to a person who has achieved actual bodhichitta and is actively striving to achieve Buddhahood. Therefore, having bodhichitta is also what determines whether or not someone has entered the Mahayana path.

You should try to generate "temporary" bodhichitta[26] all the time. Meditating to achieve bodhichitta is not the same

_____

[25] *'dun pa gnyis ldan gyi sems bskyed.*

[26] Khen Rinpoche uses the expression "temporary" to refer to the kind of bodhichitta that requires conscious effort to generate by contemplating the instructions being presented here. This "temporary" bodhichitta is different from actual bodhichitta, which occurs effortlessly and naturally in the mind

as meditating to achieve a direct realization of emptiness. Generally, in the field of meditation, shunyata or emptiness, is considered the most difficult object to perceive. Of course it is the most profound object. You have to study and have an understanding about shunyata. Shunyata, which is one phenomenon, is the object; while your mind, a different phenomenon, is the subject. Your mind has to focus on shunyata and perceive it more and more clearly. At some point, your mind can become the subject that directly perceives its object. When that happens you have become an Arya.

The process of meditating to achieve bodhichitta is different. In this case, you are temporarily generating bodhichitta as the subject in your mind and holding Buddhahood as the object. You have to temporarily generate that bodhichitta in your mind, cultivate it, strengthen, and improve it. You do not focus on some other object. You generate bodhichitta and, using many reasons, you cultivate that mind. Therefore, the main skill in this meditation is different from that used in meditation on shunyata. I will explain this another way in relation to your own experience.

In the past everybody has gotten angry. In some cases the anger that you feel toward an object or person is very strong. Sometimes that anger arises over some small thing and for little reason. The worst anger arises in relation to your enemies—toward the people you dislike or hate. When you see those people and become more and more angry, the process is very much like the one for developing temporary bodhichitta in the sense that if you want to develop and strengthen that anger you have to reinforce it by thinking things like, "He came here today, I saw him. He hasn't died yet...I wish he would die...." You may think like this even though it's very harmful to do so. "He hurt me this year, this month, last month. Not only this year, but last year he did...and said..." There are many such cases you can think of—situations that arise at work, with your family, over

---

of a Bodhisattva. At first we have to make a conscious effort to generate bodhichitta.

wealth, and so on. Not only do you think about what was done to you, but you also think about what was done to those dear to you. "Not only did he hurt me, he hurt my family too." If you think that way, supporting your own thoughts with examples, your anger gets unbelievably strong. You get so you can't sit in your chair. You have to get up and immediately do something, say something, plan something. It even keeps you from being able to sleep at night.

This process works in the same way with other mental states. First, you generate an attitude, then you make it stronger. You can develop every kind of mind in this way. Therefore, of course, you can also generate temporary bodhichitta—you can improve and strengthen it.

These are all the points in the Sevenfold Instruction for generating bodhichitta. After gaining it, you have to maintain that mind without letting it degenerate until you achieve Buddhahood. How do you do that? You have to practice two sets of causes. The first set includes four points to help you maintain bodhichitta in this life. The second set includes points to prevent you from losing it in future lives.

Maintaining Bodhichitta in This Life

The first of the four crucial causes that keeps you from damaging your bodhichitta in this life is to review the ten benefits of bodhichitta that I described already. There are also many Sutras and books that you can read to help you understand the value of bodhichitta.

The second is to rededicate yourself to bodhichitta at least six times each day. If you learn everything you need to practice, there is no problem. The only problem is laziness. The practice is not the problem.

The third crucial cause is not to allow yourself to forget or abandon the sentient beings in relation to whom you have generated bodhichitta; remember that all your activities are intended to benefit them.

The main obstacle that will come is to think, "This instruction is too difficult. I don't think I can achieve this. Even if I try, can I achieve it? It's almost impossible." Of course you can achieve it. Logicians can easily give you the reason why. You can gain bodhichitta because it is an entity produced by causes. It is a general principle of all composed things that if their causes gather together they can be produced. Therefore, if you collect all the causes through your practice, why couldn't you generate bodhichitta? Actually, right now is the best opportunity you have ever had to practice this instruction. If you had had such a chance before, you would be a Bodhisattva by now. Therefore, you shouldn't waste the opportunity that you have in your hands right now because you might not have it again in the future.

The fourth cause is to gather the two accumulations of merit and wisdom each day in order to increase your bodhichitta.

Maintaining Bodhichitta in Future Lives

The second set of causes relates to maintaining bodhichitta throughout your future lives. They include avoiding the four "black" activities that damage bodhichitta and practicing four "white" activities that keep it from being damaged. The first of the black causes is to deceive your Lama, teacher, abbot, or other knowledgeable persons by lying. The second black deed is to cause a person to regret some virtuous thing they have done. The third black cause is to speak disrespectfully to another Bodhisattva out of hatred. The fourth is to behave in a deceptive or misleading way toward others rather than in an honest and straightforward way.

The first of the "white" causes that increase bodhichitta is to avoid intentionally telling a lie, whether to save your life or even as a joke. The second is to be honest toward all beings and avoid being deceptive or misleading. The third is to regard all Bodhisattvas as the Buddha. Actually, there is a difference between Buddhas and Bodhisattvas. Buddhas have achieved the highest status. Although Bodhisattvas haven't achieved that status yet, their activities and motivation are similar to those of the Buddhas. For that reason, we should have the attitude and belief that Bodhisattvas for us are like real Buddhas. The fourth white cause is to lead whatever followers you may have to the Mahayana Dharma from the beginning, rather than to the Listeners' or Solitary Realizers' vehicle.

༄༅། །ཐེག་པ་ཆེན་པོའི་བློ་སྦྱོང་དོན་བདུན་མ། །

Part II

Oral Commentary on Lama Chekawa's *Seven Point Mind Training*

SEVEN POINT MIND TRAINING

THE ABOVE PRACTICE OF the Sevenfold Cause and Effect Instruction is one of the methods of achieving bodhichitta taught by the great Lama Serlingpa, and one of two great rivers that make up Lojong practice. The other river of instruction, as I mentioned, was taught by Buddha, passed to Mañjushri, to Shantideva, and eventually to Lama Serlingpa, who taught it to Lama Atisha. From him it passed through the lineage of Lamas to Je Tsongkapa, who then passed it through our Lineage Lamas down to the present.

From the time that Lama Atisha taught it in Tibet and for several generations of Kadampa Lamas, only the Sevenfold Cause and Effect Instruction was taught openly; this second river of instructions, the *Seven Point Mind Training*, was taught secretly to special students. These special students would in turn only teach it to their special students. Lama Atisha taught it secretly to the great Lama Dromtönpa.

Although Lama Dromtönpa taught the Lamrim openly to whomever wanted to come and listen, he taught this second set of Lojong instructions secretly to Geshe Potowa, among a few others. Geshe Potowa was a very famous, great sage and scholar who lived in the period after Lama Atisha and before Je Tsongkapa. Geshe Potowa taught this second instruction to his two great disciples, Langri Tangpa Dorje Senge and Sharawa.

Langri Tangpa Dorje Senge was a great and well-known sage. His previous incarnations included some of the greatest and best-known pandits of India: Chandrakirti, Shantarakshita, and Atisha. Shantarakshita was a great pandit who went to Tibet from India thirteen hundred years ago. There he established the monastic system, bestowing monk's vows and ordaining the first monks in Tibet. He was a great scholar of the Madhyamaka school system and wrote many commentaries on Madhyamaka.

Dorje Senge composed the great and well-known *Lojong Tsik Gyema*, or *Mind Training in Eight Verses*. My Root Lama, Kyabje Trijang Rinpoche Lobsang Yeshe, was himself the reincarnation of those great Lamas: Chandrakirti, Shantarakshita, Atisha, and Langri Tangpa Dorje Senge.

During Langri Tangpa Dorje Senge's and Sharawa's time there was another great sage named Chekawa, who at one point heard of Dorje Senge's eight-verse text on Mind Training. He traveled a great distance to central Tibet in search of Langri Tangpa to request that instruction from him, but by the time he arrived Langri Tangpa had already passed away. Lama Chekawa did meet the great Sharawa, however, who himself had also received all the Mind Training instructions from Geshe Potowa.

After practicing these instructions intensely, Chekawa gained actual bodhichitta. Later, he taught these instructions openly, feeling that if such a holy practice were kept secret, it would eventually disappear from the world. He felt that it would be a great loss for so many scholars and Dharma practitioners not to be able to hear it, so he decided to teach it to the public. Ever since then, this teaching system has spread to many scholars and practitioners.

If you don't have at least a rough knowledge of where these teachings come from a problem can arise. For example, in the past there was a rumor that has nowadays more or less disappeared. A rumor is just a rumor—it comes from a person who knows nothing about the real nature or situation of an object but makes up an idea about it, which starts a rumor. That rumor went something like this: "In India, Buddhist teaching and practice is real Buddhism, but in Tibet, what they call Buddhism is really Lamaism."

That idea came from people who didn't know how Dharma was passed down or through whom it was transmitted, and who didn't understand about the lineage of Lamas—that Dharma has been passed from Buddha Shakyamuni in an unbroken lineage down to the present. Therefore, understanding the origin and transmission of these instructions is very important.

Because of Chekawa's decision to teach this instruction openly, this second set of instructions was written down in the form of seven categories that are known as *Lojong Dön Dunma* or *Seven Point Mind Training*.

FIRST POINT:
PRELIMINARIES

THE FIRST OF THE seven points or sections of the *Seven Point Mind Training* prepares practitioners for the main practice to achieve bodhichitta. Scholars referred to this first section as the four preliminary practices or *ngöndro chö shi*, which are to contemplate 1) leisure and fortune, 2) impermanence in the form of death, 3) taking refuge, which includes considering the faults of samsara, and 4) karma and its results.[27]

Leisure and Fortune

The first preliminary practice, leisure and fortune, corresponds to the second topic of the Lamrim teachings. The first topic in the Lamrim is called How to Entrust Yourself to a Lama. This topic is not one of the four preliminary practices, but rather the foundation of all the paths and a main practice from the beginning of the path up to the highest stages of Tantric practice. Here the four preliminaries are preparations for the main practice of generating bodhichitta.

The first of the four preparations is to contemplate our leisure and fortune, which is to realize the excellent qualities of this human life. After learning and studying about it, we have to think constantly about the great value of human life. For example, we were not born as hell beings, hungry ghosts, or animals. We are free; they are not—they have no time at all or opportunity to study, to entrust themselves to a Lama, to attend Dharma teachings, to listen to Dharma, to

---

[27]Kyabje Trijang Rinpoche includes all the preliminary topics for both lower capacity and medium capacity practitioners in his word commentary to the *Seven Point Mind Training*. In this particular teaching, Khen Rinpoche emphasized the more basic Buddhist practice of taking refuge over that of considering samsara's bad qualities as the third preliminary.

practice Dharma—they can do none of these things; they don't have a chance. But we have every opportunity and that is what "leisure" means here.

Nor were we born in the god realms. Gods are constantly enjoying samsara's happiness until they exhaust their accumulated merit. When that merit is used up and they pass away, they are forced to go straight down to the hells.

We human beings have wisdom; if we do everything nicely, perfectly, we can gain correct or right view. Right view is the main instrument to cut through *dakdzin*, or grasping at inherent existence, which is the root of samsara. To cut through that ignorance you must have a sharp weapon, which is right view, or wisdom. We can study it, learn about it, and we have the ability to gain it. We also have perfectly functioning sense powers; we can see, hear, smell, taste, and feel.

Buddha appeared in this world and the Dharma system he taught still exists. We too can find a good Dharma teacher, and, if we find one, we can listen, study, think, and practice. We have the ability to do all of this and we have all of these good qualities. Therefore, we have to realize the extraordinary value and quality of this human life.

Once we realize how valuable, holy, and useful our human life is, we shouldn't waste it. We have to try to do something meaningful with it. In order to reach the goal, we have to resolve not to waste this holy human being's life: "I must do something, I must achieve some kind of goal." The best goal is Buddhahood, and we should think, "Even if I cannot achieve Buddhahood, I must at least try to achieve the Bodhisattva paths." After making that decision, we should think, "Now I have to do something."

Impermanence

Usually you think, "Today I will do something, I have to do something." Tomorrow you think, "I have to do something." A week goes by, then a month, then a year; more and more time goes by, then you wonder, "When will I do something?" You have to start right now!

Why? At this point you have to go on to the second of the four preliminaries, which is to think about the uncertainty of how long we will live. None of us knows whether we will be around tomorrow morning. Will I make it until then? Until next month? Next year? Seven more years? Ten more years? Twelve more years? Nobody knows. You can't be sure. Everybody is in the same situation. After thinking about the fact that our life may not be long and that we have no certainty about when it will end, we must decide to start practicing right away. These points relate to the second preliminary practice.

Taking Refuge

After you have made the decision to start practicing right away, what is the next step? The starting point is to take refuge. The unerring savior, the object of taking refuge, is the Three Jewels—the Buddha, Dharma, and Sangha. Take refuge in them.

What is the purpose of going for refuge in the Three Jewels? "To save myself and all beings because we are suffering—we are in a dangerous situation. Please save us. You are an unerring savior." That mind, that trust, that belief, is taking refuge. If you have that belief, you are Buddhist; if you don't, you are not Buddhist. Even if you wear monk's robes, if you don't have that belief you are not a Buddhist; the robes are the robes. If you are wearing suit pants and a shirt but you have that faith, you are a Buddhist. Taking refuge is part of the third preliminary practice.

Karma

If you go for refuge to the Buddha, Dharma, and Sangha, of course you have to follow their instructions properly. In general, their instructions are that you should not do improper activities by body, speech, or mind, but instead always try to do good things. Those are the main instructions. Once you take refuge, there are more specific instructions regarding what you should and shouldn't do.[28] Gradually, you must learn all of these.

To summarize, the first of these four practices is to realize the excellent qualities of our human being's life. The second is to think about the uncertainty of how long we will live. We have to check into this, realize it, and then start learning, studying, and practicing Dharma right now. The third point is that all Buddhist practice and knowledge is based on taking refuge. The fourth point is that if you go for refuge to the Buddha, Dharma, and Sangha, you have to keep their instructions. In the Dharma field, these instructions relate to *lendre*, which means karma's system of cause and effect. We have to study and observe karma's system. We have to try not to do improper activities and do those that are proper. Keeping the Dharma system nicely is included in this point. If you know these four, you have finished the first point or section of the *Seven Point Mind Training*, which covers the preparations for achieving bodhichitta. Once you know them well, you can go on to the second point.

---

[28]For a list of these please refer to *Liberation in Our Hands*, *Part Two*, Day 12, pages 220–226, trans. by Sermey Khensur Rinpoche Lobsang Tharchin with Artemus B. Engle. See bibliography.

SECOND POINT:
THE MAIN INSTRUCTION ON HOW TO
PRACTICE BODHICHITTA

T HE FOCUS OF THE second of the seven sections or points in the *Seven Point Mind Training* is the main instruction on how to practice bodhichitta. Bodhichitta is so holy. Many Sutras mention that from the time you generate it, all of your activities, whether you are sleeping, walking, talking, eating or working, turn into great virtues, which is a great benefit for us. To be motivated by temporary bodhichitta is extremely valuable, especially when listening to holy instructions on how to cultivate actual bodhichitta and how to maintain it throughout all your activities once you've developed it.

Buddha taught many levels of Dharma because of the many different levels of his disciples. If there are sixty people, there must also be sixty different aspirations, levels, and abilities. These teachings are mostly about a Bodhisattva's daily activities, which are unusual and great. Some Bodhisattva activities are so unusual that we aren't even ready to hear the words that describe them, much less are we able to practice them.

But what should you do when you are learning about them in class? Bodhisattva activities are so great, so unusual, so wonderful—all Buddhas achieved Buddhahood by practicing and completing these activities. Present Bodhisattvas will also achieve Buddhahood by practicing this way. You have to realize, "I know myself and my level. Right now I cannot actually or directly practice such holy and difficult activities. But some time very soon I wish to be able to practice these." This is how we should pray when we listen to teachings on such great, holy paths and holy Bodhisattva activities.

On the other hand, you should not think: "Oh no! These instructions are too difficult, I can't practice them. I have to go my own way." That is a big obstacle. Instead, try to practice the way I have explained. As beginners, we won't be able to do such holy activities because we do not yet have enough ability. But we should think, "May I try very hard to improve myself so that I can eventually practice these holy activities." Pray to the Lama, Buddha, Dharma, and Sangha: "Please help me, please bless me to be able to do this."

Earlier I described the first of the two great rivers of instruction on generating bodhichitta called the Sevenfold Cause and Effect Instruction. By practicing that instruction, you can develop temporary bodhichitta in your mind right now. Temporary bodhichitta is the mind consciousness that wants to achieve Buddhahood for the purpose of helping all mother beings. That mind is your temporary bodhichitta. You must try to develop and strengthen it. I gave you the example of how anger develops and gets stronger. Here you will be using this same method, but instead you will be developing and strengthening your bodhichitta.

In Lojong teachings the main instruction follows the second method to generate bodhichitta, which was originally kept secret and taught only to unique disciples. That instruction is called Equalizing and Exchanging Self and Others. The second section of the *Seven Point Mind Training* gives the actual method for generating bodhichitta using this approach.

Section two has five parts: 1) recognizing that self and others are the same, 2) thinking in many ways about the faults of self-cherishing mind or selfishness, 3) thinking in many ways about the benefits of cherishing others, 4) the actual practice of exchanging self and others, and 5) the practice of *tonglen* or Giving and Taking.

Recognizing That Self and Others Are the Same

The first of the five parts relates to Equalizing Self and Others, which means thinking of self and others as the same. In this practice you have to constantly think, "There is no difference between myself and others." If you don't learn this correctly you might think it is silly to say that there is no difference between oneself and others. You will think, "But there are differences; we can see differences." For example, you may be very big and tall, but I am very short and small. We can see that's a big difference, but still I say that there is no difference between us. What I mean is that you and I are in the same position or situation in the sense of wanting to be happy and not wanting to suffer.

You and I and all beings everywhere wish to be happy; none of us wants to suffer. Our wishes and goals and position are the same. So why do we still distinguish between ourselves and others? Doing that reveals a certain quality— that you are neither a real sage nor a good practitioner. Equalizing Self and Others means thinking and focusing on the situations, qualities, and wishes of beings. We are all the same in the sense of wishing for happiness and wanting to be free from suffering. Given that, it is silly if you still distinguish among beings. Therefore, we have to think again and again that we and others are the same in terms of wishing to be happy and not wanting suffering and problems.

Above I gave you instructions that when you are meditating on a specific subject you have to do practices in order to gradually collect virtue. You must also purify your bad deeds. You have to collect virtue and do purification as much as you can. These two are like watering and fertilizing your crops; they can grow better and faster. Similarly, through the power of collecting virtue and removing negative karma, you can suddenly have realizations that you didn't previously have or that you thought you couldn't gain.

After your mind has improved and become used to viewing all beings as having the same wish, you have to try to exchange self for others. You have to learn the meaning and not forget it; nor should you mix it with other ideas.

"Exchange" here means to shift your mental attitude. You have to think, "Up until now, my mental attitude has been only to care about myself, always thinking only of my own purposes. From now on, I will change my mind to think of other beings' purposes, cherishing others and ignoring my own purposes. Now I am going to switch positions." You have to start this practice with small situations and continue on to greater and greater ones. That's the meaning of "exchange" in this context. If you don't learn the meaning, you will not understand what is being exchanged.

Dakshen nyamje (Equalizing and Exchanging Self and Others) is a Tibetan term that combines dakshen nyampa, (Equalizing Self and Others), and dakshen jewa, (Exchanging Self and Others). So you start by thinking that self and others are the same, and then exchange or switch the mental attitude from concern for self to concern for others.

Thinking in Many Ways about the Faults of Self-Cherishing Mind

The second part of this second point is very important. First you have to recognize what self-cherishing mind is and then learn about its faults or bad qualities.

Some points are too difficult and unusual; even the words are beyond us. Some of you will feel, "This is silly...I'm not going to do this." There are those who think that behaving according to these instructions is cowardly or foolish. But that's not the case at all.

This Dharma center is called Milarepa Center. If you look at a painting of Milarepa, he is usually depicted as very beautiful, very nice. Actually though, he lived in a cave in Tibet. He didn't eat food nicely—he ate just enough to survive. He stayed in that cave and practiced constantly. When people happened to see him, they would say "Oh, you poor, pitiful thing!". And Milarepa would say, "It's you who are pitiful!" Passersby would talk to him from their own worldly perspective while Milarepa was seeing everything from a transcendent point of view.

The Panchen Lama Lobsang Chökyi Gyaltsen, the most famous and scholarly among the lineage of Panchen Lamas, wrote in Honoring the Lamas (Lama Chöpa):

Bless me to recognize that the chronic disease of
Cherishing myself is the source of all unwanted
    suffering,
And by blaming and resenting it,
Bless me to destroy the great demon of selfishness.[29]

Selfish mind is the worst disease. With ordinary illnesses, if you get a good doctor and good medicine, you can
be cured. But this sickness of self-cherishing has been with
us from beginningless time up to now, like a chronic illness.
When you have a chronic illness, you get all kinds of problems, one after the other. Similarly, selfishness has remained
in our mind almost permanently, resulting in samsara's
chronic problems. First, the selfish mind collects the karmic
seeds; later, that mind invites those seeds' result, which is
suffering. All the bad deeds that we collect are rooted in our
selfish mind. The results of those bad deeds are every single
one of our problems, sicknesses, and the bad experiences we
don't like—every such situation comes from our own selfishness.

When you have a worldly enemy and you think that all
of your problems are caused by him, you blame him. In Lojong practice, you can never blame other beings at all. Instead, you have to blame your own selfish mind: "That selfishness did it! That is what created it. That is what collected
the seeds. That is what produced the results. That is what
caused these bad experiences, this suffering." Therefore, if
you want to blame anyone, blame your own selfishness. As
the great Shantideva said:

All those who suffer in the world
Do so because they want happiness for themselves.[30]

and,

<hr />

[29]The *Lama Chöpa* contains a section of Mind Training verses relating to the
Sutrayana and Tantrayana paths. This is verse 8 of that section.
[30]*Engaging in Bodhisattva Activities*, ch. 8, v. 129.

Whatever hardship there is in the world,
However much suffering and fear,
They all come from clinging to self;
What use is this demon for me?[31]

The meaning of these verses is the same as the Panchen Lama's verse above, which is that all worldly sufferings and every kind of harm that you experience are the result of your own selfishness.

The mind that grasps at things as inherently existent (*dakdzin*) and the self-cherishing mind (*dak che dzin*) are like a king and his minister. They are similar attitudes and both have harmful effects. Therefore, both grasping at an inherently existent self and selfish mind are the worst kind of demons. Why wouldn't I want to get rid of them? Why am I keeping them in my mind? Although the self-cherishing mind and the mind that grasps at things as self-existent are different mental derivatives, Je Tsongkapa wrote in one of his Tantric commentaries that self-cherishing mind can be thought of as a form of grasping at things as self-existent.

As Geshe Chekawa's *Seven Point Mind Training* says, "All blame rests with one." This means that you should blame all your suffering and problems on your own selfishness.

For example, say that suddenly and for no apparent reason someone attacks you. This happens all the time. There are countless ways this can occur, with someone using a knife or a gun, or other weapons or different poisons. Sometimes accidents are related to the influence of demons or bad spirits. When those things happen we think, "What caused that?" We check for visible causes, but we don't think of the influence of demons and bad spirits. Actually though, their activity and their motivation are always to harm other beings. They constantly try to harm us, for example, by making us have a sudden accident. All of these bad situations and bad results, including bad lives—the lives of hell beings,

---

[31]*Ibid.*, ch. 8, v. 134.

hungry ghosts, and animals—are directly related to self-cherishing mind.

It often happens that in a war where many people are fighting and shooting each other, some are not killed. When they think about their survival after the fighting stops, they are shocked: "How did I manage to survive that? Such fighting, shooting, bombing, and still I didn't die. I'm alive. Impossible!" Some die even before the main fighting has begun or just as it is starting. All of these situations are a function of self-cherishing mind. In the same way, when people are served poisoned food, some get sick and others don't. This is also related to selfish mind.

Killing or taking another being's life is a natural bad deed, which means that you automatically collect negative karma just by doing it. It is not a rule made by Buddha: "Do not do it; if you do, you are breaking your vows," or "You will collect bad deeds." Deeds that are related to a rule are called *chepa*.[32] But taking another being's life is a natural bad deed that does not rely on a rule. By killing you automatically collect bad karma.

The same is true of stealing and sexual misconduct. These three are the worst bad deeds done by body. The most powerful natural bad deeds done by speech are telling lies, divisive speech, harsh words, and gossiping. The natural bad deeds done by mind are: covetousness, ill will, and wrong view. These ten are the natural bad deeds.

Among these bad deeds, killing or taking another being's life has many levels. The first level is to kill another being unwillingly. Sometimes you have to kill another being, almost without choice. But it is still a natural bad deed. Among the levels of having taken a life, doing so unwillingly is the lightest in terms of negative karma collected. As a result of having done it, you will be born in the animal realm. If you kill a person or take another being's life out of

---

[32]Buddhist ethics distinguishes between two basic kinds of bad deeds: those that are innately or naturally wrong (*rang bzshin gyi kha na ma tho ba*), for example, the ten nonvirtuous deeds of killing, stealing, lying and so forth, and those that are wrong in that Buddha prohibited them (*bcas pa'i kha na ma tho ba*).

anger, the negative karma you collect is heavier. As a result, you have to be reborn in the hungry ghost realm. The worst is to prepare to kill, using a method intended to cause your victim the heaviest suffering, and then to rejoice about it after having taken that life, thinking, "Now I succeeded, now I'm free," or something like that. Those are the heaviest bad deeds and, as a result, you have to be reborn in one of the hell realms.

We have done all manner of harm to other beings. In previous lives we gave poisonous food to destroy other beings who were our enemies or whom we didn't like. We have done many things, all of which were directly related to our self-cherishing mind. Selfish mind wants you to save and protect yourself while either ignoring the situations of others or actively trying to harm them. Because of these activities, we have collected many different types of bad deeds on many levels, and have experienced many different kinds of suffering, one after another. All of these activities are rooted in our selfish mind. For this reason it is the worst of all demons.

If you came across a demon, maybe he could harm you, make you sick, or even kill you. But if he did kill you, he has taken only one of your lives. On the other hand, the inner demon of self-cherishing mind will cut the very life force of all the Mahayana knowledges from the beginningless past up to Buddhahood. Therefore, in the scriptures this mental attitude is called the Great Demon of Selfishness. Therefore, this self-cherishing mind is the most powerful, most harmful demon, and it is still in our mind. We have to realize it. There are many examples in the scriptures, but here I've given you all the crucial points. You should pray to the Lamas and the Three Jewels, "Please bless me and help me to destroy my great demon, this self-cherishing mind."

Because we live in society and always have to associate with others—whether we are working or studying—it is very important to understand that among beings there will always be those who are financially better off than we are, those who are at about our same level, and those who are much poorer. The same is true with regard to education;

there are those who are better off, similar to us, or worse off. Physically, some have more dignity, more beauty, some are similar to us, and others are worse off.

We can meet with any one of these situations wherever we go and whomever we associate with; they are very close at hand. What do we think of when we associate with others? What will our worst demon do? If the other person has some special quality, higher knowledge, skill, or distinction, our selfish mind will almost automatically produce jealousy. If we meet a person who is at about the same level as us, you'd think that our reaction would be a little better but still it is not, because selfishness will make us competitive, racing to see who gets ahead. If we meet someone who, in terms of education, wealth, skill, status, and so on, is worse off than we are, in the best case we will ignore such a person and in the worst we will put him or her down.

Therefore, whenever we associate with others, that self-cherishing mind produces jealousy and competitiveness, and causes us to ignore or put others down. If we are jealous of another person, we collect bad deeds and we will have to experience the result. We create a bad relationship with those people. Karma's system is infallible. At some point the karma of that relationship comes around and we will experience the exact same thing. Such relationships and their results are all rooted to the selfishness in our mind. The holy Shantideva said,

> Throughout countless eons
> You have sought your own ends,
> And through such great effort
> You've achieved only suffering.[33]

Lord Shantideva is saying, "Self-cherishing, you are the worst of demons that stays in my mind. For many eons you have tried to bring me happiness and protection, but instead you bring nothing but problems and suffering." If you really want to achieve happiness and peace, the first crucial thing

---

[33]*Engaging in Bodhisattva Activities*, ch. 8, v. 155.

to do is to subdue your selfish mind. Try to abandon it. That is the instruction.

I have given a brief presentation here, but there are many more explanations about this instruction. If you really want to practice this, you have to go deeply into the subject and learn it in as much detail as you can using as many explanations as possible. No matter how long it takes—a week, two weeks, a month—you have to practice continually or until you gain that knowledge firmly. At least try to practice this subject with some regularity on weekends or when you have free time until you get a sign of having that knowledge. Only then can you receive more instruction and go on to the next step.

Here, at this teaching, I am presenting all of the instructions at once. In the future, you have to try to find a good time to practice these instructions. Even if you cannot practice them right away, you have to keep wishing to be able to do so, as I mentioned earlier. You shouldn't give up this wish even though it is a difficult practice. "Right now, I can't do it, but I wish I could. I pray that I will definitely be able to practice these instructions as soon as possible."

Have you ever seen that car commercial for the 280ZX? A little boy on his bicycle comes up to the car and says, "Wow! ZX! Wow! Someday, someday! Mmm..." I saw that commercial and thought, "That is very good. He can't buy it right away, but he is making a wish, and like a prayer, he says, "Someday, someday! Mmm...'" Therefore, you have to say about this subject "Mmm! Wow! Someday!" You shouldn't give up your wish and prayer.

Thinking in Many Ways about the Benefits of Cherishing Others

The third part of this second section is to study the good qualities of caring about or cherishing others. I've already told you about the bad qualities, functions, and results of the self-cherishing mind. Now you have to study and think about the mind that cherishes others and remember its good qualities and results. In relation to this, the holy Shantideva said,

> All those who are happy in the world
> Are so because they want happiness for others.[34]

In relation to caring about others, the holy Shantideva says in his *Engaging in Bodhisattva Activities* that both worldly and transcendent happiness come from cherishing other beings.

What does worldly happiness mean? While hell beings are constantly suffering, always experiencing being burnt, cut, and tortured, we human beings can live in a house, sleep on a comfortable bed, wear good clothes, and if we want to go somewhere in a car, we can arrange to do so. We can enjoy these things. Enjoying such things is samsara's happiness and what is meant by worldly happiness.

There is a big difference between worldly and transcendent happiness. Samsaric happiness is only happiness when compared with the tortures of the lower realms. Because it is samsaric, that happiness is mixed with sufferings and problems. Therefore, that kind of happiness is impure. Transcendent happiness is the happiness of nirvana and Buddhahood. There is a big difference between these two kinds of happiness; one is impure and the other completely pure.

The Three Levels of Motivation

You should know this for your daily practice. You can offer a pot of beautiful flowers to the Three Jewels, praying, "May I not get sick, may I not have problems, may I succeed in my every wish, and may I have a long life...." The purpose of that kind of prayer is for this life only. In the field of Buddhism, that prayer does not count for any virtue because its motivation is directed to this life's happiness. In the Dharma field, deeds done for this life's happiness are not virtue.

---

[34]*Ibid.*, ch. 8, v. 129.

In the field of Buddhism, there are three levels of motivation. The lowest form is directed toward achieving a good future life, for example, to think, "I have attained this excellent human being's life. Now I am getting old; maybe I will die very soon; I wish to have a good future life. Three Jewels, please give me your blessings, please give me the power to have this." The virtue that comes from offering a pot of flowers with that motivation turns into the lowest level of virtue in the field of Buddhism. It turns into samsara's virtue, which is impure, because a samsaric human being's life is an impure life. Therefore, you are praying for the same kind of life for the future.

Now, when you are motivated by renunciation and offer this pot of flowers to the Buddha, Dharma, and Sangha, thinking: "I'm tired of being in the world like this, always changing and suffering. I really want to be free from this cycle of suffering," you collect virtue that is pure. But it is of a medium level. The virtue of offering the pot of flowers motivated by renunciation for samsara's suffering turns into the virtue that leads to the Hinayana path's nirvana.

Another way to offer that pot of flowers is to think, "I'm suffering in this world and now I am tired. But all mother beings are still suffering in samsara too. I want very much to liberate them and place them in Buddhahood, the highest happiness. Please bless me; please give me the power to do this." Offering that pot of flowers to the Buddha, Dharma, and Sangha with that motivation yields the highest virtue in the Buddhist field, which is Mahayana virtue. If you have this knowledge and skill, your activity—in this case offering a single pot of flowers—might be the same, but by the power of the mental attitude or intention that accompanies the act you collect virtue in a completely different way. The Mahayana way is immeasurable because its object—all sentient beings—is immeasurable. Therefore, try to practice this way; it is very useful for you.

ཉྫ

QUESTION: *You mentioned that doing virtuous activities for the benefit of all sentient beings is greater virtue than doing those activities for yourself. Are activities done for yourself still virtue? Is it just that they are less virtuous than doing them for others?*

KHEN RINPOCHE: The Dharma teaches that activities done to bring yourself happiness in this life are not virtue at all. However, there is a big difference between self-cherishing mind and doing things to benefit yourself. The wish to benefit yourself can start from now and continue all the way to Buddhahood. For example, you can offer a flower to the Three Jewels for the purpose of freeing both yourself and others from samsara. Therefore, your own purpose is included there. That is not self-cherishing mind. Self-cherishing mind is an attitude that completely ignores other beings and always thinks only about your own purpose. The motivation for that attitude is related to desire, wanting to get better things, more things, larger things—like that.

ཉྫ

Another quotation from the Panchen Lama's *Honoring the Lamas*, says:

Having realized that caring for
All mother beings and wanting them to be happy
Is the door to infinite good qualities,
Please bless me to cherish them more than I do
    my own life,
Even if they were to turn against me as my
    enemies.[35]

---

[35]Verse 9; see note 29 above.

What are the characteristics of the mind that cherishes others? It is a mind that has love for all beings and wants very much to place them in a state of lasting happiness. Here, that mind is described as the main door that gives us access to worldly and transcendent happiness.

All the happiness in samsara and beyond samsara comes from the mind that cherishes other beings. Therefore, think, "Even if all the people in this city or in this country were to rise up against me, from my side I will never lose my love for them, nor will I lose my attitude of cherishing them." This is the instruction. It is very difficult to practice. When you are confronted with an actual situation, you have to practice thinking this way. In the Buddhist field, especially the Mahayana Bodhisattva field, this attitude is perfect and great. But from a worldly perspective it might seem foolish. People might think, "He has no brains."

This life's happiness, any hope for future lives' happiness, Bodhisattvas' ability to serve other beings, along with all their other activities on the Bodhisattva levels, all the knowledge, power, and goodness once we achieve Buddhahood, come from cherishing other beings. Therefore, always think of other beings.

As the *Seven Point Mind Training* says, "Meditate on the great kindness of all beings." The words of the root text here are a little bit hard to comprehend. Why should you think that all beings are very kind? First you need to understand that actions have three aspects: the subject or doer, the act or action, and the object of the action, that is, the object in relation to whom the action is done. Without a subject, an action, and an object you cannot complete a single activity. When practicing to cherish other beings, *you* are the subject, your *caring* is the action, and *all sentient beings* are the object. Without all beings you cannot complete that activity. Therefore, every being is incredibly kind and helpful in allowing you to complete these activities. The holy Shantideva said,

Why go on about it?
Notice the difference

Between the fool bent on his own well-being
And the Buddha who acts to benefit others.[36]

There are many, many quotations, good reasons, examples, and stories about this. Briefly, compare yourself to Buddha and then judge for yourself. What is the difference between Buddha and you? Buddha doesn't have any obstacles, problems, suffering, or impure qualities because he completely abandoned all of them. He has also achieved complete knowledge, wisdom, compassion, power, and activity. He has perfected all of these. "How did he do it? Why don't I have the slightest bit of any of these qualities?" Buddha achieved these qualities because he practiced cherishing other beings for many eons. We, on the other hand, have been caring only for ourselves from beginningless time and, because of that, we are still living in the same way, remaining at the same level. By checking and examining, we must change our activity and motivation from caring for ourselves to caring for others. That is the instruction for thinking about the benefits of cherishing others.

The Actual Practice of Exchanging Self and Others

The fourth point of the *Seven Point Mind Training* is the practice of actually exchanging or shifting your mental attitude. At this point, you have realized all the bad qualities of the self-cherishing mind and all the good qualities of cherishing other beings. Because of that, you have to decide, "I am going to change my mind's focus. In the past I have always considered myself as most important and ignored others. Now I'm going to switch positions. I will try to produce and maintain an attitude of giving importance to other beings while ignoring my own purposes." Practicing that, changing your mind that way, is the actual exchanging mind.

---

[36]*Ibid.*, ch. 8, v. 130.

"Exchanging mind" doesn't mean that the other being turns into you or that you turn into the other being. What it means is that your own mental attitude shifts; you exchange the focus and quality of your mind. At first it's a little bit difficult, but if you try, at some point you can definitely change your motivation, your ideas, and your thinking. When the mental attitude switches completely, instead of always thinking about yourself and ignoring other beings, you will constantly think about others and ignore your own purposes. This is the actual "exchanging mind" that you need to develop.

ཉ

QUESTION: When you were speaking about exchanging self and others, you said something about switching from a self-cherishing attitude to one of cherishing others, that we should attend to others' purposes and ignore our own purposes. Could you explain more about what this means?

KHEN RINPOCHE: You have to change perspectives. You should think, "Previously, my attitude was to cherish myself and ignore other beings. Now I am going to change. I am going to ignore my own purposes and cherish other beings." Shantideva, Lord Atisha, and those great Lamas kept this teaching secret, because if you can't learn this instruction in a proper and balanced way, your reaction might be, "Oh, this practice is impossible. I can't do it. Nobody can do it." Some Bodhisattva activities are so unbelievable that you may find them difficult to accept if you don't study the whole set of instructions. However, after learning the whole set of instructions, you can start at whatever point is appropriate to your level. You will not experience any problems whatsoever!

ཉ

The Practice of Tonglen,
or Giving and Taking

After you have changed your mental attitude, quality, and focus, you have to practice *tonglen*, or Giving and Taking, which is the fifth category. The word "tonglen" appears in many texts. *Tonglen* means Giving (*tong*) and Taking (*len*). Although the order of the syllables in this compound noun has Giving first, followed by Taking, the order of the actual practice is reversed. In relation to this, whenever there is a very crucial point involving actual practice, you need to receive instructions on it from teachers or Lamas. The Lamas' instructions for the actual practice of *tonglen* is that you have to reverse the order indicated by the syllables and do the *len* or Taking practice first, followed by the *tong* or Giving practice.[37]

Why? If somebody brings a bunch of fresh flowers, and I want to keep those flowers in this vase, first I have to get rid of the old ones and then put the new ones in. Similarly, in the world, all mother beings are experiencing samsara's general suffering and each realm's unique sufferings. They experience these constantly. If you try to give them happiness without first taking those sufferings from them, there is almost no way for them to enjoy that happiness.

For example, if someone is very sick and you bring him or her a good meal, and say, "Please eat," that person will say, "No, please take it away, please leave me alone...." Therefore, first you have to take away the suffering those beings experience. If you don't know what kind of suffering you have to take from them, your meditation and practice won't be perfect. There are general sufferings and sufferings that are unique to each particular realm.

---

[37]The instruction presented here follows this particular lineage tradition. There are others that describe a different order.

The Three Kinds of Suffering

There are three kinds of general suffering in samsara: the suffering of suffering, the suffering of change, and the suffering of conditioned existence, or pervasive suffering that covers all of samsara.

Suffering is samsara's nature, that is basic. There is no pure happiness in samsara because conditioned existence is suffering. Given that, if you get sick, another kind of suffering has occurred. That is the suffering of suffering and all six realms within the desire realm have it. It is a general suffering.

The suffering of change means that even though sometimes you may feel samsara's happiness, that happiness can quickly change into suffering. So even samsara's general happiness has the quality of suffering. Its quality of suffering is that one cannot remain in happiness very long because that happiness quickly changes into suffering. For example, when you get hungry you get a special suffering of hunger. If you eat some food and drink something, for the moment you will enjoy it and be satisfied, but later that happiness changes. Your stomach might get so upset that you have to find some Alka-Seltzer or Tums. Those are temporary medicines for the suffering of change. If you feel hot, you want to arrange something that will make you cool. First you feel cool and pleasant, and then you immediately need a shirt, a little clothing, or something to keep you warm. Immediately, it changes like that. These are among the general sufferings. There are many such situations that can quickly change, which are also the suffering of change.

The worst kind of suffering is pervasive suffering or the suffering of conditioned existence, and it cannot be realized easily. We have the nature of getting old. We don't like it, but we cannot stop it because it is our nature. In my neighborhood there are a lot of elderly people. They come to the temple to see me, saying, "Getting old is no good, getting old is no good." Nobody can stop it from happening. That is our nature, but it is very difficult to realize. We always think, "I am strong, I am young, I am capable." But that nature of getting older only gets worse. It doesn't go away, we age moment by moment. These three are general sufferings in samsara.

Samsara also has specific sufferings. The special sufferings of human beings are the problems of birth, sickness, aging, and death. Then there are those of the god realms. Although you cannot see them, gods have their own special sufferings. There are also the demigods, which you cannot see directly either but who also have their own special sufferings. And you cannot see hell beings directly but their suffering is just unbelievable. They have to endure being in places where the mountains and the water are blazing iron. They have no protection whatsoever—no shoes, no clothes, only the experience of suffering. Then there are hungry ghosts, who cannot get food or drink for many years because of their karma. Even if you put good food and drink in front of them, they cannot see it nor can they enjoy it. Animals are naturally dull and foolish; they cannot tell people what they want. Even so, they can feel suffering and a little happiness. They can do a little bit of what they want, look for what they want, but they cannot be fully satisfied. Among the unique sufferings of animals, the main one is that the bigger animals eat the smaller ones alive, and the smaller ones eat the next smaller ones and so on. The smaller animals are food for bigger animals. This is only an introduction to the general and specific sufferings of samsara's six realms.

How to Do the Visualization of Taking Suffering

As you meditate, visualize those realms and those beings experiencing suffering. Visualize them just as though you were right there seeing them directly as they experience those sufferings. Then, visualize that all of their sufferings and those sufferings' causes turn into a black light, which you then draw into yourself and dissolve into your worst demon—self-cherishing mind. All of the sufferings and their causes dissolve into that mind. You have to practice this again and again.

Sometimes you can visualize each realm one by one: hell beings, hungry ghosts, animals, humans, demigods, and gods; visualize each realm's suffering and its causes, then take them from those beings, draw them into yourself, and dissolve them into your selfish mind.

When you arise from that meditation, strongly believe that you have purified and freed all those beings of their suffering. Firmly decide that they no longer have any suffering or causes of suffering. If the virtue from just thinking that and meditating on it could turn into form, the universe would be much too small to contain it. You have to think about this great virtue and its benefits because doing so will give you courage.

The Seven Pure Practices for Accumulating Good Karma

If you are a Lamrimpa, or a practitioner of the stages of the path or Lamrim, you have to practice with a *tsok shing* or merit field at all times. There are many *tangkas,* or paintings of merit fields. You have to visualize them continually in front of you and do the seven pure practices with them in mind on a daily basis.

The first of the seven pure practices is to visualize the merit field, think about its qualities, and then make prostrations. The second practice is to make offerings. Third, confess and purify your bad deeds, and when your mind is clean, go on to the fourth practice, which is to collect virtue. The easiest and most efficient way to collect a large amount of powerful virtue is by rejoicing—rejoicing in the Buddhas' activities, rejoicing in Bodhisattvas' activities, rejoicing in the virtues of Aryas and Arhats of the three vehicles, and rejoicing in all other beings' virtues, including your own. The fifth practice is praying and requesting that the holy beings of the merit field teach Dharma. The sixth is requesting that these holy beings remain, "Please remain with me as long as possible, as long as I wish." As long as the holy beings of the merit field remain before you, you can accumulate a vast

amount of virtue by practicing these activities. The seventh
is to dedicate the merit collected through doing these practices. Dharma practitioners should do these seven pure
practices on a daily basis.

While practicing with the merit field in front of you, you
should think, "I have done the Taking practice, taking all the
bad karma and sufferings from all the beings of the six
realms. I made them pure, I made them clean." Then you
have to decide, "Now, by the power of the object of virtue,
the merit field, may it please be as I wish; may it be as I
practiced." You have to request with a prayer. That is the
meaning of prayer.

That is the general teaching for beginners on how to do
the Taking practice. Now, for more specific instruction. Not
everybody can do that kind of practice from the start because they haven't developed the habit. It is difficult for
them to practice or even to comprehend. Sometimes, if you
take all the sickness, suffering, and problems from beings
and dissolve them into your self-important mind, you might
get superstitious or have some strange idea about doing the
practice. But the teachings and texts say that it is not a bad
sign to feel scared during this practice. In fact, it is a good
sign that you are scared because it shows that your practice
is yielding a result.

When you are practicing many paths and many instructions and your feeling and mental attitude remain the same
as usual, not moving or changing, it is a sure sign that your
practice isn't helping your mind. If your mind gets shaken
up a little bit, the practice is succeeding, which is a good
sign.

If you cannot practice as explained above, Taking or *len*
practice for the beginning person is described in the *Seven
Point Mind Training* as starting with you, with your own
situation: "Practice Taking gradually, starting with yourself." How? The past is already past—what is most important is the future. You start by taking the suffering that will
come to you this evening. You have to take your suffering in
advance and dissolve it into your selfish mind. Then take the

suffering that will come to you tomorrow, next week, next month, next year, and next life.

Once this practice has become pretty good and strong, change the focus from you to your mother, father, to other beings, and later to all beings. Taking your own sufferings first and making yourself pure and clean is a good way to start, since you can do so without feeling afraid. That is a unique instruction about this practice that is specifically for the beginning practitioner.

Now the main tool or instrument you use when practicing Taking is compassion. You have to evoke strong compassion. With the power of that compassion, you start taking beings' sufferings. It might be that the doubt arises in your mind, "To have compassion toward other beings is okay, but how can I have compassion for myself?" The fact is, you already do have much compassion for yourself. To use an example that is also a great instruction, consider that you don't want yourself to have any suffering; you cannot bear it. If you do find yourself suffering, you try to remove it immediately. When you suffer in whatever way, for example, when you get sick, you think, "I am suffering! Somebody should help me. A doctor should come. Whatever is best, I want it. I want to get rid of this right now!" That mental attitude is compassion for yourself. Directing that very kind of compassion toward other beings who are suffering is a good example of practicing compassion.

In the scriptures it is written that Avalokiteshvara is the manifestation of all the Buddhas' great compassion. Avalokiteshvara's essence is all Buddhas' compassion manifested in a deity's form. In the field of ordinary persons, the strongest and greatest level of compassion is the compassion a person has for him- or herself. But the degree to which each person cares for him- or herself is not even one percent of the compassion that Avalokiteshvara has for all beings. Therefore, when Taking from yourself or from others you have to use great compassion.

There is a special instruction that is very useful when you are practicing taking the bad deeds of other beings into yourself. As I have already told you, it is a sign that your practice is succeeding if you feel scared. It is also said that this is just practicing; you are sitting on your cushion. In the beginning, the sufferings of all beings don't actually come to you. But practicing that mind is so holy and so good that you can collect a great amount of virtue by practicing this, day by day, month by month, year by year. Your mind will eventually become used to this subject and practice and at some point you can even reach the level at which you actually do take on the sufferings of other beings.

Since such situations are sometimes difficult to imagine because you cannot see them directly, I will give some examples. Buddha Shakyamuni had a cousin, the well-known Devadatta. Both he and Buddha Shakyamuni became monks. Devadatta was a great scholar and later he became very jealous of Buddha because they were close relatives. Many people paid respect to the Buddha but not to him, and so he got worse and worse.

Every day a medical doctor would offer some medicine to the Buddha. He weighed it on a scale and gave him twelve units of the medicine. Devadatta asked that same doctor for some medicine for himself. The doctor checked Devadatta's condition and gave him a small pill, but not nearly the Buddha's dosage of twelve units. This angered Devadatta: "You give twelve units of medicine to him but you give me only one! Give me twelve!"

The doctor told him, "You cannot digest it; if you take that much, you will die."

Devadatta was furious, "If you don't give it to me—!" And, pulling rank, he forced the doctor to give him the same amount that he had given the Buddha. Of course, when Devadatta took the medicine, he got unbelievably sick. Nobody could help him and he was just about to die. The other disciples told Buddha about what Devadatta had done, and that he was now very sick. Buddha said, "It's all right." He went to his cousin, and, putting his hand on Devadatta's head, he said, "He is my close relative, he is my cousin." Even if someone is like a demon and always tries to harm Buddha, he always has complete equanimity toward such a person.

Then Buddha said, "I am thinking about and focusing on you and others equally. If what I say is true, by the power of this truth may you be cured immediately." Uttering that statement, he meditated and took Devadatta's suffering from him. Immediately Devadatta was cured. Upon awakening Devadatta said, "You are my younger cousin, why do you have your hand on my head?" Like that, he started up again. Therefore, people of very high spiritual levels can take such sufferings directly.

During the time of the Thirteenth Dalai Lama Thupten Gyatso, there was a terrible smallpox epidemic in Tibet. Many people died. The Thirteenth Dalai Lama meditated on *tonglen*, and took the power of that sickness, stopping the epidemic and causing it to disappear completely. Just after that, pock marks suddenly appeared on the Thirteenth Dalai Lama without his becoming sick. In that way they can take away suffering directly.

How to Do the Visualization of Giving Happiness

At this point, you have decided: "Now all beings are clean and pure. They don't have any suffering or causes of suffering. They are pure, clean vessels. Now I want to fill those pure vessels." This is the Giving part of the *tonglen* practice.

Here let me give you a special instruction. When you are practicing Taking, you can practice taking beings' general suffering and also the specific suffering of each realm's beings. Hell beings have terribly ugly physical forms. They live in hideous and horrible places. The unique suffering of the beings in the hot hells is being tortured by heat. The emergency help that those beings need is to feel cool. Therefore, visualize that your virtues turn into a great cooling rain that extinguishes the fires of the hells and soothes hell beings. Then visualize that your Giving transforms them into human form. Emanate your virtue in the form of good homes that have everything including furniture. Then again emanate all their necessities including food, drink, and clothing.

As a second step, emanate your virtue by transforming it into a Lama that teaches those beings Dharma. As a result of their practicing, they collect virtue and generate bodhichitta and eventually reach the status of tenth level Bodhisattvas. Visualize that all their problems and sufferings come to an end.

Similarly, the beings in the cold hells need warmth. In this case, visualize that your virtues turn into warm sunlight and send it there. When the heat of that sunlight touches their bodies it removes their suffering from the cold. Then visualize that your virtue turns them into humans and then give them homes and necessities as before.

The special suffering of hungry ghosts is being unable to find food or drink. They go without food for very long periods of time. Therefore, first visualize that you emanate your virtue as medicine that restores their bodies and health. Then give them food, drink, clothes and everything else as before.

The unique suffering of animals is foolishness and ignorance. Visualize that you give them wisdom. To demigods you give armor for protection. To gods you give more enjoyments, and to humans, because of their great desire, emanate as whatever they want.

Practice at all times. As you are practicing *tonglen*, rely on the blessings of the merit field, which can be visualized extensively or with a single Buddha. An extensive version of a merit field is: visualize your Root Lama and the Lineage Lamas' group in front of you; in front of and just below them is the row of highest Tantric deities—there are four rows, one each for the four levels of Tantric deities. You don't have to visualize each and every one; a rough visualization is fine. After that come all the Buddhas. Among the Buddhas there are also many groups. There is a group of 1,001, another group of thirty-five, a group of twelve, of eight, of one and so on. In the *Three Heaps Sutra* there is a group of thirty-five Buddhas. In the medical ritual system there are eight Buddhas in a group. There are 1,001 Buddhas that will appear in this good kalpa. After the row of Sutrayana Buddhas comes the row of Bodhisattvas; then comes the row of dakas and dakinis; and in front and beneath them, the row of Dharma protectors. Together they form one huge assembly.

Beginning practitioners might not be able to visualize such an extensive assembly. If you are a rookie, visualize one figure. This means that all of the objects of virtue—the Root Lama surrounded by the Lineage Lamas, the dakas, dakinis, Buddhas, all of them—are combined in the form of that Root Lama. The outer form is the Root Lama whose essence is all Buddhas' knowledge. Therefore, if necessary, the Root Lama can emanate a whole set of the large assembly. Once the function is finished, he dissolves the emanations back into himself.

Sometimes that Root Lama is visualized in an ordinary form, at other times in Je Tsongkapa's form, or in Buddha Shakyamuni's form, but the essence is your Lama. Sometimes the main outer figure is Je Tsongkapa in whose heart is Buddha Shakyamuni and inside that Buddha's heart is Buddha Vajradhara (*Sangye Dorje Chang*). If you cannot visualize the whole set of all of these, visualize one Buddha. For you, one Buddha is better. That Buddha is inseparable from your Lama. Pray to that Buddha, "Please bless me and help me to succeed in my practice." You have to request this.

Tonglen practice is very good. "Practice" doesn't only mean sitting on your cushion. Think about it and practice it constantly, and, as the root text says, "remind yourself of the practice by reciting words during all your activities." To remind you to practice, try to do what the root text calls *tsik-ki jang*, which means to recite words about the meaning of the practice. For example, you can recite the verse from the Panchen Lama's *Honoring the Lamas*:

So then, Compassionate Holy Lama,
Please bless me that every last sin,
Obscuration, and suffering of all mother beings
Ripen upon me right now,
And, by giving away my every bliss and goodness,
Bless me to give happiness to all beings.

The first line means, "Because of that, now I am requesting you Lama Buddha Dorje Chang." The next line
means, "Please, may all mother-beings' bad deeds, obstacles,
and sufferings without exception come to me and ripen on
me, and may I practice charity toward them with all my
happiness, virtues, and knowledge." Having done that,
"Please bless me, help me to make all beings happy." You
have to request this of the merit field. If you memorize this
verse you will be able to recite the words, which will remind
you to do the main practice all the time.

Giving and Taking with the Breath

Kedrup Je was one of Je Tsongkapa's greatest disciples. He
wrote a poem about Je Tsongkapa's qualities. In it he said,
"O Lord, when even the very breath from your mouth is a
means of benefiting all beings, what then of your other
deeds that form the two accumulations?"[38]
    In the scriptures it says that we breathe in and out 72,000
times a day—sometimes more, sometimes less. When you
exhale, send all your virtues to all sentient beings. When you
inhale, draw in all beings' sufferings and problems and their
causes, dissolving them into you. Therefore, each day you
can do this *tonglen* practice 72,000 times. Since we cannot
stop breathing we can turn ordinary breathing into great
practice and great virtue. But because we are not in the habit
of doing it, we don't remember, and therefore, ordinary
breathing becomes a wasted opportunity. Now that you
have gotten the instruction, don't forget it; try to do it.
    The main instrument when you are practicing Giving
your virtue and knowledge is loving-kindness. During the
Taking practice, the main tool was compassion. Now, with
strong love, you offer your knowledge and virtue and turn
them into what beings want, what is important for them.
Your knowledge and virtue turn into the objects that you offer to them.

---

[38]See bibliography under Kedrup Je.

When you do Giving practice, you give to all beings, including the merit field. During the Taking practice, however, you cannot take suffering from the merit field because they don't have any suffering. That is the difference. During Giving practice you have to include the merit field since making offerings to them creates more virtue.

You must do this breathing exercise a little bit. In the future, if you enter into the Tantric field, it is even more useful.

ཉ༔

QUESTION: *I've heard that it can be dangerous to practice "Giving and Taking" if you aren't ready. Is it necessary to attain a certain level of understanding before you can do this practice?*

KHEN RINPOCHE: Buddha's own general instruction that appears in the Sutras says that Bodhisattvas have to practice generosity toward other beings by giving them whatever they want. You have to give everything without hesitation or stinginess. If they want your head, you have to give it. If they want your limbs, you have to give them. If they want your body, you have to give it.

But some Bodhisattvas are unable to do this. Should such Bodhisattvas still do this kind of practice? To this, Buddha answered "no." It should not be practiced by Bodhisattvas who have not yet reached the first of the ten Bodhisattva *bhumis* or levels.

The Bodhisattva path has five main divisions. The first is called the Path of Accumulation, inside of which there are three sublevels. The second path is the Path of Preparation, which has four levels. You cannot reach the first of the ten Bodhisattva *bhumis* or levels until you have finished these seven stages. When you reach the first Bodhisattva *bhumi* you become an Arya. Buddha clearly declared that Bodhisattvas who have not reached any of the ten *bhumis* should not give their bodies. If you try to do such a practice before then, Buddha said that is a demon's activity.

What does this mean? Even though someone may be a real Bodhisattva who wants to give his body to a person who asks him for it, because that Bodhisattva hasn't reached the proper level to be able to do that kind of activity properly, such a deed would be a demon's activity. Therefore, if even very high Bodhisattvas cannot give their body, head, or limbs before they reach the proper level, then it would be completely improper for persons like ourselves to do so, since we are the most beginning of beginning practitioners.

COMBINING THE TWO RIVERS OF INSTRUCTION INTO ELEVEN CATEGORIES

IN ORDER TO ACHIEVE bodhichitta more efficiently, we have to unite the two major rivers of instruction on bodhichitta into one system of practice. This system was established by Je Tsongkapa and it is the main aim of our meditation. By uniting these two rivers, the practice becomes more efficient, easier, and more useful.

The first river of instruction includes the steps from the Sevenfold Instruction: (1) recognizing all beings as our mothers, (2) remembering their great kindness, (3) wanting to repay their great kindness, (4) loving-kindness, (5) compassion, (6) extraordinary compassion or intention, and (7) bodhichitta.

The second river of instruction, which relates to Equalizing and Exchanging Self and Others, has five main steps, which were covered above: 1) recognizing that self and others are the same, 2) thinking in many ways about the faults of self-cherishing mind, 3) thinking in many ways about the benefits of cherishing others, 4) the actual practice of exchanging self and others, and 5) the practice of *tonglen* or Giving and Taking. The remaining Lojong instructions concern your daily practice once you have generated bodhichitta.

These two instructions are combined into eleven meditation topics. The eleven topics should not be taught one after the other all at once. The practitioner should be taught one topic, should master that topic in meditation, and then receive instruction on the next topic. Even though the complete instruction is being presented here, it is my hope and belief that you will practice it in the proper way. First you have to think about the ten benefits of achieving bodhichitta that were described above. Doing that will inspire you to want to achieve bodhichitta. Once you are so inspired, you are ready to practice these eleven steps.

The first step that is counted in this system as one of the eleven topics and which serves as a basis for being able to practice the others effectively is immeasurable equanimity.

There are several ways to practice equanimity. One way is to cultivate it from the perspective of all sentient beings, in which case you think, "How nice it would be if all sentient beings could be free of hatred and desire toward one another. How nice it would be if they could be free of those two powerful mental afflictions." In this context, however, you are cultivating equanimity from your own side by focusing on all sentient beings and thinking, "How nice it would be if I were free of hatred and desire toward all sentient beings." This is the basis of the practice for developing bodhichitta. You have to make this attitude firm by thinking about it with many good reasons and examples. In the beginning when you are practicing equanimity you will have to correct your mind frequently, but as your practice develops you will be able to change your old habits and eventually gain actual equanimity.

The second step is to gain the certainty that all sentient beings have been your mother many times in the past. You must try to make firm in your mind the knowledge that all sentient beings have been your mother not only once but many times. If we gain this knowledge nicely, the rest of the topics will be easier to realize and understanding will come almost automatically.

The third step is to remember that all beings have been very kind to us when they were our mother, just as this life's mother has been. Our mothers protected us from the time that we were in the womb. After taking birth we were like a worm, unable to talk, see, or do anything to help ourselves. Our mothers protected us every minute of every day.

Thinking that, you can realize their great kindness. After recalling the kindness of all sentient beings, the fourth topic is to develop the wish to repay that kindness. In this case you have to think about samsara's general condition and also each realm's specific suffering. Among all the sentient beings in samsara, how many are human beings who have good knowledge? Who has perfect renunciation, bodhichitta, and wisdom? Who has the ability to free themselves from samsara's suffering?

Many people seem intelligent and capable but most of them don't have wisdom. They don't know about good and bad deeds and most of them haven't even heard of the distinction. On top of that everyone is always busy doing something without resting. You can hear the traffic rushing along the highway twenty-four hours a day. People are always doing something, always on their way somewhere. They do not know that they are lacking in wisdom and skill about the right and wrong things to do. Sometime they will end up in the horrible abyss of the lower realms. Once there, it is very difficult to escape from that condition. Even Buddhas and Bodhisattvas can't do much to help them. Samsara's nature is like that. Therefore, it would be shameless if you just stood by and watched beings who were about to fall into that abyss and did nothing to help them. Like a mother's good child, we have to take responsibility to save beings and prevent them from falling into the abyss of the lower realms. You shouldn't waste this good chance that you have to help beings. You have to make that decision.

Usually people think that helping someone means serving beings a little bit by arranging food, clothing, or shelter. Most people can't even imagine helping beings by trying to remove all their problems and suffering and giving them unchanging happiness. That kind of attitude can only be gained through the Mahayana Dharma, especially in these Lojong instructions.

When you have finished these four topics, which are from the Sevenfold Cause and Effect Instruction, you have to start meditating on points from the instruction on Equalizing and Exchanging Self and Others, or *dakshen nyamje*. If you were continuing with the Sevenfold Instruction, at this point you would start practicing the loving-kindness that sees beings as very dear, or *yiwong jampa*. Instead of that kind of loving-kindness, in this eleven-stage system you practice the loving-kindness that checks what kind of happiness beings are lacking, which is practiced later in the ninth step.

In Je Tsongkapa's oral instruction lineage system when you finish these four topics starting with equanimity, you have gained a basic knowledge that prepares you to do the main practice of actually generating bodhichitta.

The main practice for generating bodhichitta begins with the instruction on *dakshen nyamje*. Therefore, the fifth of the eleven steps is to meditate on the sameness of yourself and others. The main point to keep in mind here is that you and others have the same nature and the same wishes. All of us are experiencing samsara's suffering and we all wish to be free of suffering. Therefore, it is improper to distinguish between our interests and those of others. We have to see them both as equally important.

The sixth step is to think in many different ways about the bad qualities of cherishing or caring only about oneself.

The seventh step is to use many good reasons and examples to think about the good qualities of cherishing other beings.

The eighth step is to do the Taking meditation with all beings. In this eleven-point system, both this step and the ninth, which is Giving, are described as including the actual practice of exchanging self and others.[39] The Taking practice is a method of strengthening and increasing your great compassion, which wishes to remove the suffering of beings. With that great compassion, you have to visualize that you are taking all the suffering from all the beings of the lowest hells up to tenth level Bodhisattvas. This practice is described in the phrase, "focusing intently on the objects of compassion." For example, when the president goes somewhere to give a speech, bodyguards accompany him. The president's main duty and that of the bodyguard are different. The president puts his effort into giving a good speech, while the bodyguard, instead of focusing on the speech, focuses exclusively on watching everyone and everything in

---

[39]The actual practice of Exchanging Self and Others was explained earlier as the fourth of the five topics in the instruction on Equalizing and Exchanging Self and Others. In the eleven-step system, the Exchanging practice is subsumed into steps eight and nine.

order to see whether there is any danger to the president. Like that, when you are taking beings' bad deeds and sufferings, you have to make a special effort to focus on all the different kinds of bad deeds and sufferings that beings experience. After that you have to visualize that all beings are perfectly clean and clear. Then you have to fill those pure vessels with good things.

The ninth step is to practice Giving, which is a way to strengthen and increase the loving-kindness that wishes to provide what beings lack. The things that you give them are described as "body, wealth, and your virtue of the three times." Your body and your wealth are general objects that you can give but in this context you have to give the most holy gift of the virtue that you have collected, are collecting, and will collect. Imagine that you turn your virtues into whatever things the sentient beings of each of the six realms need. Your mind will eventually become used to this by practicing again and again. Often you will see or hear something that will remind you to practice, and this way your knowledge of the practice will get better and better.

At some time when you get sick, you will think, "Now my *tonglen* practice is succeeding, this is a sign that my *tonglen* is improving." Try to be happy about your sickness by thinking that way. You can also think, "One kind of bad karma that I collected has ended. Now I don't have to experience the suffering result of that karma anymore. This is the actual blessing of the Three Jewels." You can get outer medicine from doctors, but this practice is an inner medicine that reduces the suffering and greatly increases the happiness of Dharma practitioners.

After doing the Giving part of the *tonglen* practice you have to relax a little bit. You should think, "While meditating, I gave all my knowledge, virtues, and wealth to sentient beings. I took away all their problems, sicknesses, and difficulties and dissolved them into myself. But did this actually happen or not?" When you check, you can see that you only imagined that you did this. Although you can collect a huge amount of virtue by meditating this way, you didn't actually produce this result. Therefore, you have to think, "I must take responsibility for making this result actually happen."

Having this extraordinary intention is the tenth step, which has to be practiced after you have completed both parts of the *tonglen* practice. This extraordinary compassion or intention is the main cause that immediately precedes actual bodhichitta. After you achieve extraordinary compassion, you can easily achieve the eleventh step or bodhichitta, which is the mind that wishes to attain Buddhahood for the benefit of all sentient beings. When you develop that attitude, you become a Bodhisattva and can be called a spiritual son or daughter of the Buddhas. This makes you worthy of being prostrated to by other beings. There are many, many good results that you gain all at once when you succeed in generating actual bodhichitta. This is the complete set of points in the unique oral instruction for developing bodhichitta.

THIRD POINT:
THE METHOD OF TURNING BAD EXPERIENCES
INTO CAUSES FOR ENLIGHTENMENT

THE THIRD SECTION OR point of the *Seven Point Mind Training* relates to "the method of turning bad experiences into causes for the path to enlightenment." This means that if something bad happens to you, you use your meditation to prevent it from turning into actual bad causes. You have to transform those bad causes into good causes. If you have some problem or suffering, you have to turn it into causes to strengthen your practice, your knowledge, your bodhichitta, and your Bodhisattva activities. This is the main point of the third section.

Renunciation, or *ngenjung*, can be either very steady and firm, or it can be the kind that arises and disappears quickly, like a water bubble. Without steady renunciation, whatever good or bad things you experience can cause you to lose your virtuous mind and practice.

If something good happens to you—for example, you become very rich or you get a good position—you become very happy. You are so thrilled that you forget your daily practice and lose your virtue. On the other hand, if at some point you have a problem or you get sick, you immediately give up your daily practice. First you will quit your daily practice and because of that, you will quit trying to make progress in your practice. How do you respond when something good or bad happens to you? You have to check your mind.

These situations definitely happen all the time. Sometimes we experience happiness and good things, but most of the time we have difficulties and problems, which shake and destroy our daily, virtuous, practicing mind. They shake us and we lose our virtuous thoughts and knowledge very easily.

What should you do in those cases? You have to have skill, instructions, and be in the habit of practicing the instruction. You must try to change the good or bad things that happen to you into good causes that will strengthen your practice. That way, your practice can develop and your bodhichitta can become firm and steady.

Turning Bad Experiences into Good Causes by the Power of Mind

Within this section there are two categories on how to change difficult conditions into good causes. One is to change them with your mind, that is, through your mental attitude. Having done that, the second way is to change them into good causes through activities of body and speech. The first section has two parts: changing bad experiences into good causes with your behavior and changing them by generating correct view, thinking about them, and applying that right view.

Some obvious examples of bad situations are health problems, money problems, family problems, career problems, social problems—any bad situation. When we have such experiences we usually look for their causes outside of ourselves. When we get sick we think, "Oh, I went out to a friend's house for dinner. There must have been something bad in the food or drinks." We always think that something outside ourselves was the cause of the problem. We never think of the inner causes at all. It is the same way with other bad experiences; we very easily blame other people, other beings, other things like food and so forth. But those are just temporary or incidental causes. Temporary causes don't have much power.

When the Buddha was in India, many people tried to poison him. They would invite him to a meal and offer him poisoned food and he would knowingly accept. He would tell his disciples, "Today we are going to such and such a place to eat. First, let me enjoy it; do not eat it before I do." Poisoned food could not hurt him at all because of the power of his goodness, because he had done the Giving and Taking practice for so many, many eons. The poison could not harm him, or even his circle of disciples. His power could completely protect his circle. Why? Because he didn't have any inner or mental poison. The inner causes of the selfish mind along with its seeds were completely gone. Because of that, temporary causes could not harm him. Temporary causes can harm us very easily because we have very powerful inner causes within our minds. The power of the inner and outer causes come together very easily and as a result we get badly hurt.

Bad situations or experiences do not come from the outside. You have to realize and think to yourself, "I created this; I arranged this all by myself. I planted the causes of this." All of these bad causes are the result of karma. Who collected those karmas? "I did it by myself. So, if I want to blame anyone or anything, I should blame myself, not others." Anyone who is trying to realize his own faults is doing good practice. That itself causes one to become a Bodhisattva and to achieve Buddhahood. Therefore, in that way, you can turn bad situations into good causes.

For example, if your room gets dirty and you want to clean it, you have to sweep it with a broom or use a vacuum cleaner. Similarly, we have a countless number of causes of suffering. We collected them many times. Our minds are very rich with the causes of suffering. Those causes remain in our mind.

The general cause and effect system is that when the result comes out, its root will disappear. Then you have to plant new seeds. If you get sick while practicing, you have to realize that the sickness is a good thing—it came to you at the right time. You can turn it into good practice. If the causes of that sickness had ripened in another realm, the suffering would be much heavier, would last much longer, and at that time we would not be able to help ourselves. We would just suffer. But now you are in a position to help yourself when you are experiencing the suffering. You have to do it.

How? By rejoicing. Usually, Bodhisattvas rejoice by thinking, "This sickness is a very great kindness for me. It came to me right now. Because of that, a bad deed has disappeared from my mind. Now I don't have that bad deed anymore. It is through the kindness of that sickness that I was able to remove it." You have to rejoice about that. It is appropriate to practice this way and get used to it.

From a worldly perspective, you will not feel suffering very heavily because that feeling of experiencing suffering is one kind of mind. Generally, we have three different feelings (*tsorwa*): pleasant, unpleasant, and neutral. We can change these feelings with the mind. We can change a suffering or unpleasant feeling into a pleasant, happy one.

Say, for example, that there are three people who are each carrying some money; the first one is a Bodhisattva and the other two are ordinary people. If the Bodhisattva is robbed, he will enjoy it, thinking, "Great! He took my money!" With that experience, he practices *tonglen*. But if the others are robbed they will suffer. The same thing happened in the same way to each of them, but only one really felt happy about it, while the others got upset or angry. Their suffering was created by the mind.

If you have received this instruction and put it into practice, you won't get the least bit upset when you get sick. You can rejoice and collect great virtue in the meantime. "Oh good, I got really sick." It is by the power of the merit field— the Lama, the deities, and Bodhisattvas. I got sick due to their kindness and blessings. In the past I practiced *tonglen* and, at that time, I prayed to them and requested that the sufferings of other beings ripen on me. They helped me; now the actual result has come to me. Very good, now I have succeeded." Instead of suffering, you are rejoicing and by doing that you collect great virtue.

These are not difficult practices; you can definitely do them. You do not have to postpone practicing by thinking, "someday...sometime." You have to know that if you practice these instructions, you can automatically turn every sickness and problem into causes for making progress in your practice of bodhichitta.

Generally, if you get sick or have some serious problem, it upsets and worries you. Sometimes it tortures you. But if you do this practice, such things cannot torture you. You won't get upset. You won't feel worried. The holy Shantideva said,

And the other benefits of suffering are
Loss of pride through dissatisfaction,
Compassion for samsara's beings,
Dread of evil, and love of good.[40]

Generally, suffering is suffering; bad situations and bad things don't have good qualities. But through them, Bodhisattvas and practitioners of this subject develop many good causes and other good qualities. For example, getting sick is upsetting, which tames your pride for the time being. You feel, "I'm sick, I'm not feeling well, I can't do that today, I can't go there," let alone, "I can't fight today." Being sick definitely blocks pride.

When you get sick you suffer, which causes you to be able to sympathize with the situation of other beings. If other beings get the same sickness, you can realize, "Oh, they must be very upset because that sickness is terrible. I remember, I know how it feels." Thinking that, you can feel compassion for them. Therefore, suffering can cause you to activate love, compassion, *tonglen*, and many other good things.

Now, this is a most crucial point. If you get sick or have some problem, you won't like it. That experience is a result. "I don't like the result but I like the causes." Silly, right? We collect bad deeds automatically in many things we do, some of them deliberately and others unintentionally. We don't much think or care about it. But when we experience even some small, unpleasant result, we don't like it and we feel upset. If you experience some suffering and you don't like it, you are getting the instruction: "If you don't like me, don't collect my causes." An ordinary person can't comprehend that instruction, but if you are a practitioner, especially if you are practicing in the Mahayana Buddhist field, you can easily catch the meaning.

---

[40]*Engaging in Bodhisattva Activities*, ch. 6, v. 21.

Turning Bad Causes into
Good Causes through Right View

We have learned how to turn bad conditions into good causes with that mind focusing on general objects. What is a general object? What is a specific object?

When we practice meditating on emptiness or shunyata, we are focusing on the actual nature of phenomena. At that time we have to recall how the general object appears to our mind and remember how the mind usually holds that object. How does the mind hold its object? Why does the mind hold the object that way? Thinking like this, try to realize what the real nature of all phenomena is.

How do we realize the nature of all phenomena? With our mind. What kind of mind should you have? For that, you have to study about shunyata, which is absence of self-existence. You have to gain that knowledge. On the one hand there is the mind that grasps phenomena as self-existent; on the other hand there is wisdom. Grasping at self-existence has its object and wisdom has its object. Grasping things as self-existent and wisdom are opposites, and therefore, mutually exclusive. Of course, grasping at things as self-existent is a mistaken mind—the most mistaken of minds—because its object does not exist. That mind apprehends its objects in a mistaken way. Since wisdom is an unmistaken mind, its object, which is self-existentlessness, is something that does exist. Wisdom apprehends that object unerringly.

There is an analogy that is very useful for teaching beginners about how the mind that grasps at self-existence is mistaken. When it gets dark out, you might see a piece of rope or a rubber hose on the ground and think, "Oh, there's a snake!" Immediately you get scared. You might run inside and yell to someone, "Come quick! I saw a snake! Help!"

You then go outside with a flashlight and your friend asks, "Where? Where? Where?"

And you say, "There! There! There!" as you point with the flashlight.

Before you see what it is with the flashlight, you have a very strong mistaken mind that is firmly fixed on its misapprehended object. The misapprehended object is that "snake." Actually, there is no snake, but a rope that appears to you as a snake. But your mind gets scared and strongly believes that what is there is a snake. Then you and your friend go there with the flashlight and discover that what you thought was a snake is only a piece of rope. Then you let out a sigh of relief and say, "Wow," because you just saw the actual quality of that object. As a result, that mistaken mind automatically disappears because its object has disappeared.

Similarly, your ignorance grasps all things and beings—you yourself, your heaps, your body, everything—as self-existent or independent phenomena that arose without causes and conditions. When you see something or someone, when you meet or talk to somebody, you appear to one another as independent phenomena or people. Because of that, your wrong view holds each of you as independently existing persons. But actually, neither of you is an independent or uncaused object.

"Independent" means not relying on causes. An object is produced, and a label is ascribed or given to it. When all the causes come together, the result is that object. Then the mind follows the name of that object. But actually, an independent person or object does not exist. Although ignorance recognizes all objects as independent, wisdom recognizes that nothing exists independently or without causes. All things rely upon something else.

Therefore, you have to learn to think about your bad experiences this way: "All of these bad situations appear to me as problems, they appear to me as obstacles blocking me. But no real enemy or self-existent sickness exists. Their nature lacks self-existence. The way a thing appears to me and its actual quality are completely different. Therefore, I do not have to be worried about it. It appears to me as a problem, it appears to me as an enemy, but it is not an independent sickness, it is not an independent enemy. I don't have to worry."

You have to think that all phenomena and all of those "bad results" are like an illusion. That is the method of applying right view to turn all bad experiences into the main causes of a Buddha's omniscience. Correct view is the wisdom that perceives the real nature of phenomena, and that wisdom is the main cause of a Buddha's omniscience. With study we can awaken and gain that wisdom right now. Then, without losing that wisdom, we have to progress by making it firmer and firmer in our minds.

There is a verse from *Engaging in Bodhisattva Activities* that is very useful for you, so don't forget it. Generally people get upset and unhappy when they have problems or difficulties whether they are general or specific. Because they get upset, they often become completely desperate, which can disturb the mind, causing them to become like a crazy person. This happens to many people. But the holy Shantideva said,

> If there is any remedy at all
> Why be upset about it?
> But then, if there is no remedy
> Why be upset about it?[41]

If you get those kinds of problems, you have to check immediately to see whether or not you can change them. Is it possible to change the problem or not? If you can do something about it, why are you upset? Why don't you try to change it? This is almost too obvious. Instead of getting upset or desperate, try to do something to remove or change those problems. If the object is changeable, we can definitely change it if we try. There is no need to get upset, to suffer, to get desperate, or to yell. There are many ways you can practice.

Therefore, during your meditation, you can use your mind to change whatever problems you encounter into good causes. In this way, you can do everything without taking any action by body or speech.

---

[41]*Ibid.*, ch. 6, v. 10.

Turning Bad Experiences into Good Causes through Taking Action by Body and Speech

You can also change problems by taking physical and verbal action. How? Through *jorwa*, which means taking action. The general meaning of *jorwa* is preparation, but in this case it refers to taking action—the actual method of changing those sufferings into good causes.

Tsok sak is the first important point. *Tsok* means virtue, *sak* means to collect. If you want to remove obstacles and change suffering and problems into good causes, you must collect virtue.

The second is *drip jang*. *Drip* in Tibetan means obstacles and bad deeds, *jang* means to get rid of them. Collecting virtue and getting rid of bad deeds are not mutually exclusive. Each of them has both functions of purifying the mind and collecting virtue. However, when the main purpose is to collect virtue, this is *tsok sak*, and when the main purpose is to get rid of bad deeds, it is *drip jang*.

How can you collect virtues and get rid of obstacles and bad deeds? When you wake up in the morning, clean your shrine area or the room where you keep holy images and objects. You clean it and you clean them. After that make offerings of water, flowers, incense, light, or whatever you have. Then make prostrations, do recitations, meditations, and so on. You should do this on a regular basis if you have time. Even if you are busy, you can still do an abbreviated version.

Removing bad deeds is done mainly with the Vajrasattva meditation. But there is not necessarily just one way to purify. For example, you can recite the *Three Heaps Sutra*, which is a great Sutra for purification. It is both incredibly useful and very easy. At the beginning of the Sutra you take refuge. Then, as you make prostrations, you recite the names of the thirty-five confession Buddhas. You continue by reciting the confession, in which the heaviest negative deeds a person could do are listed. The next section relates to the kind of motivation with which you confess your bad deeds in front of those Buddhas, and finally, there is a section on promising to restrain your mind from doing bad deeds in the future. All of these are contained in the *Three Heaps Sutra*. By reciting it, you can cleanse yourself of bad deeds.

Je Tsongkapa practiced this Sutra in a very good and holy place in southern Tibet. Usually, 100,000 times counts as one set. He did one hundred such sets of 100,000 recitations of that Sutra, while prostrating and confessing to each of the thirty-five Buddhas. He made one huge boulder, which was his prostration board, very smooth and clean. Eventually, all thirty-five Buddhas appeared in front of him.

If you have the mental attitude: "I want to get rid of my bad deeds; I am now going to do this next activity for the purpose of purifying myself of negative karma," you can use every activity you do as an antidote to your bad deeds.

If you have a good instructor and learn the instructions, all Buddhist practice becomes like a ball of candy; no matter where you taste it you can experience the sweetness. Therefore, every practice can be done for the purpose of collecting virtue or purifying bad deeds. The only thing we are lacking is faith, understanding, and instructions. That is the problem. From the Dharma's side there is no problem—everything is ready. If you've received the instructions and cultivated the skill, you can collect virtue and purify your bad deeds.

The third step in the category of taking action by body and speech is practicing giving to demons and bad spirits by offering them food along with performing rituals and reciting mantras. There are many such rituals. Giving them food is one way to turn bad causes into good causes. To do this, you need special knowledge. Why? Demons are always trying to harm you and influence you to behave negatively. Whenever you get sick, or have a problem or accident, try to prepare and offer food ritual cakes or *tormas*. Then, using your concentration, perform the ritual and offer them these *tormas*. If you invite them with holy mantras and rituals and offer these ritual cakes, they cannot ignore you; they must definitely come and accept them. In those rituals, there is an instruction for them that says: "You must eat this, you must accept it and enjoy it, and now you must change your mind from an evil one into a good one and support and protect Dharma practitioners. Don't harm them." Since those mantras and rituals are holy, those beings have no choice but to accept them.

Because we are practicing Lojong, when we are addressing those demons we have to make our request not with an ordinary attitude, but with a Bodhisattva's attitude. For example, we have to think, "You have been extremely kind to me. You did a very good job. It is because of your harmful activity, because you made me sick, because you made me have an accident, that I was able to strengthen my Dharma practice, knowledge, and bodhichitta. Thank you. Please take and accept this *torma*. And please continue to harm me in the future, make me sick, give me problems, whatever you can." From your side, you have to say this with complete sincerity. If you sincerely request that of them, they will definitely change. If you say it with any insincerity at all, as if you were deceiving or tricking them, they will definitely cheat or trick you. These are real and actual situations. This is still another way that you can change those bad influences or bad causes into good ones.

The fourth point is that you have to arrange offerings and then, with a ritual, offer them to the Dharma Protectors in thanksgiving or appreciation. It is like saying, "Thanks for your help and protection," and, "Because of your help I succeeded in turning those bad causes into good causes. In the future, please help me in the same way." This is an activity for Bodhisattvas and practitioners. This is the attitude you must have. You have to practice requesting in this way to the saving Three Jewels.

How? If you get sick, you usually pray to the Three Jewels, "I got sick. Please bless me, save me, protect me, and remove this sickness. Make it go away as soon as possible. Please, may I not get sick in the future and give me a long life." That is how people ordinarily pray. But practitioners of this holy subject will not pray that way. Instead, if they get sick, they pray, "Please, Three Jewels, if it is good for me to be sick, give me more sickness. If it is good for me to die, may I die. If it is good for me to be cured and live a long life, then please give me that power." Even though this is very unusual, they actually pray that way. These instructions are very holy and powerful. I especially believe and hope that they will help you. Please don't forget them.

Everybody has problems sometimes, general, specific—many things can happen. At those times, remember to do this practice. You are a practitioner—a person who is interested in and practicing Dharma. There are people who have never heard the holy Dharma. Between them and you there should be a *big* difference. You may get the same kind of sickness as another person, but there should be a big difference in your feeling and attitude about it. Other people will experience heavy suffering and become very sad, upset, and worried. But you won't worry. By practicing this you will easily be cured, although that should never be your motivation for practicing, "By practicing this, I will be cured." Never. Needless to say, you might get a good result through your practice, but it is only incidental. These are the four points of turning bad causes into good ones through taking physical and verbal action.

In summary, there is a sentence in the root text that says,

Immediately apply to your practice whatever is
   unexpectedly encountered.

FOURTH POINT:
A SUMMARY OF HOW TO PRACTICE
THROUGHOUT YOUR LIFE

ONCE YOU HAVE GENERATED bodhichitta, you
have to continue practicing Bodhisattva activities on a daily
basis.

The Five Strengths

The fourth section of this Lojong instruction teaches the five
strengths to be applied to your daily activities throughout
your whole life. Your whole life's practice, both your specific
daily activities and the general values you live by, should
fall into these five categories or five strengths.

The Strength of Intention

The first strength is the strength of intention. Among the five
strengths, this is the most important for beginning practitioners. *Penba* is the Tibetan word that is translated here as
"intention." It means to make a decision when you are about
to begin a particular activity, especially in relation to what
that activity is and for how long you will do it. For example,
when you are getting ready to meditate you might think,
"Right now it is two-thirty in the afternoon. I absolutely will
not get up from my cushion until four P.M." If you make such
a strong decision before you sit on your cushion, you will try
to keep the practice for that long. If you don't, you may feel
like stopping after a little while to get up, make some coffee,
and relax. We do this all the time.

The most important time to make a firm intention is
when you wake up in the morning. You should think, "By
the blessing and power of the Three Jewels, I did not die last
night. I woke up this morning feeling refreshed and wonder-

ful. It is because of their blessing that I can now get up again." The longest span of time you can consider is from now until you achieve Buddhahood. You make a decision that covers that period by thinking, "From now until I achieve Buddhahood, I will always do activities that are causes for developing my bodhichitta. I will do Bodhisattva activities." If you can't behave perfectly according to that intention, you can think, "For the rest of this life, I will always do activities to develop my bodhichitta." If you can't do that, think, "I will try to do such activities until the end of this year." That is also a relatively long time. If you can't do those activities nicely for that long, think, "I will at least try to do them until the end of the month," or finally, "From now until I go to sleep, I will try to collect pure, clean, great virtues." So when you get up in the morning, focus your attention on a particular span of time and make the determination to do all your activities during that day with bodhichitta. The power of that motivation should stay with you and influence you throughout the whole day. Even if you accidentally do something wrong, those things can turn into good virtue by the power of that motivation.

The instruction here is that you should develop the habit of having this intention as soon as you wake up in the morning: "Now I won't waste any more time. I will not waste the rest of my life. I will not waste the rest of this year. And most especially, I will not waste this day's twenty-four hours on meaningless activities." Make the firm decision, "I must try to make sure that all my activities are meaningful."

What should you do? "I must defeat my main enemy." Who is your main enemy and where can he be found? Your enemy is your own self-cherishing attitude, and this enemy is still in your mind.

Your intention is what determines all the activities that you do throughout the day. It provides the focus for everything you do, leading you along the Hinayana way, the Mahayana way, or in all the opposite ways. Therefore, if you start the day with a pure motivation, it will lead you in the right direction throughout all your activities.

Everything you do within a twenty-four-hour period is very important. You can finish several activities even within just a few minutes. For example, in America you don't get lice as often as you might in India, which makes things a little bit easier for you, but you do get many other kinds of bugs. If you want to remove bugs you have to make the decision to do so. That decision leads you to take action. Similarly, before you can make lunch or dinner, you have to decide what you are going to cook. That decision takes you into the kitchen where you open the refrigerator, take out some ingredients, prepare the food, and then finally enjoy the meal. These are relatively small activities.

So even from the time you wake up and start putting on your clothes, you need to have a good motivation. Tibetans often carry prayer beads. If you are a yogi and a serious practitioner you can tie one or even three or four knots on the string of your prayer beads to remind yourself of the most important and special things you need to do each day. Or, you can make lists or leave notes for yourself on your refrigerator. This is a very good habit to get into.

In general, most of what we do is for the purpose of getting food and clothes. Also, we are constantly thinking about how we can become famous. But yogis and yoginis should not focus at all on those things. Instead, you should think, "I must practice in order to benefit all sentient beings and try to achieve Buddhahood." Then do your daily practices with that motivation. Even though you may in fact do all your daily spiritual practices, if you don't make a strong decision first thing in the morning, you won't feel the need to do them with any intensity. But if you do make a decision in the morning, it will carry you through the day and your daily practice will become stronger, which is why the strength of intention is so important.

The Strength of White Seeds

The second strength is called "the strength of white seeds." In this case, "white" refers to virtuous deeds and "black" refers to bad deeds. Here, white seeds refer to the strong seeds of the Mahayana path, those virtues that will bring you Buddhahood someday. The strength of white seeds means you have to collect many virtuous seeds on a daily basis. It is a strength or power that comes from collecting virtue.

The way to develop this strength is to bring to mind temporary bodhichitta and keep yourself from losing it. You must also improve your bodhichitta by doing activities that will help you collect merit and remove bad deeds and other mental obstacles as much as you can. This is the best way to improve your bodhichitta.

You can collect merit and remove obstacles by doing practices like the ritual for the preliminary practices known as *Jorchö*.[42] In Tibet, whenever we received instructions on the Lamrim teachings, we would first recite the *Jorchö* ritual, which is a set of six preliminary practices and a very powerful practice. Whenever you hear or practice Lamrim instructions, you first have to do these six preliminary practices. Each part of this ritual has a complete method for collecting virtue. If you do this recitation, you will complete a set of virtuous practices. The purpose of this ritual is to collect virtues so that you can develop your bodhichitta and make it firm and steady.

All these activities should be directed toward achieving Buddhahood, not toward this life's happiness. Usually we do virtuous deeds for the purpose of this life's happiness. This means that because of our bad thoughts, we are taking a great practice and turning it into a cause that will only bring a small result. Therefore, activities that are done only for this life are foolish activities. It is very important not to practice that way. If you are doing great activities, their focus and aim should be directed toward the ultimate goal.

Generally, after a cause produces a result, the cause's power is exhausted. Then that result becomes a cause that produces another result, and so on. But if you collect virtuous seeds motivated by bodhichitta, or the wish to attain

---

[42]See Appendix C of *Liberation in Our Hands, Part One*, pp. 249–270 for a translation of this ritual. Days Four through Six of this volume are instructions on how the ritual is performed.

Buddhahood for the benefit of all beings, when those virtues produce their good results, not only will you enjoy those good results, but their good causes will not be exhausted. This is an unusual exception; not only will those causes not disappear, they will develop more and more until you attain Buddhahood. By the power of that bodhichitta motivation, they won't decrease or be exhausted. Once you achieve Buddhahood, they will *never* be exhausted. That is why those virtues are called the great strength of white seeds. You have to collect as many of these as you can every day.

What should you do on a daily basis? Think about how you can use all your activities to develop your bodhichitta. Everything you do, everything you think about, should be done to improve your bodhichitta.

Can you turn drinking tea and eating lunch or dinner into ways that develop your bodhichitta? Without studying and learning these skills, you might think, "No, eating is eating and drinking is drinking. They are done only to remove hunger and thirst." But this is not the case. To develop bodhichitta and to help all sentient beings, you need to have a strong body. The body's strength comes from daily food. Therefore, you should think, "I am eating this food to keep my strength from degenerating so that I can continue to practice to be able to help all sentient beings." By eating this way, you are developing your bodhichitta. That is the meaning of the strength of white seeds.

༄༅

QUESTION: *You talked about turning everyday activities like drinking tea and eating food into good causes by thinking, "I need a strong body, so I'm going to eat this food." I spend a lot of time taking care of my baby boy and, in some ways, it seems to take me away from my practice. I have to change diapers, wipe the floor, and so on. How can I turn that activity into good causes?*

KHEN RINPOCHE: You can definitely use those activities. As I have taught you, it is very important to think about and practice loving-kindness, compassion, and patience. Therefore, you cannot lose patience helping your son. You have to practice loving-kindness toward him all the time, along with compassion, and so on. Therefore, you can think, "As soon as possible, may I be able to act toward all sentient beings in the same way I am now acting toward my son." This will automatically develop your bodhichitta.

First you have to have the skill and instruction. After that, you must not allow yourself to forget them. And when the right time comes, you have to put your knowledge into practice immediately. This is the most important thing. If you practice this way, all the activities you mentioned will turn into Bodhisattva activities. You know about recognizing that all beings have been your mother, about remembering their kindness, about the need to repay their kindness. So why shouldn't you be able to do this?

ᘰᘰ

The Strength of Repeated Practice

The third strength is the strength of repeated practice. You gain this strength as your mind becomes used to daily practice. Even when you are doing a difficult job, it will get less and less so with repeated practice until eventually it becomes easy to do. This is because your mind has become used to it so that it is no longer a problem. In relation to this, the holy Shantideva said,

> Nothing at all remains difficult
> For one who practices repeatedly.[43]

There is no knowledge, activity, or object of the mind—whether it relates to the ordinary world or beyond the

---

[43]*Engaging in Bodhisattva Activities,* ch. 6, v. 14.

world—that doesn't get easier once your mind is used to it. Everything is difficult to do at first, even simple jobs. But when your mind gets used to it, everything becomes easy.

For example, if you are a smoker you have a powerful urge to smoke every day. That habit becomes very strong in your mind. Even though you may think it is a bad habit and want to quit, it isn't easy to do. I know a man in New Jersey who is both an alcoholic and heavy smoker. In fact, he did quit drinking alcohol but couldn't stop smoking. Even though he tried to quit, he didn't succeed. He then began to have lung problems and went to a doctor. The doctor told him, "You have to stop smoking now or else you won't get better." But he replied, "No way, I can't quit! I stopped drinking, but I can't stop smoking." The habit had become too firmly fixed in his mind.

Similarly, you can get into the habit of thinking about the problems and suffering of other beings and think again and again about taking responsibility for removing their problems and suffering. If your mind becomes habituated to that kind of practice, you can develop a strength that causes your virtues to be greater and more powerful. That is what the strength of repeated practice means.

Most of your physical activities can be included in the four of walking, sitting, standing, and lying down. The strength of repeated practice is to turn all of these activities into causes for developing your bodhichitta. It means you have to practice this way on a continuous basis.

Dharma practice doesn't mean just sitting on a cushion with your eyes closed like a rabbit. Sitting isn't the only way to practice. You can turn all of your ordinary activities into Bodhisattva practice. If you gain bodhichitta and are practicing to develop and strengthen that mind, you have to act like a Bodhisattva. A Bodhisattva is like an elephant. With their large bodies and great strength, elephants can work more efficiently than other animals. And, whether an elephant is walking on the road, sleeping, or just standing, its elephant nature never changes; it always remains an elephant. Similarly, you should never lose your bodhichitta no matter what you are doing. If you can do this, all your activities automatically turn into Bodhisattva activities. It won't matter what you appear to be on the outside or what kind of activity you are doing, your mind will always have the nature of a Bodhisattva.

You can read about the Buddha's former lives in the Jataka tales. He gave up his body many times to feed hungry beings. Sometimes he gave his head, sometimes his limbs, his wealth, or his kingdom. He gave many such things without the least hesitation. This is how he and many Bodhisattvas practice the perfection of giving. Right now, we cannot do activities like these. It may even be more difficult for us to give ten dollars to a beggar than it would be for a Bodhisattva to give his eyes or one of his limbs. Bodhisattvas give such things very easily and happily. They think, "Today I got a great opportunity; I met a beggar!" Immediately, they will cut off part of their body and give it away without a second thought in order to satisfy the person who asks for it. You can achieve this ability by starting to practice generosity with small things. Later, after you give greater and greater things and your mind becomes used to it, you won't have any problem giving special objects.

Instead of being a problem, giving brings great joy to a Bodhisattva. After they give something, they rejoice with an incredible sense of happiness. They are overjoyed just to hear someone's voice asking them, "Please give me such and such." Then they give whatever is needed. All these difficult activities are accomplished through a process of habituation. If your mind becomes used to doing them, you won't have any problem. But if your mind isn't used to them, it will be very difficult for you to give even small things. Therefore, it is very important to practice in a way that your mind becomes used to doing such activities.

When engineers or carpenters first try to make a car or a piece of furniture, it is very difficult for them. They aren't sure how to make such things. What measurements need to be taken? How should they cut the materials? How do the parts fit together? After they have become used to their skill, an image of the whole structure and process appears in their mind even before they start to make the object. After they begin working, they don't even have to think about it; they can finish putting the object together very easily and quickly. This is because their minds have become used to the work.

Similarly, it is very difficult to practice the perfection of giving from the beginning by giving your body and your life. But after your mind has gotten used to this practice, it will be easier than it is now for you to give someone an onion or a potato. If someone asks you, "Give me a potato," you will say, "Sure. Here, take it." Later, you can give your body even more easily than that.

How many points are there in Je Tsongkapa's shortest Lamrim prayer, *Source of All Goodness*?[44] If you are not familiar with this prayer, it is difficult even to count the number of points it has.

These days most people travel by car. But in old Tibet people rode on horseback. When you ride a horse, first you put your left foot in the left stirrup, and then you swing your right leg over its back and put your right foot in the other stirrup. Great practitioners and Lamas could finish a complete *shar gom*[45] or scanning meditation on all the Lamrim topics in the amount of time it takes to mount a horse. It is hard for you to imagine how this is possible, but they could do it because their minds had gotten used to that subject. Like a powerful machine, they could finish a scanning meditation within that short period of time.

Is it easy or difficult to drink a cup of tea? You might think it's easy, but you still can't finish it all at once or in just a few seconds. It takes a certain amount of time. You can't

---

[44]*yon tan gzhir gyur ma.* A fourteen-verse prayer requesting the Lamrim Lineage Lamas to bless you to achieve realizations of the Lamrim topics. The name of this prayer, which means literally "source of all good qualities," derives from the opening words in the first verse. A translation of all fourteen verses can be found in *Liberation in Our Hands, Part One,* pp. 265–266 as well as in *Preparing for Tantra* (see bibliography under Tsongkapa). *Preparing for Tantra* includes an English translation of Pabongka Rinpoche's commentary on this prayer.

[45]*shar sgom.* This is a practice in which you briefly review the meditation topics of a particular set of instructions. For a more detailed description of this type of meditation, see *Liberation in Our Hands, Part One,* Day Six, note 92.

take another mouthful before you swallow the first one. Therefore, if you aren't used to drinking tea, it can be difficult even to finish a whole cup. On the other hand, if you're a big tea drinker, it will be very easy!

The Strength of Removing Obstacles

The Tibetan word for this strength is *nampar sunjinpa*, which means to ruin, remove, or get rid of. Therefore, it is the strength or antidote that removes obstacles. Obstacles are the problems that interfere with your practice or with your thoughts about collecting virtue. For example, getting angry is always bad. Therefore, if you get angry you have to practice the strength of the antidote, which in this case would be patience. Patience is the direct antidote to anger. Patience doesn't come easily. You have to try to gain it using reasons. You should think, "A negative attitude has come to my mind. I must fight it."

How do you do that? If you experience anger often, you can think of the last time you felt that way, whether it was last week, last month, or earlier this year. "The last time I got angry I fought with another person. I did bad things, said bad words, and thought very bad thoughts. I planned very bad things. Because of that, I had no peace." Thinking about anger in relation to your own particular situation is more efficient and powerful than just thinking about it in general.

However, if you know the general qualities of anger and patience, you can think about them as well. This can help you to realize how such bad activities produce bad results. Then you will decide, "Now I must stop myself from getting angry. Anger only brings me problems and leads to bad results."

If you get angry about something, it immediately destroys your happiness and peace. Not only can an angry person not be at peace, even the color of his face will change. If you are angry as you try to comb your hair nicely and make it shine, even the appearance of your hair changes. It looks as if it is about to catch on fire! Anger immediately destroys not only your happiness, but that of those around you as well.

Therefore, you have to use reasons like these to stop your anger. Think of the good qualities that come from practicing patience. If you fight against anger and practice patience, that very activity is a good deed that will bring you unbelievably great virtue. One way to stop anger, then, is to consider the negative qualities of anger; the other is to consider the positive qualities of patience. If you practice patience this way, you are practicing a general form of this strength, or the strength that removes obstacles. You can abandon anger and stop yourself from getting angry. At some point, you can even get rid of anger from the root, which is very lucky for us.

In the Lojong practice, however, this strength doesn't only mean to apply a general antidote to obstacles like anger. It refers specifically to the antidote for self-cherishing mind. A Bodhisattva's worst obstacle is the self-cherishing mind. A Bodhisattva's main aim is to help other beings. If he develops a selfish mind, he loses the strength of the mind that wishes to think about and help other beings. Thinking about the welfare of other beings and selfish mind are exact opposites. What should Bodhisattvas and practitioners do when that selfish attitude makes its way into their mind? They have to stop it immediately before it arises or just as it is about to come up. They must not give it any opportunity to arise.

For example, the self-centered mind is described as being like a stray dog. In this country there aren't as many, but in Tibet there are a lot of stray dogs. Since they don't have an owner that will feed them, strays have to find food on their own, so they go from door to door looking for something to steal. If they get a chance, they sneak into houses and take whatever food they can find.

So if a stray comes to your door, you have to stop it before it has the chance to steal anything. There's no use trying to chase after it once it has already come inside and made off with something. You have to stop it from the beginning. Similarly, if the self-cherishing attitude is about to come into your mind, you have to think, "Oh, here comes that thief!" Then immediately try to stop it. Stop it as you would a stray dog. That is the main method and meaning of this fourth strength of removing obstacles. It is the antidote that destroys your obstacles immediately.

The Strength of Wishing Prayer

The fifth strength is the strength of wishing prayer. The word *mönlam* or wishing prayer is very well known. But the benefits of a wishing prayer cannot easily be seen. If you work hard to build a house, you will eventually see the result. Similarly, any material object that can be made will become visible once it has been produced. But the results of purely mental activities like prayer cannot be seen in the same way, yet the extent of their power is much greater than that of activities related to physical objects. Therefore, you have to have the strength of wishing prayer.

Generally, you have to make a wishing prayer whenever you finish any virtuous activity. A wishing prayer is like a tailor. If you get a bolt of good cloth, you can make clothes with it. Although you are the person who wants to wear the clothes, you can't use the cloth without making it into something that you can wear, like a suit, a pair of pants, or a coat. The cloth is there and you are here. The important thing you need at that point is a tailor or seamstress. That tailor can join you and that cloth together so that you can enjoy it. Similarly, you are the subject or agent; your virtues are like the bolt of cloth. To experience the result of those virtues at an important time, you need to do a wishing prayer. Like a tailor, the strength of a wishing prayer arranges all your virtues properly. The Tibetan expression for this is *tsamjor*, which means to join. Therefore, you need to do wishing prayers all the time so that you can get the good result of your virtues when you need them. That is the fifth strength.

How should we pray and what should we pray for if we are practicing this Lojong teaching? At night when you're ready to go to bed, you have to take whatever virtue you collected that day and turn it into causes that will increase your bodhichitta and bring you Buddhahood as soon as possible. You have to pray, "May all the virtues I collected today turn into those two causes." Whenever your prayer is associated with some particular virtuous activity that you did, it is a dedication prayer as well as a wishing prayer. In this case you are dedicating whatever virtue you collected during the day as a cause to develop your bodhichitta and bring you Buddhahood as soon as possible.

These are the five strengths we must develop over our lifetime in relation to our daily practice. We have to be ready to use our knowledge of them, so that when the appropriate time comes we can put them into practice.

The Five Strengths as Practiced at the Time of Death

There are two sets of five strengths. We finished the set that relates to your daily activities, which should be practiced throughout your life. The other set is made up of the five strengths that a person should practice at the very end of this life when he or she is about to die. The names of the five strengths to be practiced at the time of death are the same as in the previous group. The five strengths to be practiced at the time of death are also known as the transference instruction or *powa* of the Lojong tradition. The root text of the *Seven Point Mind Training* states:

> The Mahayana transference instruction
> Is to practice the same five strengths and
> To give special importance to your physical position.

Generally, we can use whatever ability or wisdom we may have to benefit our present life, but it is more important to work for the purpose of future lives. Therefore, we have to practice these five strengths in order to do something for our future lives.

There are several kinds of *powa* or transference practice that can be done at the time of death. Another person can perform a *powa* ritual on your behalf, or you can do it yourself. *Powa* means to transfer or promote the mind from this life to a good future life. The aim is to promote this life's mind to a Buddha's paradise, such as Tushita, which is Maitreya's paradise; or Kechara, which is Chakrasamvara's paradise; or Sukhavati, which is Amitabha's paradise, and so on.

In certain other *powa* teachings you have to meditate with strict concentration to move your mind from your heart up through your body to the crown of your head. Your mind operates in conjunction with airs in the body. As you raise the mind along with its air, you have to make certain special sounds, such as *hik!* and *phet!* Most people think this kind of *powa* is an unbelievably great practice. When a person achieves certain signs related to this practice, such as an itchy sensation or a small hole on the crown of the head, it is thought to be very extraordinary. But Kyabje Pabongka Rinpoche said in relation to this, "You can experience these signs just by reciting *hik!* and *phet!* continually, without even practicing any of the *powa* instruction's meditations properly. These signs can come just from meditating on the body's airs. There is nothing remarkable about them." Although these practices are beneficial, you can't always be sure whether they will be effective in sending your mind to a heaven or a good life.

The Lojong *powa* instruction, however, doesn't use any of these meditation techniques. You just calmly lie down and pass away while generating bodhichitta. And yet practicing these five strengths is much more profound and effective than other *powa* practices, and will definitely lead you to a heaven or a good future life.

The Strength of Intention as Practiced at the Time of Death

It is very easy to practice the five strengths. You have to practice bodhichitta every day, and try to develop and strengthen it all the time. By doing that, you will become used to having that attitude. You shouldn't forget bodhichitta during any of your daily activities. If you succeed, just remembering bodhichitta when you are about to pass away will definitely cause you to attain the kind of good future life you wish for. By doing so, it is impossible to fall into a lower realm. You can be sure of that.

As I explained before, intention generally means to make a decision about how long you will do a certain activity before you start it. There are many ways you can make this intention. For example, you might think to yourself, "I won't eat any food today until I finish doing all of my rituals." You can even make an intention about food: "I won't stop eating until I finish thirty-five *momos*!" When Buddha Shakyamuni sat down under the Bodhi tree, he resolved, "I will not get up until I achieve Buddhahood." This resolve helped him to achieve enlightenment very quickly.

In this Lojong instruction, the strength of intention at the time of death is for you to think, "I am going to die very soon. After that, I will enter the *bardo* or intermediate state. During these times, I will never let go of bodhichitta."

To be able to do this you have to start thinking from this moment on, "I'll never give up practicing bodhichitta until I reach Buddhahood and I'll never forget to practice bodhichitta for the rest of this life." If you can make that decision and keep practicing it, you won't forget it and it will come to you at that very important time.

When kids play outside with other kids, you don't have to teach them to call "Mommy!" or "Daddy!" if somebody is beating them up. Immediately they will yell, "Mommy! Daddy! He beat me up!" That's because the child's mind has become used to thinking of its mother and father all the time. Similarly, if you practice bodhichitta every day, you will definitely remember it when you are about to die. Doing so will bring a guaranteed *powa*, a definite promotion of your mind.

The Strength of White Seeds as Practiced at the Time of Death

The highest result a practitioner can achieve is to reach Buddhahood within his or her lifetime. Even though you may not be able to do this, you still must try to achieve some level of the path. If you can't do that, you must at least make sure to die without having any regret. "I couldn't achieve Buddhahood within this life or even the beginning levels of the path. But I still don't have any regrets, because I did everything I could with my life." Every Dharma practitioner should at least have this kind of attitude. If you have no regrets, you won't worry when death comes.

When you are about to die, the worst kind of attitude is to feel attachment for your possessions. The tenth limb of dependent origination is "existence," which refers to a form of karma. This karma is activated by desire, and this desire can be for anything, including your wealth. When you are about to die and realize that you are going to leave your possessions behind, your attachment can make you upset at the thought of who will get your things after you die. This thought will activate a bad karma and cause you to fall into a lower realm's rebirth.

Therefore, just before you die your mind should be clear and clean. The way to do this is to free yourself of whatever strong desire you may have for your wealth and possessions. In America there is a good system of making a will so that you can dedicate your wealth before you die. This allows you to give up your attachment to your wealth. You can rest assured that your wealth will be enjoyed by the people you have dedicated it to.

Here the Lojong instruction explains that you should give away your wealth and other property by making offerings to "higher" objects, such as the Three Jewels, and by practicing charity toward "lower" objects, like beggars, spirits, and other needy beings. So you should offer some of your wealth to holy objects and also decide what part to offer to a monastery, to your children, and to other relatives, and so on. By making these arrangements you can remove all your attachment for material objects.

Tibetans and Mongolians have a custom of holding a religious service in which offerings are made to the Three Jewels when someone dies. Sometimes they also practice charity toward needy persons. While these activities are done in order to collect virtue for the benefit of the deceased person, they aren't nearly as beneficial as if the person had done them directly while he or she was still alive. If someone develops the motivation to do a particular virtue himself, the benefit will be much greater than if they are done by someone else on his behalf after his death.

The harmful effect of attachment is easy to understand. If you are a secretary at a company and you love that job, your desire will keep you in that position. You won't think of being promoted to vice-president or president. But if you don't remain attached to your present job, you will definitely want to reach a higher position and later another one higher than that. Similarly, at the end of this life when you are just about to go to the next life, it is very important that you not have any desire for this life's family or property. You shouldn't think, "Oh no! I'm leaving my bank account!" Those desires pull you down and send you to the lower realms. The important thing is to prepare nicely by not having attachment for what you are leaving behind. Focus your mind only on the future.

During the Buddha's time, there was a monk who had a good sage's bowl. Because of attachment for his bowl at the time of his death, he was reborn as a snake. Since the snake was near the monastery, Buddha told his disciples to take it to the forest. When they did, the snake became angry. By the power of karma, the snake's anger caused the forest to catch on fire, burning up the snake along with the forest. The former monk's anger then caused him to be reborn in the hells. As a result, that monk's three bodies from three successive lives were all burning in three separate fires at the same time. His first body as a monk was burning in the cemetery. The body of his rebirth as a snake was burning in the forest fire. Also, before that body was finished burning, he quickly fell into hell, where his body was also being burned by fire.

There is also a story of a man who had a large amount of gold. When he was alive, he buried that gold underneath his house. After he passed away, he was immediately reborn as a snake living near that gold. When the man's relatives discovered the snake in the house, they asked the Buddha what they should do. Buddha told them to dig the ground under the house. There they found the gold and wondered what they should do with it. So they asked some other sages, who told them to offer the gold to the Buddha and ask him to do prayers for them.

Another story relates that there was once a woman who, because of attachment for her former body, was reborn as a worm that crawled around inside the corpse of its former life. There are many stories like these. Therefore, when you are about to die, don't allow yourself to have any attachment for material objects or your own body. Think only about your spiritual practice. Also, try to collect as much virtue as possible and pray strongly to be able to increase your bodhichitta.

When the time comes to go to the next life, the only thing you should do is collect as much virtue as possible. It is more powerful at that time because your mind is thinking about and seeking your future life's purpose. Therefore, the virtuous activities done at that time are much greater.

You should also think, "I practiced the highest mind of bodhichitta as much as I could during this life, generating it, developing it, and doing all the related practices. In all my future lives, I will maintain those attitudes and activities continually until I reach Buddhahood." This is a very powerful virtue.

Strength of Removing Obstacles as Practiced at the Time of Death

The third strength to be practiced at the time of death is the strength that removes obstacles. This strength is an antidote for your bad deeds. Just before you go to your next life, you have to make a strong confession of all your bad deeds generally and especially the ones you collected during this life. You have to try to purify yourself with a very strong mind. Doing that acts as an antidote.

The Tibetan word for purification is *shakpa*. In Buddhism, the confession or purification practice doesn't mean simply admitting to another person, "I did a bad deed." There are two types of bad deed that you collect when you do something like killing another sentient being or stealing someone's property. One is the actual bad deed itself. Right after you do a misdeed, you also collect a second fault—that of concealing your bad deed. If you verbally admit your bad deed, you can remove that fault of concealment. That is the purpose of verbal confession; but this alone doesn't remove the actual potential or force of your misdeed.

Therefore, the purification practice has four elements. First is the basis, or the holy object before whom you make a confession, which means your Lama and the Three Jewels. The second element is to feel sincere regret for the bad deeds you have done. Third is the attitude of restraint in which you think, "If I can cleanse myself of this bad deed, I will never do that sort of thing again." The fourth is the action you do as an antidote for your bad deeds.

One practice you can do as an antidote is to meditate on emptiness. Or you can recite holy Sutras, like the *Heart Sutra* and the *Three Heaps Sutra*, which, though short, are very effective for practicing purification.

The three heaps referred to in the title *Three Heaps Sutra* are (1) the heap of making prostrations to the thirty-five confession Buddhas, (2) the heap of confessing misdeeds, and (3) the heap of dedication. If you recite this Sutra every day for a month, you will easily memorize it. Anyone who considers himself a Buddhist should at least be able to recite one Sutra from memory. Two good Sutras to memorize are the *Heart Sutra* and the *Three Heaps Sutra*.

When you recite the *Three Heaps Sutra*, you should also do full-length prostrations. There are three recitations that are traditionally done during one session relating to purification of bad deeds. The first is the *Three Heaps Sutra*, which is also known as the *Bodhisattva's Confession of Transgressions*. The second is a recitation called the *General Confession*.[46] The *Three Heaps Sutra* mentions various specific bad deeds that you have collected. The *General Confession* refers to bad deeds in more general terms and is only about one third as long as the *Three Heaps Sutra*. The third recitation is a prayer called the *Leading Conqueror*,[47] which is not even one page long.

Another powerful method of purification is the Vajrasattva meditation and mantra recitation. If you recite the Vajrasattva mantra twenty-one times, it keeps your former bad deeds at their present level and prevents them from further increasing in strength. Otherwise, your bad deeds would increase by an unbelievably great amount.[48] This is like removing the "interest" of your karmic debt. Depending on how intensely you do the practice, it can also eat up some of the "principal" from your bad karma. Being able to do that is a great benefit.

If you are a Tantric practitioner, the most efficient form of purification to do just before you die is a self-initiation ritual. But you cannot do this ritual yourself until you have finished a *lerung*[49] or "fitness" retreat. If you haven't completed such a retreat, you can request a Lama to give you the initiation again. This will enable you to restore your Bodhisattva vows and Tantric vows. Other methods of purification can remove bad deeds but they cannot restore your Bodhisattva vows and Tantric vows. The self-initiation ritual is more efficient because it removes bad deeds and restores broken vows.

If you go to a Lama privately and ask for instruction, he or she may give you some teaching, but it is not the same as receiving the kind of detailed explanations you receive in a

---

[46]*spyi bshags.*

[47]*rtso rgyal ma.* This prayer consists of ch. 2, vv. 47–53 of Shantideva's *Engaging in Bodhisattva Activities*, which describes the act of taking refuge.

[48]This relates to the second of the four principles of karma, which is that karma becomes magnified (*las 'phel che ba*) over time. See *Liberation in Our Hands, Part Two*, p. 234.

[49]*las rung.*

public teaching. Kyabje Pabongka Rinpoche always used to say, "I give you very detailed instructions when there is a formal teaching, including quotations from various Sutra and Tantra scriptures as well as other holy books. But you don't keep them in your mind. Instead, you bother me between classes with all kinds of small questions that just take up my time." Therefore, the best instructions are the ones you receive in a formal class setting.

Practicing purification regularly—whether by reciting the Sutras I mentioned, taking self-initiation, or receiving an initiation from a Lama—is important, but it is especially important when you are about to die. If you don't purify yourself at that time, your bad deeds and mental obstacles will block you and prevent you from going to a Buddha paradise, even though you may otherwise be ready to go there.

The Strength of Wishing Prayer as Practiced at the Time of Death

In the Lojong *powa* practice, this strength doesn't mean to pray to be born in a Buddha paradise. The main object of your prayers in the Lojong practice is to wish, "May the suffering of all sentient beings and the causes of their suffering ripen upon me." It also means to pray that you and all beings succeed in developing actual bodhichitta. In the Lojong tradition the object of your prayers is to achieve the aim of the Giving and Taking practice.

The Strength of Repeated Practice as Practiced at the Time of Death

You have to practice bodhichitta continually during your life so that you become used to generating it. This will enable you to do the Lojong *powa* by meditating on bodhichitta as you are dying. You can't find any practice better than this. If you can pass away with bodhichitta in mind, there is no way you will go to any of the three lower realms. Even if you wanted to go there, you couldn't. The door would be shut.

*Assuming the Proper Physical
Position at the Time of Death*

If your mind is focused on bodhichitta when you are about
to pass away, what should your physical posture be? You
have to lie down in the same position as Buddha Shakyamuni did when he passed away. This means to lie down on
your right side in what is called the lion's reclining pose.
Place your right hand under your right cheek and rest your
left hand on top of your left thigh. This posture alone is very
beneficial for being reborn in a Buddha paradise.

The main practice of a beginning practitioner—known
as a person of small capacity in the Lamrim tradition—
includes meditating on leisure and fortune, taking refuge,
and karma.[50] Therefore, a practitioner of this level should
try to pass away while generating the mind of taking refuge.
A person of great capacity,[51] however, should pass away
while trying to generate bodhichitta.

How is it that passing away while meditating on
bodhichitta causes you to be reborn in a Buddha paradise?
For example, when Geshe Chekawa was about to pass away
he told his attendants, "Quick! Arrange some offerings. I
have been praying to be reborn in Avichi hell[52] to benefit all
sentient beings, but I don't think I can go there because I
keep having visions of heavenly realms."

Geshe Potowa was also one of the great Kadampa Lineage Lamas. Religious histories say that he was one of Je
Tsongkapa's former lives. He also passed away in the same
manner as Geshe Chekawa.

There is a story of a mother and daughter who fell into a
river and were carried away by the rapids. As the current
pulled them under to their death, the mother and daughter

---

[50]See *Liberation in Our Hands, Part Two* for a discussion of the practices relating to a practitioner of lesser capacity.

[51]That is, a Mahayana practitioner who is cultivating bodhichitta and the six
perfections.

[52]The worst of the eight hot hells.

each felt great love for the other. As a result, they were both reborn in Maitreya's Tushita paradise.

Hloka is a region of southern Tibet. After flowing south from Lhasa, the Brahmaputra river turns east and winds around the back of a group of mountains. As it continues in that direction, it reaches a place where a famous temple, called Ja Sa Hlakang, sits on the riverbank. The temple houses a huge image of the Eastern Buddha Vairochana. No one knows how or where this image was constructed. On its western side is a large ring that was used to tie a rope so that it could be transported to this temple. The temple itself is quite large and beautiful.

The entire fourth month in the Tibetan calendar is considered holy, because the fifteenth or full-moon day of the fourth month marks the day Buddha was born and also the day of his enlightenment. On this day, the Tibetan government would send messengers from Lhasa with grain to spread on the roof of Ja Sa Hlakang, which was flat, unlike most roofs in this country.

In Tibet, the cuckoo is thought of as the king of birds. Tibetans are very fond of this bird and when they hear its song, they always say something respectful like, "The cuckoo is singing." The cuckoo comes to Ja Sa Hlakang on this day, along with many other kinds of birds. People say—and everyone can actually see—that before the cuckoo enjoys water and grain from the temple roof, no other bird will land there. Only after the cuckoo finishes and flies off to a nearby tree do all the other birds come down to eat. The name *Ja Sa Hlakang*, or "Temple of the Place of Birds," was given because of this unusual event that began long ago and continues to the present day.

Right at the location of Ja Sa Hlakang, there is a kind of ferry boat for crossing the river. Called a *kowa*, it is made from many yak skins that are sewn together and stretched over a wooden frame. Although the boat can hold a good number of people, one day it was carrying a load that was much too heavy and so was about to sink. Among the passengers was one of those government messengers I just described. Wishing to spare the others, he jumped into the water. But because of this noble attitude, he didn't die and a rainbow appeared above him. These examples show that if you have even temporary bodhichitta when you are about to die, you are certain to be reborn in an excellent place in your future life. Therefore, you have to practice bodhichitta all the time. Once you have it, develop it in your mind and make it stronger and stronger.

How do you make bodhichitta a mental habit? To become used to bodhichitta, always do activities that benefit all sentient beings. To benefit all sentient beings means you continually strengthen the wish that all sentient beings be freed from suffering and achieve a state of happiness. It is to help bring this about that you must awaken bodhichitta all the time.

It isn't enough just to wish that all beings achieve happiness, you must take responsibility yourself, thinking, "I myself will take the responsibility to benefit all sentient beings." Whenever you do any activity, your main purpose should be to make this result come about. The main purpose of all your activities should be to achieve that goal.

This is the starting point, which you can do any time. You can even do it today five or six times, whether you are doing some spiritual practice or any other regular activities. Do them without forgetting your main purpose. This is how you will eventually become used to having bodhichitta in your mind.

These instructions on the two sets of five strengths are very useful. Once you've received them and learned how to practice them, you will know everything about how to live this life and how to go to a future life.

FIFTH POINT:
SIGNS OF HAVING MASTERED THE LOJONG INSTRUCTION

THE FIFTH SECTION OF the *Seven Point Mind Training* relates to how you can determine your level of mastery in this practice. It allows you to know whether or not you have achieved the level that is the goal of the Lojong practice. About this, the root text says:

> All Dharma teachings are based
> on one underlying thought.

"All Dharma teachings" means all those that were taught by the Buddha. Their underlying thought means that the Buddha had only one intention when he taught all 84,000 heaps of Dharma. The purpose and main point of every one of these teachings was to tame, subdue, and eliminate the self-cherishing mind and the belief that a real self exists.

What is self-cherishing mind? What is the belief that things exist from their own side? Buddhist logic, as I mentioned earlier, is a very subtle way of using sharp reasoning to make fine and detailed distinctions. Therefore, we can use logic to distinguish even the slight differences between these two minds. However, the general explanation and one that Je Tsongkapa also gave is that self-cherishing mind is a form of the belief that one has a real self. Therefore, the essence and main goal of all Buddha's teachings is to counteract both self-cherishing as well as the belief in inherent existence.

Tik gyaba is a Tibetan expression that means to "draw a line." This is done, for example, when you are starting to construct a mandala. In Tibet stone masons would split huge rocks to make a pillar, a slab, or whatever form they wanted. Before cutting the stone they would take measurements by marking lines on it with black ink. That way they could cut the stones very precisely. Carpenters also had to mark lines on big pieces of wood before cutting them into whatever boards they needed because they didn't have lumber that was already cut to size in a sawmill.

Namtik is a Dharma term that literally means "a line in the sky." Sometimes you can see a huge white line cutting all the way across an autumn sky at night. Similarly, there is a line that divides Dharma from non-Dharma. But this is a line that only you can determine for yourself. If hearing and learning Dharma instructions helps you to subdue and reduce your mental afflictions, then your Dharma is increasing, which means that the knowledge you gain from studying the teachings is real Dharma. But if your mind only becomes harsher, no matter how many teachings you listen to, nothing you do will help. In that case, your activities are not real Dharma; they are actually non-Dharma.

Devadatta, Buddha's older cousin, had unbelievably extensive knowledge of Dharma. He could recite many volumes from memory, but all that learning and understanding turned into bad knowledge because of his jealousy toward Buddha. Due to his motivation, all of his knowledge turned into poison for him. Therefore, in general, what distinguishes Dharma from non-Dharma is whether or not it helps to remove your suffering and mental afflictions. In the context of this Lojong instruction, it especially refers to what helps remove the mental afflictions of self-cherishing and the belief in an inherently existent self.

Many people like the idea of meditation. They go to a cave or retreat place and stay there for a long time, practicing and practicing, meditating and meditating. After some time they may say, "Nowadays, I am having all kinds of very good dreams," or "While I was meditating many bright lights came and dissolved into me." But these kinds of experiences are not important. You can measure whether your meditation and retreat practice were successful by comparing your mind now to what it was like before you started. Did it become softer and gentler, or did it become more hardened and insensitive? The best sign of success in meditation practice is if your mental afflictions are reduced in number and power. If you can manage to do that, there is no need to ask anyone else whether your practice is succeeding or not.

Continued meditation can at some point bring certain miraculous powers such as being able to fly in the sky. Is that so wonderful? Vultures too can fly in the sky. Just being able to fly is not such a great thing. It would be much greater to subdue your mind by making it better and reducing your mental afflictions.

People cannot pass through the ground. If you try to go in the ground like a mouse, you will only hit your head. But if you practice with a good motivation and achieve the meditative state of quiescence (*shamatha*),[53] you can also achieve what are known as common goals,[54] such as certain miraculous powers. You can then fly in the sky like a bird, go underground as easily as a fish swims in water, or even walk on the surface of water the way people walk on the earth.

Followers of non-Buddhist traditions can also achieve the state of quiescence and along with it these common powers. But since they don't have the motivation even to achieve nirvana, their attainments become causes that further their circling in samsara, and cannot bring any real or lasting peace. Therefore, achieving common miraculous powers is not a definite sign of successful practice. We can't tell for sure if such powers are a good or bad sign; whether they are real or false. But we can be sure that our meditation practice has been successful if our mind changes from renunciation to actual bodhichitta.

Great scholars and sages of previous times called this Lojong teaching the scale that measures whether something is Dharma or non-Dharma, which means that by studying it you can determine whether something is real Dharma or not. Therefore, the indication of whether or not you have

---

[53]See Appendix for a discussion on how to achieve quiescence.
[54]Spiritual powers that are common to Buddhist and non-Buddhist traditions. They include the ability to make single objects appear as many, or many as one, to make objects disappear, to levitate and travel through the sky, and to accurately perceive the thoughts of others.

practiced Lojong successfully is that your self-cherishing mind and your belief in inherent existence are reduced. For example, when Sir Edmund Hillary climbed Mt. Everest, he planted a flag on top of the mountain as a sign of his efforts. This is what the fifth category is about—recognizing the signs of whether your Lojong practice has been successful or not.

Another line from the root text states:

Pay attention to the more important
of the two witnesses.

A witness can be someone who testifies in court about what they saw in order to support or deny some claim. Here the Lojong mentions two witnesses you can have in relation to your spiritual practice: yourself and others. The most important of these is the first, that is, you witnessing your own actions.

Logic uses a technique for analyzing these four categories (*mu shi*) in relation to two qualities: (1) something that has the first quality but not the second, (2) something that has the second but not the first, (3) something that has both, and (4) something that has neither.

Can you find an example of someone who is a human being but not a Buddha? You yourself might belong to that category. Although I can't be certain whether or not you are a Buddha, you can know that about yourself. That is an example of the first category.

An example of the second category would be a being who is a Buddha but not a human. A Buddha's sambhoga-kaya or enjoyment body, which is a deity body, would be an example of this.

Is there anyone who is both a human being and a Buddha? One possible answer would be Buddha Shakyamuni.

What about the fourth category? Usually, in logic it is easiest to find an example of something that includes neither of the two qualities in question. Here, a rabbit would be a good example since it is neither a human being nor a Buddha.

Now let's examine a different situation. Suppose you don't have any genuine spiritual knowledge and you don't practice Dharma nicely, but you pretend to be a great logician, sage, Lama, or Bodhisattva. Showing that kind of outer appearance can fool others into believing that you are a pure and kind-hearted person. This is one of four categories that exist among the two qualities of (1) only appearing to be spiritually ripe on the outside, and (2) actually being spiritually ripe on the inside.

The mango is used to illustrate these four categories. In India, they say there are fifteen different kinds of mango. Some are very good, others are not. Some mangos look ripe and ready to eat on the outside, but on the inside they are not yet ripe; they're still very green and sour. This type of mango is like the person who pretends to be pure but isn't. This represents one of the four categories, that is, the person who seems spiritually ripe on the outside but isn't ripe on the inside. The other three categories are: a mango that looks unripe on the outside but actually is ripe on the inside; a mango that both looks ripe and is ripe; and a mango that doesn't look ripe and actually isn't.

The pretender I described above is like a cat that hides and deceives its prey. Some cats lie very still as though asleep, and won't move even if a rat or mouse comes very close to them. When they are sure they will catch their prey, they will suddenly attack. They trick the rat or mouse in order to get food, because they aren't actually sleeping. Similarly, the common person who doesn't know much about Dharma can be tricked into thinking that a so-called Dharma practitioner is truly a great sage. If you are a Mahayana practitioner, you shouldn't deceive people this way.

The second type of person is spiritually ripe on the inside, but appears to be unripe on the outside. The sage Tilopa's mind was completely ripe on the inside; he had already achieved ultimate Buddhahood. But those who lived nearby called him "beggar Tilopa."

Tilopa acted this way deliberately to spiritually tame Naropa. But, generally, you shouldn't appear unripe on the outside while your mind has become completely ripened spiritually on the inside since it hurts your ability to help other beings. They won't come to you; they won't think you're a great sage. They might even collect very bad karma by speaking disrespectfully about you, like those persons who referred to Tilopa as a beggar. Therefore, by being outwardly subdued you won't cause others to think badly of you.

The Tibetan word *trel-yö* means to have a sense of modesty or propriety. It's a kind of awareness where you think, "Oh, I shouldn't do that because if someone sees me they will get upset or confused, and will think badly of me." This awareness keeps you from doing bad things. Here it especially means to avoid behaving in a way that causes others to have bad thoughts about you. Therefore, if you are spiritually ripe on the inside, you have the most important thing. This makes it easy for you to behave well.

Bodhisattvas will do anything that benefits sentient beings. They won't care if this brings them a bad name, requires them to do something bad, like being caught and imprisoned by police. If it benefits other beings, they will happily give up their lives.

Since we have to live among other human beings, it is not good if they lose respect and faith in us because of our activities. Therefore, by behaving properly at all times, we should try to prevent that from happening. Otherwise we can damage our reputation. When you check your mind in relation to the activities you have done, you should avoid having to be ashamed of yourself: "I did very bad things; I shouldn't have done them, but I did." Instead, you should behave in such a way as to be able to rejoice, "Oh, I behaved well. I did the right thing. I did many good things."

The next line of the root text says:

Always keep a happy mind.

This means, for example, that if you become wealthy, as a Mahayana practitioner you shouldn't always think, "I must try to increase my wealth by investing it in business." Nor should you constantly think about how to protect your wealth from loss or from being wasted. Usually, these aren't considered improper activities. But thinking about and planning what to do with your wealth causes you to busy your mind with many thoughts. Most of the time your plans will fail. Then you will just have that many more thoughts and it will disturb your happiness. Your mind won't be at peace. Therefore, try to avoid thinking too much about such things.

Even if you don't have much wealth, don't exert yourself too much in trying to acquire material things. As a Mahayana practitioner how should you think? "Although I don't have much, at least I don't have that much to worry about either. Rich people have a lot of wealth, but they also have more suffering and more things that disturb them. Instead of being happy and contented, they have more mental suffering." Therefore, whether rich or poor, Mahayana practitioners should use their circumstances as a method for developing their bodhichitta.

If something good happens, realize that this comes as a result of your previous good motivation and positive deeds. Thinking this way helps to develop your bodhichitta. Even if something bad happens, recognize those experiences as burning up your former bad deeds, one by one. "No one other than me created these situations. They are the results of my own bad deeds; therefore, I have no choice but to accept them."

Real Bodhisattvas even enjoy bad experiences. They think, "Now one of my great bad deeds is finished! I got the result! It's finished!" You also have to practice being satisfied with what you have, thinking, "That's enough for me."

If somebody praises you or if you become famous, as a Dharma practitioner you shouldn't react by getting particularly happy about that. And if somebody scolds you or you develop a bad reputation, you shouldn't get discouraged. Don't be concerned about these kinds of circumstances. If you practice this way, you won't let that happiness puff you up with pride. And if something bad happens, you won't put yourself down and feel discouraged. You should maintain an even mind in either case. Your mind won't become disturbed no matter what experiences you meet with. This is a very important quality in a Dharma practitioner. The next line of the root text says:

> If you can practice even when distracted, you have gained mastery.

After hearing and gaining knowledge of these Lojong instructions, you have to be able to remember them all the time so you can put them into practice whenever a particular situation arises. If you learn how to apply this instruction, it will eventually become a habit for you. You have to check yourself, "Am I acting properly or not? Am I thinking properly or not? Am I speaking properly or not?" Always try to maintain recollection and alertness about these points.[55]

Sometimes you will forget and not be able to keep them. You will lose your recollection and alertness. But if you have gotten used to the usual practice, you will be able to keep yourself going in the right direction. For example, some people who ride horses are rookies while others are very advanced. Rookies have to sit carefully and concentrate very hard when they are riding, otherwise they might fall off. But master riders can't be thrown by the horse even if they are thinking about something else, because they are accustomed to riding.

In Tibet, there were warrior horsemen, much like American cowboys, who would fight, shooting at one another as they rode their horses. While the horses were galloping, the warriors would hide their bodies behind one side of the horse with one leg in the stirrup, and then shoot with their guns resting between the horse's ears. They never fell off and didn't even have to think about being thrown. Similarly, if you practice the Lojong instruction continually until you become used to it, someday you can also become a champion. You won't make any mistakes, even when you are thinking about other things.

---

[55]These two mental factors are also described in the context of cultivating quiescence on pp. 263–264 of the Appendix.

Suppose somebody suddenly calls you stupid, accuses you of doing something wrong, or says you're a criminal. If you are a champion in Lojong practice, those words won't hurt you. But if you are a rookie Lojong practitioner and somebody talks to you that way, you won't have strict control of your mind; you will instantly lose your temper and become angry. But, after practicing a long time, you can tell whether you have become a champion or not. If somebody says something bad to you and it doesn't disturb you or make you angry, even when you are not meditating or thinking about the practice, you have reached a good level of mastery. As the root text says:

> The measure of mastery is that self-cherishing has been turned back.

For example, we have a practice of meditating on impermanence. We have to die at some point, and nobody can stop that from happening. That impermanence isn't about the disintegration of outer things, about them breaking, tearing, or getting old. Our impermanence is something that is caused by karma. When our karma is exhausted, we have to die. One of our lives is then finished. This is the meaning of impermanence. Everybody has to experience this condition. It is our nature.

Thinking again and again about this condition and meditating on impermanence, we might decide, "Now, maybe my practice on impermanence is okay. Maybe I can go on to the next meditation topic."

If you want to know whether you are ready to move on to the next meditation topic, you have to check your mind to see whether your desire for this life's happiness has decreased or if you don't think about it very much or at all. If desire for this life's happiness doesn't come into your mind and you are constantly thinking only about the happiness of future lives, you have reached a high enough level of proper meditation on impermanence for you to move on to the next meditation topic. You can also know if you have gained the proper result of practicing renunciation. Along with the desire for this life's happiness, you have to overcome all desire for *any* form of samsara's happiness.

A Mahayana practitioner's main practice is to subdue the self-cherishing mind and develop an attitude of cherishing others. Again and again you have to think about other beings' happiness and constantly do things to help them. All your thoughts, words, and deeds should be of benefit to others. Don't think only of your own purpose any more. When you come to have this attitude, you have gained mastery. Instead of thinking only of your own happiness, you reverse that attitude and think of the purpose and benefit of other beings. The next line of the root text says:

There are five great signs of having trained.

This line refers to the five qualities of being (1) a great ascetic, (2) a great being, (3) a great spiritual practitioner, (4) a great Vinaya-holder or vow-keeper, and (5) a great yogi. If you have these five qualities, you have gained the five great signs that show you have completed the practice.

Sometimes the practices are very difficult, which is why not everyone can do them. If you don't think of your own happiness and always think only of other beings' aims, then it's possible that you may not achieve any purpose of your own and you may not do anything that benefits yourself. Because of that, you may sometime experience suffering and other problems.

When rookies experience suffering and problems in this way, they immediately lose all the strength and power of their practice. But champion Mahayana practitioners will think, "Oh, now my practice must be pretty good. This is a sign that I am succeeding. These problems and obstacles mean I am doing something right; otherwise they wouldn't come."

Therefore, no matter what kind of bad situation occurs, you shouldn't allow it to disturb your mind and shake your equanimity. If your patience becomes strong enough to keep your mind from getting disturbed when something bad happens, then you have achieved the sign of a "great ascetic."

If your mind changes so that you really do care more about others than yourself, you have achieved the mind that is the sign of a "great being."

"Spiritual practitioner" is a person who tries to stop bad deeds and who collects virtue as much as possible. Therefore, if you can practice without ever straying from the ten Dharma activities,[56] you have achieved the sign of a "great spiritual practitioner."

The ten Dharma activities are described in detail in Sutras and other major Dharma scriptures. One of these activities is to memorize the Sutra and Tantra scriptures. If you can't memorize the scriptures, at least you should read them whenever you have time, and try to grasp their meanings.

Another of the ten Dharma activities is to give the oral transmission blessing of the scriptures to others. This blessing is the unbroken continuum of oral recitation from the Buddha's time. To receive this blessing for the entire hundred volumes of the Kangyur collection of scriptures is very difficult. When I was fifteen years old, I received the oral transmission blessing for the sixteen volumes of the *Perfection of Wisdom Sutras* from Kangsar Dorje Chang. To receive such a blessing properly, you have to sit and listen to the recitation attentively; you can't fall asleep.

It takes a long time to finish just those sixteen volumes. Many others have listened to all one hundred volumes of the Kangyur. I very much wanted to do so, but my teacher wouldn't allow it because he thought I was too young. Because I insisted strongly, he let me hear the sixteen volumes of the *Perfection of Wisdom Sutras*.

Another important activity is to try to learn the meanings of the scriptures in order to gain knowledge of them. Doing these ten Dharma activities in relation to the holy Su-

---

[56]According to one traditional list from the *Perfection of Wisdom Sutras*, among others, the ten are (1) to copy scriptures, (2) to make offerings, (3) to practice charity, (4) to listen to Dharma, (5) to memorize Dharma, (6) to read Dharma, (7) to teach Dharma, (8) to recite Dharma, (9) to think about the Dharma's meaning, and (10) to meditate on the Dharma's meaning.

tras and Tantras will keep you busy. By doing this, you will automatically collect great virtue and at the same time avoid doing bad deeds. This will make you a "great spiritual practitioner."

There is another reference to ten Dharma activities in the following verse from the beginning of Lord Maitreya's *Jewel Ornament of Realization*:

The purpose of composing the treatise is
To easily gain a realization of the Sutra's meaning,
Which consists of ten Dharma activities,
So that by keeping in mind that meaning,
Those with intelligence can directly perceive it. [57]

Actually, a Vinaya-holder is an ordained person who does not break any vows and observes them properly. But even if you are not ordained, you still have to keep the morality of refraining from the ten nonvirtuous deeds. There are also the two other classes of vows: Bodhisattva vows and Tantric vows. The main purpose of all the vows is to subdue and control your mind.

If you do these practices nicely, your mind will become subdued and you will be at peace. Vinaya, or *dulwa* in Tibetan, literally means "subduing." "Holder" is the person who subdues his or her mind. If you can do this, you have achieved the sign of a "great Vinaya-holder."

A great yogi or yogini is one who joins his or her mind strictly and one-pointedly to the perfect Mahayana paths. If you can do this, you have achieved the sign of a "great yogi" or "great yogini."

If you practice this Lojong instruction, you can gain these signs, and doing that means you have succeeded in your practice. If you practice a part of some other instruction for a very long time—even for your whole life—you won't be able to achieve any of these five great signs. To gain them, you must practice this very Lojong instruction, which

---

[57]Ch. 1, parts of vv. 2 and 3. In ch. 1, v. 3 of the *Abhisamayalamkara* the ten Dharma activities refer to the ten topics within the first chapter.

teaches Equalizing and Exchanging Self and Others along with Giving and Taking. These two practices are the main focus of the Lojong teaching. While there are other categories in the instruction, their purpose is to help you improve your practice of these two. For example, the five great signs described here indicate whether or not your practice has been successful. The purpose of these other categories is just to give you a way of checking your progress.

SIXTH POINT:
THE EIGHTEEN LOJONG PLEDGES

THE SIXTH SECTION OF the *Seven Point Mind Training* covers the eighteen pledges of the Lojong instruction. Pledges, or *damtsik* in Tibetan, are similar but not identical to vows. Bodhisattva vows, for example, are vows that you promise to observe when you repeat the words of the vow ceremony in front of the merit field that is made up of your Lama along with the Buddhas and Bodhisattvas. A pledge, however, does not require a promise to be made in the context of a formal ritual.

Literally, *damtsik* means something that cannot be ignored, given up or abandoned; it is something that must be kept. In that sense it is like a vow. The pledges are very important and you must keep them even though it may be difficult to do so. If you want to achieve Buddhahood you must keep them.

On the other hand, if someone says he doesn't want to achieve Buddhahood, then there isn't much you can do. You can't force him to do something he doesn't want to do, in which case I might say, "Well then, it's okay for the time being if you don't keep them." It is a Buddhist tenet that every sentient being will eventually become a Buddha. Of course, I don't actually mean that you don't need to keep the pledges. What I'm saying here is that I can't force you to keep them. If every single sentient being without exception will achieve Buddhahood at some point, it logically follows that sooner or later everyone will have to keep the pledges since no one can attain Buddhahood without keeping them.

Why will all sentient beings definitely achieve Buddhahood sooner or later? Because all sentient beings have the "spiritual lineage" [58] or *rik* of a Buddha. It is like being a

---

[58] *rigs*. This is synonymous with what has popularly come to be referred to as

prince. When a king dies, his subjects have to find a successor to rule the kingdom. Similarly, we have a Buddha's lineage in our mind. There are many other terms that relate to this spiritual lineage. One Sanskrit term is *sugatagarbha*, or *dewar shekpay nyingpo*[59] in Tibetan, which means "Buddha's essence." The term we use most on the debate ground is *rangshin nerik*[60] or "innate spiritual lineage."

Some scholars of other systems describe a crucial element of *sugatagarbha* incorrectly. They understand it to mean that sentient beings already have the nature of a Buddha and that this nature is temporarily covered or obscured by the stains of bad deeds. They say that once those stains are removed, a sentient being then becomes an actual Buddha.

In the Gelukpa system we have a term *bakchak goshi*,[61] which refers to the subject or individual that is tainted by the traces or imprints left by our good and bad deeds. Karma is collected when a deed is completed. The seeds of those good and bad deeds are then deposited in the mental continuum. The individual who is related to that mental continuum is the subject tainted by those karmic traces. Each being is the subject that holds his or her own karmic traces. But a Buddha does not collect bad deeds, nor is a Buddha a receptacle or holder of karmic traces or seeds. Given that, how could we say that we are already Buddhas? A Buddha cannot be a subject that is tainted by karmic traces. This is actually a subtle point that has serious implications if it is not properly understood.

There are eighteen Lojong pledges. The first three are referred to in this line from the root text:

Always train in the three general principles.

Buddha-nature.
[59]*bde bar gshegs pa'i snying po.*
[60]*rang bzhin gnas rigs.*
[61]*bag chags bsgo gzhi.*

1.

*Do not let your Mind Training practice
conflict with other precepts.*

The first of the three principles relates to the Hinayana system of vows. There are three Buddhist vehicles: the Listeners' vehicle, the Solitary Realizers' vehicle, and the Mahayana vehicle. Among these, the Mahayana vehicle is the
highest level, because the other two are part of the Hinayana
tradition. If someone asks you, "What level of Buddhism do
you practice?" you might answer, "I do Mahayana Lojong
practice, not Hinayana practice." Although this might be
true, it is completely wrong to think, "I am a Mahayana
practitioner; therefore, I don't have to practice the morality
taught to Listener disciples in the Hinayana's Vinaya system."

For example, without good reason and without performing a special ritual, a monk's Hinayana vows do not allow him to cut even small branches and grass, or dig the
ground more than four inches. A monk shouldn't think, "I
don't have to observe those vows because I am a Mahayana
practitioner." Therefore, this pledge means that you can't
use the Lojong practice as a justification for breaking even
minor Hinayana vows; you have to keep all of them as
strictly as you can.

2.

Do not let your Mind Training practice become reckless.

The second principle might be a little difficult for most
Westerners to understand because they don't believe in
ghosts. Actually, though, there are many different classes of
hungry ghosts and other spirits. Some of them stay near us;
others remain in a tree or by a rock as their main dwelling
place. Certain *nagas* or water spirits also live in springs or
other bodies of water and guard them. If we feed these *nagas*
nicely, the water will remain clear and abundant. But if we
don't, the *nagas* will move and the spring may dry up. This

actually happened in Tibet and Tibetans strongly believe it; but I don't know if you will believe it or not.

Because of this belief, ordinary Tibetan people usually don't like to cut trees for fear of disturbing the spirits that dwell there. However, it is possible for someone to think, "I am a powerful Mahayana practitioner; I don't have any self-cherishing mind. Therefore, I don't care what might happen to me. I'm not afraid of any spirit. Give me the saw, I'll cut down that tree." If you do that, you are using force against those spirits, harming them, and causing them to lose their habitat. Actions motivated by this kind of pride is what is meant here by reckless behavior. The purpose of Lojong practice is only to benefit other beings. Therefore, we can't use it as a justification to act forcefully against others.

3.

Do not let your Mind Training practice be partial.

The third principle is to be impartial when you practice the Lojong instruction. Since you have to practice Exchanging Self and Others, Giving and Taking, patience, loving-kindness, and so on, you shouldn't think, "I can practice patience with my relatives and friends, but not with my enemies," or "I can practice patience with human beings, but not with other kinds of beings." Distinguishing among beings is a major enemy of Lojong practice. Always practice by focusing equally toward all beings.

4.

Change your aspiration but remain natural.

The main subject is, of course, cultivating bodhichitta and Bodhisattva activities. Generally, a Bodhisattva's practice involves training in the six perfections. Here, it means especially to train ourselves in activities that subdue our own mind.

What are we taming? On the one hand, we are trying to tame our selfish mind; on the other we are trying to develop loving-kindness, compassion, and bodhichitta. So a Mahayana practitioner's main goal is to put a stop to self-cherishing mind as soon as possible and to perfect the practices of loving-kindness and compassion.

In this pledge, "change your aspiration" means we have to try to change our motivation and way of thinking. Generally, our mind is very hardened and difficult to tame. First, we have to recognize this about ourselves and then we have to learn how to tame our mind.

The way to tame our mind is to check and see if it is getting better, remaining the same, or even possibly getting worse. We shouldn't let our mind remain at the same level. Although it was previously hardened and mostly following a selfish way, we must not let it remain at that level; we must make it go in a more noble direction. A noble mind is the opposite of a selfish one; it is a mind that cherishes others and thinks about their happiness. One focus, then, is to try and tame our selfish mind; a second is to cherish others.

Because it is difficult to change the mind, Lamas have a skillful instruction that relates to this point. Generally speaking, is it possible to abandon the selfish mind and gain the attitude that cherishes others and tries to benefit them? Of course it is, because both attitudes are impermanent, or caused entities. Buddhist logic shows us that any impermanent entity, because it is caused, is capable of change. If the mind couldn't be changed from self-cherishing to cherishing others, it would be pointless to try. But since impermanent things are changeable, why couldn't you also change your mind? You can be sure of this and you can tell yourself, "Of course I can change. I can change my mind."

How long does it take to make a change in the mind? In the best case, it can be changed within twenty-four hours. A medium level of effort is to try and change it within a month. You should think, "Even if it takes me a whole month to change my mental attitude, I have to do it." The weakest level of effort is to think, "Even though it will be very difficult, still I must change myself within a year."

As a Mahayana practitioner, you can look back to the time when you began to practice Dharma—possibly many years ago—and check if your mind's level and direction has changed or not. You can check whether your mind has become spiritually subdued or not. You know whether you have tamed your mind and how much listening to Dharma teachings has benefited it.

Here Lamas use a rock as an example of an object that doesn't easily change. Some houses have pretty gardens out front, but in the back there may be some huge rocks. Those rocks don't change at all. Instead, they stay hard. Don't be like that huge rock that remains the same, always hard and never changing shape. But, actually, even rocks are changeable. Generally, you can't talk to a rock or cause it to change. But sometimes it is possible for a rock to listen to you and change right in front of you. I realized this when I visited Italy and saw Michelangelo's sculptures. He carved such beautiful statues. Some are completely finished, yet others have parts of the rock left unfinished because he didn't live long enough to complete them. They are all examples of how he could change rocks into exactly what he saw in his imagination. The rocks listened to him! They didn't show any hardness. If ordinary rocks can change this way, why not your mind?

What tools do you need to change your mind? You need bodhichitta, renunciation, and recognition of impermanence. After generating and improving your bodhichitta, you have to use that attitude to tame your mind and do activities that benefit all sentient beings.

But to gain bodhichitta, first you need to develop renunciation. To help sentient beings and liberate them from their suffering, you have to practice the bodhichitta that causes you to think, "How can I free other beings? What kind of suffering and problems do they have?" Before you think of other beings' suffering and problems, you have to realize the nature of your own samsaric suffering. Without examining your own suffering and problems, you can't realize what the nature of other beings' suffering is really like. Therefore, you need to develop renunciation in order to gain actual bodhichitta.

You also need to meditate on impermanence as a method for changing your mind; this is what will help you to realize and understand your own impermanent and changeable nature. If you continually think about your own impermanence, at some point you will have a realization of that topic and receive the blessing of having achieved that knowledge. Knowledge of impermanence has the power to change you and urge you to do something that will benefit your future lives. It will also compel you to begin doing something right away so that you won't have any regrets later. If you don't act immediately, your level will remain the same and later you will regret that you didn't do anything. By then it will be too late.

Once you gain knowledge about this subject it will cause you to start practicing right away, because you are impermanent. This knowledge changes your attitude immediately and later becomes even stronger. When that awareness of impermanence urges you to do something, you will ask yourself, "What should I do?" This will lead to the renunciation that makes you think, "I must free myself from samsara's general and special suffering." If this awareness becomes very strong, it will change your mind and cause you to develop very strong renunciation.[62]

But you have to develop this kind of renunciation further by thinking, "Although I can free myself from samsara's suffering, all sentient beings—who are my mothers—will continue to suffer in samsara the same way that I have. Therefore, it is selfish for me to wish only to free myself from samsara's suffering and not to think about the suffering of other beings. I must also change my own renunciation and

---

[62]One method of developing renunciation is to contemplate the Four Arya Truths (*'phags pa'i bden pa bzhi*), commonly referred to as the Four Noble Truths. First you contemplate the suffering nature of samsara and realize that its causes are karma and the mental afflictions. Then you investigate whether it is possible to be liberated from samsara and whether there is a method or path which leads to that liberation. Renunciation is the sincere wish to achieve liberation that is gained after contemplating these topics.

start thinking about removing other beings' problems and helping them to become free and happy." This kind of thinking leads to bodhichitta. Therefore, the three knowledges of impermanence, renunciation, and bodhichitta are tools that you have to learn to use, one at a time, in order to change your mind.

You can go to Dharma classes, listen to teachings, and gain many kinds of knowledge, but whatever knowledge you do gain you have to *use* to tame and change your mind. Even though you may have listened to a lot of Dharma teachings and have a lot of understanding, unless you use that knowledge to change your mind, it won't benefit you at all. This is what often happens to some people.

Whenever Kyabje Pabongka Rinpoche taught Lamrim, there was always a huge number of disciples. At one teaching in particular, there were eleven thousand students. Among them was a certain monk who had not studied the main subjects of the monastery's curriculum. He went with us to the teaching and heard Kyabje Pabongka's explanation of different Lamrim topics such as the bad qualities of samsara and the good qualities of nirvana. One point in particular was about the main roots of samsara—ignorance, hatred, and desire, which are symbolized by a pig, a snake, and a rooster in drawings of the Wheel of Life. Kyabje Rinpoche taught us about the bad qualities of these mental afflictions and how to get rid of them. But that monk didn't grasp this part of the teaching too well. Later, he came to a lunch that had been arranged by a sponsor where all kinds of fancy foods were prepared for us, including some nice ham and eggs and so on. But this monk said, "I won't eat eggs or pork." When asked why, he said, "Because I have abandoned the three poisons." Then, rolling his eyes upwards and looking very pious, he generated what he believed to be very strong renunciation.

Some of my companions at this meal were very great scholars. We talked about this and had a good laugh. He thought that you could abandon desire and ignorance just by not eating eggs and pork! Actually, he helped us by giving us a good example. This monk had not understood the

teaching on ignorance, hatred, and desire and their antidotes, because if he had, he wouldn't have said what he did.
Therefore, it is improper for practitioners and scholars to
appear outwardly subdued without gaining the knowledge
that changes the mind inwardly. This is a very dangerous
characteristic that can confuse others. It also sets a very bad
example.

You have to develop and increase spiritual knowledge
within your own mind. Improve your mind by making it as
noble and knowledgeable as possible. You can do this by
applying antidotes when you experience problems and suffering. If you do it that way, your mind will be perfect and
will stay that way because you will have done the job nicely,
having laid the proper foundation.

As you practice, gain knowledge, and improve your
mind, try not to show it outwardly; remain natural, the same
as usual. Doing that is a great way to progress spiritually.
Nobody should know what kind of knowledge you may
have developed in your mind. This is what great beings like
Shantideva, Arya Pantaka, and Chandrakirti did.

Shantideva

The Indian saint Shantideva lived at Nalanda Monastery,
where he studied every subject and used that knowledge to
tame his mind. By doing this he became a great and unusual
Bodhisattva, but he never revealed anything on the outside.
Therefore, monks at the monastery gave him the nickname
"Three Thoughts," because everyone believed that all he
thought about was eating, sleeping, and going to the bath-
room. Actually, it wasn't the monks' fault that they saw him
that way. A monastery's necessities come from people who
have faith in the Dharma and the Sangha. They support
monks with donations in order to help preserve and spread
the Buddha's teachings in the world. The monks' main job,
however, is to study, practice, and develop their own
knowledge of these teachings. They can also teach others

and compose religious books, which are ways of helping to preserve the Buddha's teachings in the world.

Shantideva's fellow monks thought that since he wasn't doing any of these activities, it was improper for him to accept any of the offerings made by the monastery's benefactors. They also feared that these donors might lose faith in the general Sangha if they realized a "useless" monk like Shantideva was living at Nalanda. So the monks discussed the situation and decided that Shantideva would have to be expelled.

A monastery is run according to a system designed to maintain peace and prevent fighting and disputes. So it wasn't that easy for the monks to force Shantideva to leave; they had to find a good reason for expelling him. After holding a meeting, the monks agreed that each week a different monk would be assigned to give a teaching to all the other monks. They made a list of which monk would teach each week. This way Shantideva's turn would eventually come up and surely Three Thoughts wouldn't be able to teach a thing. Then it would be easy to get him to leave Nalanda.

One week after another passed as each monk on the list gave his teaching. Finally, it was Shantideva's turn. All the monks whispered and talked among themselves, "Next week is Three Thoughts' turn. What will he do?" When his day came, a huge, high Dharma throne was arranged in the teaching hall, but no staircase was placed beside it. They wanted to make fun of Shantideva even before he began his teaching by making it impossible for him to get up on the throne. A special announcement was made in the nearby towns and cities that there would be a great teaching and that everyone should attend. So all the monks, the monastery's supporters, and many townspeople came to hear the teaching.

When the time came for Shantideva to teach, he entered the hall and did three prostrations before the throne. It is customary for the teacher to make three prostrations to the Dharma throne before sitting on it in order to request permission from the Lineage Lamas to teach and to subdue one's own pride. As Shantideva made his prostrations, everyone murmured, "Now he'll really make a fool of himself." But when he finished prostrating and arranging his robes, he suddenly appeared on top of the throne without anyone realizing how he got there.

"How did he do that?" No one knew. Instead of looking like a fool, Shantideva surprised everyone. He could do this because of his knowledge. After sitting on the throne, he asked the audience, "Today should I teach something that Buddha, Bodhisattvas, and other monks have already taught, or would you like to hear something new?" Surprised by this question, the monks thought, "Maybe he can teach a topic that has already been taught." So they said, "Give us a new teaching."

Shantideva agreed and said, "I have composed three texts. One is called the *Compendium of Training*,[63] but there isn't enough time to teach that today. The second is called *Anthology of Sutra Passages*[64] but this is too short. So, I will teach you the medium-sized one, *Engaging in Bodhisattva Activities*."[65]

Then Lord Shantideva began to teach. The main subject of the first chapter is the characteristics and benefits of bodhichitta. Because it is very difficult to gain bodhichitta, first you must purify your mind-vessel by clearing away bad deeds, which is the subject of the second chapter. Other chapters teach about the ritual for cultivating bodhichitta and taking the Bodhisattva vows, as well as how to practice morality, effort, and the remaining perfections. In all, there are ten chapters.

In the middle of the tenth chapter, while he was still teaching, he slowly began to rise up into the air. Shantideva continued to teach even as he floated higher and higher. Only certain monks who had achieved the special power to hear sounds at a great distance could still hear his voice, but

[63]*Shikshasamuchaya*, see listing in bibliography under Shantideva.

[64]*Sutrasamuchaya*. Although this work was not translated into Tibetan, it is referred to in ch. 5, v. 106 of *Engaging in Bodhisattva Activities*.

[65]*Bodhicharyavatara*, see listing in bibliography.

most of the others couldn't hear him anymore. After some time, even those special monks couldn't hear him any longer. Meanwhile, Shantideva completely disappeared before the teaching was finished. He never returned to Nalanda Monastery.

In our Sera Monastery, we have a special chanting style when reciting the tenth chapter of *Engaging in Bodhisattva Activities*. The scholars and sages who developed the melody for the chant had in mind the image of eagles enjoying their flight in space, so the chant gives you the sense of soaring through the sky. Because of the way Shantideva disappeared, the tenth chapter of this text ends abruptly. It doesn't have a summary or conclusion like most other books do. It just ends with this verse:

I prostrate to Mañjughosha,
Whose goodness makes my mind virtuous.
And I prostrate to my Spiritual Teacher,
Whose goodness makes that virtue grow.

At first, no one knew where Shantideva had gone. Later, a rumor reached Nalanda that he was staying in the south.

Unlike scholars nowadays, those of long ago could listen to a teaching once, remember everything they heard, and then write down all the verses and make a book from them. This is what some scholars did with this particular teaching. Some versions contained extra words, making the volume longer. Others had made shorter versions of what was said. This caused some disagreement about the exact length of the text, to say nothing of the meaning. When the monks heard that Shantideva was staying in the south, they wanted to ask him about the correct length of his *Engaging in Bodhisattva Activities* and also to locate the other works he had composed.

Several messengers were sent to apologize to Shantideva for the measures that had been taken to expel him from Nalanda. They also told him that some scholars had written down versions of his work that contained a little over a thousand verses, while others had put together versions with fewer than a thousand verses. Shantideva said, "I taught exactly one thousand verses." The messengers also asked about the other two texts he had mentioned, the *Compendium of Training* and the *Anthology of Sutra Passages*. He said, "You can find them in the ceiling of my room at Nalanda. I wrote them on some rolls of paper and put them there." After the messengers returned, the texts were found and preserved.

The way scholars and sages compose books is different from the way ordinary people do. When ordinary beings write something, they sometimes get stuck and think, "Now, what should I write?" For example, an anthropologist might have to go to others and ask for information or ideas, or he might read other materials and do research. After writing a book, he might be able to tell you about the main subject, but not necessarily be able to repeat the whole thing word for word. He may or may not remember something he himself wrote if someone were to read it to him. He might even ask, "Did I write that?"

But the method great spiritual scholars use is very different. First they compose the entire work in their mind. If it is necessary to teach it, they are ready to do so from beginning to end. Shantideva composed his books this way. That is what "knowledge" means. Although he was a great Bodhisattva, he didn't show any outer sign, which is why he was called "Three Thoughts" and was made to experience such problems at Nalanda. Therefore, Shantideva's behavior is a good example to follow.

Arya Pantaka

Arya Pantaka, or Pakpa Lamchung in Tibetan, was one of Buddha's disciples who became a great sage. His story is very beautiful and can be found in the collection of Buddha's teachings or Kangyur. Buddha said about him, "Among my disciples, Arya Pantaka is the one most skilled in teaching." Earlier in his life, though, he had been very stupid.

When the Buddha was alive, there was a nunnery nearby. Every two weeks a monk was sent there to teach. One monk had the duty of asking the Buddha each time who among them should go teach at the nunnery. Then that monk would announce who was scheduled to teach and also inform the nuns. One time Buddha appointed Arya Pantaka to go and teach.

When the nuns were told that Pantaka was going to teach them, they held a meeting, saying, "I think Buddha is putting us down by sending Arya Pantaka to teach us. We know his background." So they also made a high throne without stairs, and thought of questions to ask him in order to make fun of him. But Arya Pantaka surprised the nuns in the same way Shantideva had the monks at Nalanda. Again, this happened because Arya Pantaka's mind was completely filled with knowledge, while his outer manner was very humble and subdued.

Chandrakirti

Chandrakirti was also a great pandit whose knowledge was not recognized by the other monks at Nalanda because he kept quiet about himself and didn't show anything outwardly. He also had a nickname like Shantideva and the monks wanted to expel him. One administrator, however, who knew of the monks' plan, was aware of Chandrakirti's high level of knowledge. He told Chandrakirti, "Most people have little understanding, but I know you are the greatest scholar here. Everyone else is bothering me and complaining about you. Now you must accept the duty of monastery caretaker."

The caretaker's main duty is to arrange for all the food and other material necessities of the monastery. Nalanda owned a herd of cows that provided milk for the monks. During the daytime, the cows had to be taken out to graze, but one day Chandrakirti forgot to let the cows out. So that evening, when it came time to offer milk to the monks, the cows had no milk to give.

When Chandrakirti's assistant asked what to do, Chandrakirti said, "Don't worry. Tell the young monks to bring their buckets." Then he led them to a huge boulder nearby, and after drawing a picture of a cow on it, he proceeded to milk the picture. They got even more milk than usual, which was then offered to the monks. Of course they were all amazed and after that no one could criticize him. Chandrakirti was able to do this because his inner knowledge was very high. But he wasn't very famous among Nalanda's pandits, since he kept this knowledge hidden.

All of us who follow this teaching have to practice like this. We shouldn't try to give the impression of being a great practitioner or claim that we have special powers or some high level of realization or that we can see spirits or subdue demons. Those great scholars and pandits never did that and those of us who are disciples of this lineage tradition should not do so either.

Khenchen Ngawang Drakpa

In the Gelukpa tradition, the display of spiritual powers is not allowed. When Je Tsongkapa was living at Ganden Monastery, he had a disciple, the great scholar Khenchen Ngawang Drakpa, who is recognized as having been one of Kyabje Pabongka Rinpoche's previous incarnations. Khenchen Ngawang Drakpa established Gyalrong House at Sera Mey Monastery. Although he had the ability to found many monasteries in his native region near the eastern border of Tibet, he wanted to remain near Je Tsongkapa in order to continue his study and practice. Even Je Tsongkapa could not directly order him to leave, much less the other scholars at Ganden. There was no other way to get him to leave Ganden Monastery except by expelling him as punishment for some infraction.

Every two weeks, monks have to gather for Sojong, a purification ceremony to restore any vows they may have broken. At that time, Gyaltsab Je, another of Je Tsongkapa's famous disciples, was serving as the administrator in charge of discipline at Ganden. It is customary to strike a special board, called a *gendi*, to summon the monks to the main hall. Gyaltsab Je instructed the monk who beat this board, "Tomorrow morning, beat the *gendi* one hour earlier than usual." The other monks, except for Khenchen, were told that Sojong would be held early.

So the next morning when he awoke, everybody had already gone to Sojong. Because monks are not allowed to miss this ceremony, he rushed to get there. But by the time he reached the hall, the door had already been closed and he couldn't get in. He knew that if he didn't attend, the administrator would later ask why and he would have a big problem. So he went up an outdoor stairway to a second-story window that was covered by a huge curtain and climbed through the window. Since it was too high for him to jump from the window into the hall, he used his spiritual powers to float down to the floor of the main hall, making his way into the Sojong ceremony.

Gyaltsab Je knew that Khenchen Ngawang Drakpa hadn't arrived when he closed the main door of the hall. So after the Sojong ceremony ended, he sent for Khenchen. When he arrived, Gyaltsab Je asked him, "Why did you miss Sojong this morning?"

Khenchen Ngawang Drakpa responded, "I went—I was there."

"You were *not* there! I know, because I counted heads and yours was not among them."

"No, truly, I was there."

"I myself closed the door. You weren't there when I closed it. If you attended, how did you enter the hall?"

Of course at this point Khenchen had to tell the truth, so he said, "I came to the door, but it was locked and I couldn't get in. So I went upstairs and came down through the window."

At this Gyaltsab Je pretended to be angry, demanding, "How could you! Showing miracle powers is a violation of our Gelukpa system! We can't show *any* miraculous powers. What a mistake! You can no longer stay at this monastery, but must leave now and go back to your homeland!"

Khenchen Ngawang Drakpa then went to Je Tsongkapa and told him what had happened. Je Tsongkapa told him, "Don't worry. Take this rosary and go to your region and establish a monastery wherever there is a suitable place. When you finish each one, leave a single bead there as a holy object. You will be able to use up all one hundred and eight of these beads. You can do it. You have the ability."

So Khenchen Ngawang Drakpa went back to eastern Tibet and started building monasteries. He named the last one *Datsang*, which means "Now Complete." He built these monasteries, taught in them, and established them very well. The point of this story is that you cannot show any miracle powers in the Gelukpa lineage system.

If you show everybody that you have a wishing jewel or a lot of money in your *jola*,[66] you won't have it for long. Someone will immediately take it from you. There is a similar danger in trying to show others that you have great spiritual knowledge. Keeping quiet about yourself is the best way to behave generally, and especially when it comes to your knowledge.

If you have knowledge and become a great scholar, you will acquire a reputation. Then everybody will want to seek you out, show you respect, and make offerings to you. This will make you very busy and at times you may end up thinking and acting like a big, worldly businessman. If you do that, you yourself will be ruined and you will waste your good opportunity. Then you won't be able to help others either; you won't be able to subdue their minds, teach them, or lead them nicely. That is the danger. But if you keep quiet about yourself, you can avoid those kinds of problems.

When some people teach Dharma or do some other kind of spiritual activity, they need to make a big announcement about what they are doing. Actually, the activity may be quite small, but they have to make a big announcement. This too is a very bad quality.

How should we be? Be like the candle inside a pumpkin on Halloween. It shows light inside the pumpkin, but not

---

[66]A Tibetan-style cloth shoulder bag.

much outside. Like that, your knowledge should be very bright on the inside, but not show much on the outside. This is the best way to be. There is a Tibetan expression: "Hide your spiritual qualities like a light inside a pot." All of these comments relate to the fourth pledge of changing our attitude but remaining outwardly natural.

ཉༀ

QUESTION: One of the Bodhisattva vows is that, if we have special powers, we should use them to help other beings. If we aren't supposed to show special abilities to other people, does this mean that such activities must be done secretly, so that they don't know?

KHEN RINPOCHE: Anyway, what kind of powers do you have? You have to examine the situation to see what is best. The main point here is that you should not make a show of any special abilities. When farmers in Tibet try to sell a goat's head or a yak's head, they put it on a table in the marketplace for people to see. When people ask how much it costs, the farmer will tell them whatever amount he thinks he can get for it. Sometimes farmers carry a whole skinned pig or sheep carcass on their shoulder, yelling, "Wanna buy a whole pig? Wanna buy a whole sheep?" If someone is interested, they will ask, "How much?" and then maybe buy it. If you have some spiritual power or knowledge, you can't announce it like this, as if you were in a marketplace.

Sometimes people might really want the benefit of your knowledge. Even if they do, you still must check to see if the person is a proper disciple for you to teach. If they are, you can help them. Otherwise, you can't. It is also improper to teach those who lack faith.

QUESTION: It would seem that if I did develop bodhichitta on the inside, my outer manner would also change. A person's outer manner shows itself in relationships with others. If my mind changes for the better, it seems to me that my outer manner would also improve. Given that, how do we go about keeping this fourth pledge?

KHEN RINPOCHE: Automatically, you can get a sign in your mind of what your level of knowledge is. You can see for yourself what is happening in your mind. Although you don't have to show your spiritual knowledge through your outer manner, generally you should behave nicely in your everyday activities. If you act this way, people will realize that you have a good mind. This can lead them to the hope that you will help them. Then they will come and tell you their problems and wishes. You can check what is a proper way for you to help them. "Keeping the same outer demeanor" doesn't mean that you shouldn't help others.

For example, the great Indian yogi Tilopa was called "the beggar Tilopa" by local people. When Naropa was searching for him, he asked different people, "Where is the great sage Tilopa?" Nobody could tell him because they didn't know about any sage named Tilopa. They all said, "Around here we only know a beggar Tilopa; we've never heard of any great sage Tilopa."

So one day Naropa asked someone, "Where is the beggar Tilopa?"

And the person replied, "He comes here sometimes, but he's not here today."

Then another day a large arrangement of food and offerings was prepared for a service at a main temple. Tilopa came and sat outside the temple and began preparing his own food. He built a small fire and placed a pot of live fish beside it. He then took fish from the pot and began to cook them over the fire.

Someone told Naropa, "That is the beggar Tilopa."

Naropa went over to see if it was the Lama Tilopa, but the man looked like a real beggar. When he took another fish from the pot and started to cook it, Naropa said, "Oh, don't do that! You mustn't cook it!"

Tilopa replied, "This is my regular food. Why can't I cook it?"

"No, that's a very bad deed. You can't do that."

"All right," said Tilopa. Then he threw the cooked fish into a nearby pond. When the fish landed in the water, it came back to life and happily swam away.

Then Naropa thought, "This isn't just a beggar; he has great spiritual powers. Maybe he *is* the real Tilopa."

As soon as Naropa thought that, Tilopa declared, "Yes, I am Tilopa." Then he continued to do more "bad deeds" as before.

This time Naropa thought, "Maybe he isn't the real Tilopa after all."

So Tilopa said, "No, I'm not him." At this point Naropa realized that Tilopa was clairvoyant. Naropa continued to check this way for many days, trying to determine if this was really the Lama he was looking for.

༄༅

5.

Do not speak about the faults of others.

This pledge teaches you about proper speech. It means that you should not speak about or describe others' faults.

6.

Do not be concerned with others' business.

If you want to examine anyone's faults, check your own. Ask yourself in relation to your activities of body, speech, and mind, "Am I doing the right things or not? Am I saying the right things or not? Am I thinking the right things or not?" Check your own activities, not those of others. If you continually examine others' activities, you will definitely find many faults, especially if you examine an ordinary person's behavior. But most of the time our mind perceives things in a mistaken, inaccurate way. If our mind is mistaken, what we perceive about objects will also be mistaken. For example, Buddha had a disciple named Udayi, or Charka in Tibetan, who stayed with him and served him for twelve years. Even so, Charka would say about the Buddha, "I didn't see any good qualities in Buddha except that he had a halo of light that extended four feet from his body." He continually saw nothing but bad qualities in the Buddha. It doesn't matter whether a person actually has a particular bad quality or not; a mistaken mind will still perceive something as bad and believe it to be true. This hurts others and also badly hurts oneself.

Your Lama and fellow practitioners can also serve as examples. If you check your Lama wrongly, you might think, "This Lama talks very nicely in class, but he never practices the teachings himself." You might also perceive him in many other ways and think things like, "He is very greedy and stingy," "He is a short-tempered person," or "He is very strange." You may have similar thoughts about your friends and fellow practitioners. "Some of them are very friendly, but others are very unfriendly." They appear that way to you. If you aren't careful, you may not be able to find a single pure person anywhere in the world. Everyone will appear to have one kind of fault or another. This is one of the worst qualities you can have and it is a very important point to understand.

Buddha taught about this in the Sutras. Dharmakirti also taught it in his root text on logic, the *Commentary on Valid Cognition*. Many sages and scholars have explained the meanings of those root texts. Although these are difficult subjects, I will describe this one point. Suppose I asked you, "Could a ghost be standing right in front of you watching you, listening to you, and checking what you are doing?" You can't answer with a definite "no," because that would mean you determined with certainty through unerring cognition that no ghost is present. That kind of certainty is very difficult to achieve. But you can't answer with a definite "yes" either. About this point, Dharmakirti's root text states:

Non-occurrence of correct cognitions

Results in a non-occurrence in relation to an absence.[67]

Before you can recall having seen a ghost in front of you, first you must have actually seen a ghost. Being able to remember that perception is a second step that can only come after the first step. Therefore, without perceiving a ghost with unerring cognition you cannot have a memory of having perceived it. Similarly, if you look at another person and ask yourself, "Does he have renunciation or bodhichitta or correct view?" You can't answer with certainty either, "Yes, he does," or "No, he doesn't," because you don't have any correct cognition about whether he does or does not have any of these types of knowledge. So if you say, "No, he doesn't have any of those knowledges," that "no" can't be said with any certainty whatsoever, because you don't have an unerring cognition in relation to the object. You can't tell whether that person is an actual Bodhisattva or a great sage.

For example, when Naropa first saw Tilopa, he appeared to be a very poor beggar. But actually Tilopa was a great yogi who had already achieved Buddhahood. Asanga also first saw his Lama Maitreya as an injured dog, even though that dog was actually Maitreya. Therefore, if we say that someone is not a Bodhisattva when he or she actually is one, we commit a grave error and collect a very heavy misdeed.

---

[67]*Commentary on Valid Cognition (Pramanavarttika)*, ch. 1, v. 3. The cryptic root text of Dharmakirti's treatise cannot be understood without referring to commentarial literature. These lines are the first reference to the third type of valid reason recognized in Buddhist logic, called *ma dmigs pa'i rtags* or in Sanskrit *anupalabdhi*, an argument based on the non-apprehension of something. The first line, "Non-occurrence of correct cognitions" refers to someone who does not have the capacity to perceive certain types of objects. Gyaltsab Je's commentary uses the example of someone who cannot perceive a ghost or spirit. The second line, "Results in a non-occurrence in relation to an absence," means that because such a person can't perceive a ghost, it follows that he can't assert that ghosts exist because he lacks the subsequent cognition (*bcad shes*) that follows the first moment of cognition (*tshad ma*). The fundamental concept here is that the first moment of correct cognition is always followed by successive cognitions. These are what enable someone to assert the existence of the object of their correct cognition. The non-occurrence of the first correct cognition—in this case, perceiving a ghost—would make it impossible for this person to assert or deny the existence of ghosts.

Similarly, you can't be sure whether someone is really a demon or not. Demons can very skillfully give the appearance of being gentle and nice, but actually their main purpose is to deceive others. This might lead you to think and say about someone, "He is a real Bodhisattva—a very good person and a great sage." If you make everyone else believe this and you also believe it yourself, all of you will end up going in the opposite direction of the Buddhas because you are believing in a demon. Gyaltsab Je Dharma Rinchen, Je Tsongkapa's successor, wrote about this very important point in his logic commentary, *Clarifier of the Path to Liberation*:

> Because one can never be sure about who is a holy being, to criticize such a person is described everywhere in Sutras and Tantras as a perfect cause for having to be reborn in the terrible lower states. Therefore, intelligent people should be extremely mindful about this point as though it were a fire pit covered over with ashes.[68]

So, be careful when describing other beings as holy Bodhisattvas or as demons with bad qualities, since it is like a nice covering of ashes over a fire pit. If you walk over one, you will fall into the fire and get burned.

When Buddha Shakyamuni was alive in India, there was a rich family that was deceived by some charlatans. These false sages told the family, "You must kill Buddha and his great disciples." When they asked how to do this, they were instructed to arrange food that contained a deadly poison. They were also told to prepare a concealed fire pit just inside the gate of their home so that anyone who tried to enter would have to walk across it and fall into the fire. Then they were to invite the Buddha along with his disciples to come to their house the next day to recite prayers and have lunch.

Buddha agreed to go, but just before leaving he said to his disciples, "Today, no one can enter that place before me." Then, without saying anything else, Buddha went ahead of

---

[68]*Clarifier of the Path to Liberation* (*thar lam gsal byed*), p. 28. See bibliography.

the others. When he reached the fire pit it turned into a lake that immediately became covered with many lotus flowers sturdy enough to support a person's weight. So the Buddha and his disciples were able to cross the pond safely and enter the house. After realizing that they could not harm the Buddha or his disciples, the family felt extreme regret and confessed what they had tried to do. Buddha responded to them by saying, "I struggled for many, many eons to overcome these kinds of difficulties; such small things cannot harm me at all. Don't worry about me."

The above two pledges have to do with being restrained in our speech and being careful about how we perceive others.

7.

Remove your worst mental affliction first.

Why is it that we remain in samsara, experiencing all of samsara's different kinds of suffering one after the other? What is the source of these problems? Who created them? We did. We arranged them all perfectly at a previous time. How? Our own mental afflictions motivated us to collect many bad activities of body, speech, and mind. These are the causes that make us experience suffering endlessly.

If you don't like to experience suffering, you have to try to stop planting its causes. There is no result that can come without causes. Because our suffering is caused by the mental afflictions, we have to learn how to remove those afflictions. The instruction relating to this pledge is that you should eliminate your strongest mental affliction first. Although you have to remove all the mental afflictions, you should start with the one that is the strongest in you.

Which of your mental afflictions is the strongest? Is it desire, hatred, or ignorance? If you have very strong desire, you should practice its antidote first. If hatred is the stronger affliction in your mind, practice hatred's antidote. By terminating the strongest mental affliction first, you will gradually be able to remove the others easily. That is the way to destroy them all.

In the yard at the temple, there are many dandelions in the summer and many leaves in the fall. One fall, I raked all the leaves on a Thursday, but there were more on the ground on Friday. So I raked them again on Friday. Then on Saturday morning, because of the wind, there were even more leaves than before. There is one particular area in a corner by some steps where a lot of leaves gather. First I tried raking them, which is easy with the ones that pile up in front. But it is difficult to rake just the few that are left in the back. So I set aside the rake and picked those leaves up one by one. That was much easier and the yard was left very clean.

There are two types of obstacles that are to be abandoned by the Buddhist path: those that are abandoned by the Path of Seeing and those that are abandoned by the Path of Meditation. As I was picking up the leaves one by one, I thought to myself, "This is like practicing the antidote to the obstacles that are to be abandoned by the Path of Meditation."

The main form of this kind of obstacle is the mind that grasps at self-existence. There are two forms of this mistaken belief: the first kind is a belief that ascribes self-existence on the basis of bad reasoning, which is conceptual or acquired wrong view.[69] This kind of mistaken belief, which is conceptual, is easier to remove than the second kind, which is innate grasping at self-existence.[70] If you meditate on the emptiness that is the real nature of samsara's suffering and its causes, eventually you will be able to achieve a direct realization of this emptiness.

Once you have reached the Path of Seeing, in which you perceive emptiness directly, all conceptual forms of wrong views are eliminated. However, just perceiving the real nature of things directly once does not remove the innate form of grasping at self-existence. Innate grasping at self-existence

---

[69]*kun brtags.*
[70]*lhan skyes.*

is not removed at the Path of Seeing, but at the Path of Meditation. This means that you can't abandon the innate grasping at self-existence just by seeing the real nature of things but you have to meditate continually on each antidote to the various types of innate grasping at self-existence. You have to practice over and over in order to abandon those obstacles one by one.

Each of the Bodhisattva levels—from the first to the tenth—has three types of innate grasping at self-existence. The lower levels have rough forms, and as you advance through the levels the subtlety of innate self-grasping increases. The most subtle form of grasping at self-existence is not abandoned until just before you achieve Buddhahood.

To sum up, you can abandon some of the mental afflictions by having a direct realization of emptiness. But for other mental afflictions, you have to apply each one's particular antidote. And, as stated by this pledge, first you should abandon the strongest mental affliction, that is, the one that disturbs your mind most often.

8.

Give up all hope of achieving results.

When you go to a store, you can buy whatever you want by showing your dollar and exchanging it right there for whatever you need. While this is true for ordinary things, you can't do the same thing with virtues and the results of virtue. For example, you might think, "Oh, tomorrow I have something very important to do. I have to go to a meeting with my boss or with some businessman. I really want this meeting to go well so that I can reach my goals." Because of that, you may pray: "Namo Gurubhya, Namo Buddhaya, Namo Dharmaya, Namo Sanghaya." It's very possible that when you go to the meeting the next day it will be a failure. Then you will come home disappointed, thinking, "Well, I failed; my prayers didn't help me. Taking refuge didn't help me either." This shows that your attitude toward the Dharma is like that of a shopper at a store.

This point is especially important for a Dharma person to understand. What about the situation I just described? Doesn't it help to pray for results? It does help. Sometimes it helps directly and brings what you want right away, while at other times it might take a long time to see a result. When you fail at something, it means you got a bad result. You collected the cause of that bad result at some earlier time. That cause and result represents one set of karma. You collected a bad deed at some previous time and its result has now occurred. When you took refuge in the Buddha, Dharma, and Sangha and made prayers to them, you collected a new form of virtue. Its main result will come later. That cause and result is another set of karma.

Sometimes your prayers do help right away. Generally speaking, your prayers definitely always help, but you won't necessarily get positive results immediately, a hundred percent of the time. But, this shouldn't matter to you when you're practicing, praying, or meditating. You should think, "The results will definitely come. Whether it is sooner or later depends upon the strength of my virtue, practice, faith, and effort. The goals will come to me, but it will take some time." If you have this attitude, it won't matter to you whether results come quickly or not. You should have the kind of determination that makes you think, "I will never give up my practice to achieve the ultimate goal." By achieving the ultimate goal of Buddhahood, temporary goals will automatically come as well.

The main point is that you should never think of your spiritual practice as something that can be traded for beneficial results the way a shopper exchanges money for things in a store. Otherwise, you are in great danger of developing a wrong view about your practice and losing faith in the holy objects.

9.

Avoid poisonous food.

Of course, no one thinks that you should eat food containing poison. But here "poison" specifically means self-cherishing mind and the wrong view of grasping at things as self-existent. These are a Mahayana practitioner's main obstacles. "Eating poisonous food" means doing activities of body, speech, and mind with a selfish motivation. If we do this, we cannot practice Mahayana Dharma properly. Therefore, Mahayana practitioners have to try to abandon this kind of poisonous food.

There are two technical Buddhist terms that relate to the wrong belief in a self: the "transitory-collection view that perceives an 'I'"[71] and the "transitory-collection view that perceives things as 'mine.'"[72] These two forms of grasping at self-existence are the main leaders of samsara's wheel. The first one focuses on you and believes that you are an independently real self. The second one focuses on your five heaps and believes that they are independently real things belonging to that self. This twofold grasping at self-existence has a very tight hold on you. It makes you think, "I am, I am, I am." "I shouldn't be poor." "I shouldn't be foolish." "I shouldn't experience any bad situations." It also makes you think, "I want to have a long life." "I want good health." "I want to be wealthy." "I want to succeed in everything."

You need to have a pure motivation. The best kind of motivation is renunciation, bodhichitta, and the right view of emptiness. Therefore, the meaning of this pledge is that you shouldn't do even virtuous deeds with a selfish motivation and the wrong view of grasping at self-existence.

Most people who don't know about this instruction will go to a temple when they get sick or experience some prob-

---

[71] *ngar 'dzin pa'i 'jig tshogs la lta ba.*

[72] *nga yi bar 'dzin pa'i 'jig tshogs la lta ba. 'Jig tshogs* refers to five heaps that are a "collection" of entities and "transitory" in that they pass away from moment to moment.

lem and pray, recite mantras, do prostrations, or offer flowers. They will pray that their problem will go away and that they gain happiness. In one respect, these kinds of activities are generally considered virtuous. But since their motivation is mixed with self-cherishing mind and the wrong view that grasps at self-existence, these activities are ruined and wasted. It is like putting poison in food. You must avoid that kind of motivation from the beginning, because it turns your virtuous activities into poisonous ones.

While it is easy to hear and understand this instruction, it can be very difficult to actually maintain the proper motivation in your various activities. You have to remember this point and have the right motivation when you are preparing to do some activity. First stop your self-cherishing mind, then try to generate bodhichitta.

If you say, "I'm going to the temple today. I am going to see holy places, holy images. I'm going to do prostrations and make offerings." If someone asks you why, you might answer, "To help all beings." But it isn't so easy to help all beings; you have to have enough power and complete knowledge. To gain this knowledge and power, first you yourself have to achieve Buddhahood. After that, you can help beings with activities that will benefit in a complete way. Therefore, when you are planning to do some virtuous activity you should think, "I am going to do this good activity so that I can achieve Buddhahood for the benefit of all beings. At that time I will be able to do the things that help beings in many ways." That is a Bodhisattva's daily attitude and the way a Mahayana practitioner should prepare to do activities.

10.

Do not be patient [with your mental afflictions].

Generally, being patient is a noble person's quality. This pledge doesn't mean that you shouldn't be patient with others; that is definitely the right thing to do. It means that you shouldn't be patient toward the mental afflictions that come into your mind, nor should you allow them to increase and get stronger. You shouldn't think, "Now I'm going to be visited by a huge fit of anger. Come on in! Welcome! Make yourself at home! Get really angry!" Stop your mental afflictions, don't welcome them into your mind.

There is an instruction for what high government officials should do if they get a problem from some political enemy:

Instead of showing anger to a disturbing enemy,
A skillful person greets him with an artificial smile.

This quotation means that you have to be very careful and clever. How? When you see and talk to an enemy, even though you know that he is your enemy and someone who makes trouble for you, you shouldn't show him a dark or angry expression. Instead you should smile and be pleasant. Normally, people change their expressions when they see their enemies or their friends. If you are very skillful, you should show the same expression to both; you shouldn't smile at your friends and frown at your enemies. You should smile and behave politely even toward your enemies. This is how to show yourself to be a noble person. This kind of advice describes a politician's way of being polite and noble. Scowling and being unfriendly to your enemies will only bring you an immediate bad result.

The spiritual way of being polite and noble is to *sincerely* and warmly greet the people that you meet. You should receive them with compassion and love and say, "Hello, how are you? Please come in and sit down. Is there anything I can do for you? Do you need any help?" These words should be a genuine expression of your true feelings. They shouldn't be an act, like a politician. This is what it means to be noble and good in the spiritual sense.

While this is the way you should behave toward other beings, you can't be that way in relation to your own mental afflictions. If you are tolerant and lenient with them, they will only come to your mind more and more, and with greater and greater strength. They will control you, defeat your noble quality and completely destroy it. Therefore, when the mental afflictions come into your mind, you must immediately take action to stop them by applying the appropriate antidote.

Again, it isn't enough just to hear this instruction. First of all, after hearing and developing knowledge about it, you shouldn't forget it. When a situation arises, right then you have to use this instruction and apply the proper antidote. Otherwise, the teaching cannot help you. For example, when you find yourself starting to get angry, you have to try to stop it; don't welcome it into your mind. The way to stop anger is to think about its bad results.

You have to remind yourself: "Anger is very bad. I know about its bad results. I shouldn't welcome it. I must stop it." Some of the bad results of anger are very easy to understand. The first is that an angry person's face will change color immediately. You don't like to see it in others, so naturally others won't like to see it in you. If anger is something that you and others don't like to see in a person, why should you welcome it into your mind? Therefore, tell yourself that you must stop it from entering your mind.

Anger also immediately disturbs everyone's peace and happiness. During the time that you allow yourself to become angry, there is no way you can remain happy or have peace of mind. Your anger also disturbs others. If another person who has good self-control realizes that you have become angry, he will think, "Oh, this person has gotten angry. I think I had better go away for the time being. I'll come back to talk with him another time." But if the other person is short-tempered, he won't go away and the two of you will burn each other with your anger. Then the situation will only get worse. Sometimes anger can bring about a very bad result that you can hear and see. These are the kinds of bad results that you can easily understand.

In a spiritual and philosophical sense, anger burns away our virtuous deeds. Some of them can be burned away completely, down to their roots. Other virtuous deeds can have their power weakened and their amount reduced by anger. Just as a huge pile of hay can easily be burned by a single match, if you let even a slight bit of irritation or anger grow in your mind, it will immediately burn and destroy a huge amount of virtuous deeds that you collected in the past. This type of bad result is difficult to understand without studying Buddhist philosophical teachings.

How is it that anger can completely destroy some virtues and only diminish others? As I mentioned earlier, good deeds that are collected for one's own benefit alone are weaker in strength and smaller in amount. But virtuous deeds collected with the wish to benefit all other beings are immeasurable. Therefore, anger can only reduce their power somewhat; it cannot destroy them from the roots. Those virtuous deeds are countless because you collected them for the sake of all beings who are also countless.

For example, the easiest mantra to learn and recite is *Om Mani Padme Hum*, which is the mantra of Avalokiteshvara, the Buddha of Compassion. If you recite this mantra once to benefit yourself, that virtuous deed is very small. But if you recite *Om Mani Padme Hum* for the benefit of all sentient beings, the virtue of that recitation is measureless. It is this latter kind of virtue that anger cannot destroy from the root.

In short, you have to practice noble activities of body, speech, and mind toward everyone. But you shouldn't welcome any of the mental afflictions—weak or strong—into your mind.

11.

Do not engage in bitter quarreling.

Some people think it is cowardly not to become angry and defend themselves against the criticisms of others. But in the Mahayana Dharma, it isn't cowardly. A person who does not get angry or does not try to defend him- or herself is considered a great hero or heroine. In the Mahayana field, a great hero is someone who can defeat the mental enemies, which is very difficult to do; an ordinary person cannot do it easily, if at all.

During a political campaign, you often hear candidates openly criticizing and complaining about one another. If you are a candidate and your opponent criticizes you, you have to come back with a stronger, sharper, and worse criticism of him. A politician has to try and silence the enemy's mouth with his own words. If you don't, you are not considered a hero. People will think you are foolish and incapable of coming up with a response. They will think your campaign is worthless.

In the Mahayana Dharma field, however, the Bodhisattva who can tolerate the complaints and criticisms of others is considered a hero. The ordinary person will think, "I can't bear this. If I practice patience, others will think I am stupid and a coward." Practicing patience and other virtues are very difficult. You at least must develop an understanding of these instructions. Eventually, you also have to try to practice them.

If you cannot tolerate someone's criticism and feel it necessary to respond, you should do so very reluctantly and with a sense of having no other alternative. This will lessen the bad deed somewhat. The opposite attitude, for example, would be for you to kill a deer and then think, "What a great thing I did today. I shot a deer. Now I can enjoy the meat for a few days." A slightly better reaction would be, "It's wrong to kill a deer. It causes the deer incredible suffering; it causes death. Although I don't like what I did, I only did it so I could get some food." In the second attitude, the antidote is mixed with the bad deed; therefore, the bad deed is not as strong. The first attitude lacks any antidote. A person who thinks that way actually takes pleasure in what he did, making that kind of bad deed heavier and stronger. In the Mahayana Dharma field if someone tries to argue with you, you should forget about it; that is a hero's reaction. How do you forget about it? If you actually are a bad person, then that is what you are whether someone says so or not. If you are a good and noble person, it doesn't matter whether someone says you are good or bad; your actual good quality will still be there. Dharma practitioners should have this kind of knowledge. It doesn't matter what anyone says about them. They won't argue back with harsh words.

If you observe the following four principles, you are worthy of being called a spiritual practitioner: (1) not to respond to harsh speech with harsh speech, (2) not to respond to anger with anger, (3) not to respond to criticism by criticizing, and (4) not to respond to being beaten by beating.

Normally if someone says, "You're an old dog!" you might answer, "Oh yeah? Well you're a thief!" Then the accusations increase and get worse and worse. If someone tries to beat you one time, you might try to hit him back twice. In hockey, that is exactly what the players do. When two players are fighting and one hits the other once, then the second one tries to hit the first one twice.

When I watch professional athletes on television, sometimes I think they are very skilled at their sport; at other times their behavior seems ridiculous. If two athletes are doing their job for pay, they are both employees. How silly of them to hit each other. It is worse than going on strike against an employer. At least a strike has a purpose, like a pay raise. But when two athletes beat each other to the ground, there is no point at all; it's just foolish. It would be much better if they just played fairly and tried to protect each other from physical harm.

12.

Do not wait along a back alley.

This pledge refers to behavior that politicians often engage in. For example, if you have an enemy, you won't like his attitude or activities. So you say to yourself, "I know what I have to do. I will get my revenge. I will wait for a good opportunity to harm and defeat him. When the time comes, I will definitely get the better of him." Sometimes thieves or muggers hide in a quiet, back road, waiting until some unsuspecting person comes by. Then they suddenly attack and mug that person. You shouldn't be like this, waiting for an opportunity to harm your enemy.

This kind of attitude and motivation is especially bad, because you have to hold it in your mind for a long time. During that time, the power of the bad deed gets stronger and heavier. This is like a politician who hates his opponent from the bottom of his heart, but smiles and greets him warmly when he sees him. Although his face is bright and smiling, his mind is dark. Mahayana practitioners should not involve themselves in this kind of deception.

In the worldly arena of politicians and businessmen, a person who knows how to act this way is admired and thought of as skillful. But in the Dharma field, this is one of the worst kinds of behavior. It shows how the worldly and spiritual realms are in direct opposition.

The contradiction between the worldly and the spiritual comes from the difference in attitudes and activities such as these. It does not mean that it is improper for a spiritual person to be in the world associating with others, talking and working with them. Buddhas and Bodhisattvas come back into the world even after they have achieved nirvana and Buddhahood. Sometimes they come back as an ordinary human being in order to help others. When they do, they have to associate with others by talking and working with them. This kind of behavior is not in contradiction with the Dharma. The worldly things that are in contradiction with Dharma practice, nirvana, and Buddhahood are the kinds of negative attitudes I described above.

13.

Do not strike a vital point.

When you spend time with others, you can observe their attitudes and behavior and learn about their faults and what bad activities they may have done. Many businessmen and government officials get into trouble when the people who work with them see them doing things that are wrong. But as a Mahayana practitioner who works with others and sees their faults, you should not expose these faults in front of others or criticize them publicly.

This pledge also applies to how we should treat demons, ghosts, and certain demigods. Some demigods are good, but others have very bad minds. Demigods with very bad minds are what we usually call demons. But there are also many human beings that are demons. A demon is any being whose main purpose and attitude is to harm others, to destroy their happiness and the source of their happiness. The activities of demons are to harm and kill other beings.

In my lifetime, I can say Mao Tsetung was the greatest demon. Even though he was a human being, he was an unbelievably bad demon. He tried to sabotage the source of beings' happiness—the Dharma. Thousands and thousands of temples were destroyed because of him, and huge numbers of learned scholars and practitioners of the Dharma were killed. He took many lives and took away peoples' right to pursue happiness. You can't find any actual demon as horrible and powerful as that human demon was.

Buddhism classifies all beings into two types: Buddhas and non-Buddhas. Beings that are non-Buddhas are further divided into those of the six realms:[73] the three lower realms and the three higher realms. There is no seventh realm. Anyone who is a sentient being must belong to one of these six realms. Therefore, demons too must be included in these six realms. Some demons can be human beings, some demigods, some worldly gods, some animals or *nagas*, and some hungry ghosts. Since the condition of hell beings is so bad and they can't do anything except experience extremely heavy suffering, they don't have the opportunity to harm others much.

You might think it is proper for a great sage or holy being to perform rituals and recite powerful mantras to destroy, defeat, and control demons. But as followers of the Mahayana Dharma, we shouldn't do that kind of activity. What can we do? We have to pray and recite mantras in or-

---

[73]See p. 37 above.

der to help decrease those demons' bad mental attitudes and transform their minds so that they develop good attitudes. We should pray that they develop bodhichitta as soon as possible, and that they gain the knowledge that makes them want to help other beings instead of harm them. That is your duty as a Mahayana practitioner.

14.

Do not displace a dzo's load onto an ox.

In Tibet, a *dzo* is the best animal farmers can use for plowing their fields. A *dzo* is the male offspring of a *yak* and a cow. It has a gentle disposition, doesn't tire easily, and is easy to feed. It is very strong and can carry a much larger load than an ox. Therefore, you shouldn't try to put a *dzo's* load onto an ox, because it will only cause a problem for the ox. Similarly, if you work with another person—for example, as police officers often do—and you do something wrong, you shouldn't put the blame on your partner. There is no worse way of giving him a bad name and trouble.

15.

Do not practice wrongly as if doing worldly rituals.

The purpose of these instructions is to help the Mahayana practitioner subdue the self-cherishing mind. If you are trying to subdue your selfish mind all the time, you won't do the worst thing when you find yourself in the kinds of situations that are described here; you will practice patience. If you are a great scholar and sage, you should do activities that will benefit other beings.

If your practice is motivated instead by the selfish wish to become famous, or to stop the harmful influence of demons, then you are behaving like someone who does rituals for achieving some worldly purpose. Sometimes a person's sickness can be caused by the influence of bad spirits and demons. Medicine won't help to cure this type of illness; the only thing that will help is to satisfy the harmful spirit and do what it wants. This can be accomplished through special prayers and rituals, and by offering *tormas* to the spirit. This is what is meant here by "worldly rituals." However, your practice of the Lojong teaching should not be polluted by selfish aims and used to serve this kind of purpose.

16.

Do not try to be the fastest.

If you are a Mahayana practitioner and own something jointly with someone else, such as another family member or a business partner, it is wrong to try and act quickly so that you can get it all for yourself. When something is being divided up and distributed to a group of people, you shouldn't try to get the best part for yourself and leave the rest for everyone else.

17.

Do not turn a god into a demon.

Suppose somebody asks you, "What are you doing these days?"

You might answer, "I am practicing to reduce, subdue, and destroy my selfish mind."

"Oh, that's very good. Does it help? Is it getting weaker?"

"No, it's getting worse."

If a demon is trying to harm you, you have to take refuge in the divine protectors who can save you. But if the protectors themselves turn into demons for you, then you won't be able to get any protection. Therefore, you shouldn't let your practice turn into something that hurts you instead of helps you. If your efforts at spiritual practice only make your mind worse, then you are "turning a god into a demon" and there is no way that you will be able to tame your selfish mind.

18.

Do not seek others' misery as a way to be happy.

Suppose a Mahayana Dharma practitioner says, "I want peace and happiness." Then somebody asks him, "You haven't found peace yet?"

"No."

"But you do want peace and happiness?"

"Yes."

"So, what's the problem, what's bothering you?"

"My enemies."

"What do you want?"

"I want them to die very quickly." This kind of attitude is the opposite of what a Mahayana Dharma practitioner should have. You shouldn't think that the way to find peace and happiness is through the destruction of your enemies. That is the worst kind of selfish mind. If you think that way, you are not looking for real happiness and peace at all. Instead, you are actually looking for suffering—the opposite of peace—because you are collecting its causes by wanting your enemies to suffer and die quickly.

If you want to make a delicious cup of coffee, you first put water and coffee into a coffeepot. If you then add some hot pepper, the result will be something that will taste terrible—it will be undrinkable. This is because the causes you collected were for a result that was the opposite of what you wanted.

These are the eighteen pledges that must be kept as part of your main practice. They are special instructions that you cannot abandon if you want to practice the real Mahayana Dharma. Practice each of them daily, remembering them at the proper time and in whatever situation may arise. At first, you won't be able to practice them nicely. But you should at least remember them and try to practice them, even if you can't keep them successfully. If you try to keep them, of course you will eventually get better and better. But if you don't try at all, they will always be beyond your reach.

SEVENTH POINT:
THE TWENTY-TWO LOJONG PRECEPTS

_____

THE LAST SECTION OF THE *Seven Point Mind
Training* includes the twenty-two precepts that Lojong practitioners should observe.

I.

Do all yoga practices with one thought.

There are many spiritual practices that you can do, each one
with its own special purpose. You have to integrate all of
them with the main practice that recognizes the equality of
oneself and others and exchanges concern for oneself with
concern for others. You have to make sure that every one of
your practices is based on this attitude.

Recognizing the equality between oneself and others is
taught using only one reason, which is that I and all other
beings are the same in that we both want happiness and dislike suffering. It is very important for Mahayana practitioners to think this way.

Generating desire and aversion in our mind is a useless
and foolish thing to do. Desire comes from thinking that our
wish to find happiness entitles us to seek every kind of
goodness for ourselves alone. Aversion is a feeling of total
disregard toward others, causing us at times even to rejoice
at their suffering, and making us think, "They got what they
deserve." But for ourselves, we feel great satisfaction when
something good happens to us, and this causes our desire
for happiness to increase.

Allowing ourselves to have feelings like these is considered very wrong in the Mahayana field, because our situation and that of others is the same. None of us wants suffering and problems and we all want happiness and peace.

Therefore, when you or someone close to you experiences something, don't react in a way that makes the situation worse. If you have the ability to do so, try to make others happy, try to make them feel better. You are breaking the main root of the Mahayana attitude if you let yourself generate desire and aversion because of the distinctions you make between yourself and others.

Exchanging oneself and others doesn't mean that you should change your identity and become others while others change theirs and become you. That kind of change is not possible. In this case, exchanging self and others means to remove other beings' suffering and share your happiness with them. All your spiritual practices and activities should be based on this attitude. In fact, all Mahayana practice, including recitation and meditation, is actually based on this attitude from beginning to end. You must realize this, otherwise you won't be able to achieve the proper result. If you understand this point, you will see that all your activities of body, speech, and mind have to be motivated by this attitude—whether you are meditating, making offerings, reciting prayers or whatever. This attitude is included in the thought, "I want to achieve Buddhahood in order to benefit all beings," which is the starting point of all Mahayana practice.

For example, you had a good lunch today, right? If you ate with others, you probably talked with them and enjoyed your meal together. But did you base those activities on the attitude that recognizes the equality between oneself and others and then exchanges concern for oneself with concern for others? It may be that it didn't even occur to you to think about this at all. But by doing so you can turn eating into an act of great virtue.

From the beginning you must have the proper motivation: "I will help all sentient beings and serve them. To be able to do this, I want to achieve Buddhahood." After dedicating yourself to the service of all beings, you need to have good health to do this. Good health comes from eating properly, so that you can make your body strong. With good health, you can do everything. You have to think similarly with regard to all your other activities as well. If you can do this, you won't waste a single movement of your body; every one of them will turn into virtuous activity.

At first it is very difficult to gain this kind of holy attitude, because we are not in the habit of thinking this way. It is easy to just hear this instruction and afterwards maybe say, "That was very interesting." But the best way of showing interest is first of all not to forget an instruction that you have just heard. Second, when the appropriate time comes, apply the instruction right away.

If you recite mantras and prayers, or hold a ritual for the benefit of other beings, all such activities should be based on the attitude that exchanges self and others. This should be your main motivation.

2.

Respond with one antidote when overwhelmed by obstacles.

In Tibet, doctors would first check their patients and then give them medicine and instruction. If the medicine and instruction didn't help they would try a more radical treatment, called *tarsek*, which includes blood-letting and moxibustion. The attitude of exchanging concern for oneself with concern for others is like this kind of radical treatment in that it is the most efficient antidote for all the mental afflictions.

If you think to yourself, "I want to achieve Buddhahood, I want to achieve nirvana," and wonder, "Why can't I achieve Buddhahood and nirvana today?" You have to realize, "I can't achieve these goals right now because there are many obstacles and mental enemies that I have to fight with." If you want to fight with these enemies, what kind of weapon do you need? The basic weapon you need is the attitude that exchanges concern for oneself with concern for others. You have to develop this attitude very strongly in your mind. If you practice this, you can help your own mental illnesses and problems, as well as those of other beings.

3.

Two activities: one for the beginning and one for the end.

This means that there are two important things that you should do at the very beginning of any activity and at the end. The first important thing you have to do at the beginning of every activity is to correct your motivation. Then, after you finish your Dharma activity, the second important thing is to dedicate your virtue. It is also important for you to check your body, speech, and mind throughout the day to see whether your activities are in accord with the motivation that you formed early in the morning right after you woke up.

A beginning practitioner should at least be motivated by an attitude of renunciation. But because this instruction is a Mahayana teaching, your motivation has to include bodhichitta in addition to renunciation. This means you should think, "I want to achieve Buddhahood for the purpose of helping other beings." Why doesn't this attitude include the wish to help oneself? The desire to help oneself is included in renunciation. Renunciation is the wish to free oneself from samsara's suffering. But it isn't enough just to free yourself from that suffering. Others also need to achieve happiness. This is what it means to understand the equality of oneself and others.

Wanting to help other beings shouldn't be just to help them in some small, temporary way—for example, by giving them food, shelter, or other material necessities. When you help others, it should be to provide them with the kind of firm and unchanging happiness that cannot be lost. This means you have to free them from samsara's suffering, from all obstacles, and lead them to a state of ultimate happiness. This should be a happiness from which you can never be separated once you achieve it. The nature of this kind of help and happiness is not temporary; it is a permanent result. This is the kind of motivation you should have. You should think, "I want very much to achieve Buddhahood. If I achieve Buddhahood, I will have all the knowledge, power,

and skill to give others the highest help, which is to lead
them to ultimate happiness. For that purpose I am going to
do this or that activity." With this attitude you can listen to a
Dharma teaching, contemplate or meditate on its meaning,
or do any other kind of spiritual activity.

Buddha's teachings, especially his Mahayana teachings,
are unbelievable. You have to catch the real quality of Buddha's teaching. As I mentioned earlier, if you have a piece of
candy, you will taste the sweetness of the sugar no matter
where you bite it. Buddha's teaching is like that as well.

A practitioner is not someone who just sits on a cushion
with his eyes closed, without changing his mental attitude at
all. A rabbit can sit very straight and still for a long time.
You could say it knows how to practice austerities, since it
can sit this way even without using a cushion. But you can't
call that meditation, because a rabbit lacks any kind of
proper motivation. Therefore, a Mahayana practitioner is
someone who starts by developing a good motivation and
then makes sure that all his activities follow that motivation—day by day, week by week, month by month, year by
year. You shouldn't think, "Oh, I haven't been able to do any
practice for a week, for two weeks, or even a month." Saying
this shows that you think practice only means to go and sit
on a meditation cushion in front of some holy objects, and
then close your eyes as you think about some subject or recite some prayers. Everything you do at all times can be
Dharma practice. Even sleeping and getting up from your
bed in the morning can be great practice. If you have the
right skill and recollection, you won't let those activities go
to waste.

You can turn enjoying coffee and breakfast in the
morning into great Mahayana practice. If you understood
this, you could never say, "I haven't been able to practice for
a whole week." You would know how unbelievably silly it is
to say that. Therefore, you should understand how it is possible to practice all the time.

You always have to remember that you and others are
equal. Because of that, you have to try to do something to
benefit others. Your motivation should be: "I am doing my

general practice, especially my daily practice, and most especially what I am doing right now because I want to help all beings." If your motivation is good, you can collect a great amount of virtue with each step that you take as you leave your house to go to a Dharma teaching. You should be thinking, "I want to achieve Buddhahood in order to help other beings. Because of that, I need to hear Dharma instruction and learn its meaning. Therefore, I am going to this Dharma class today."

Why do you collect so much virtue by doing this? If you see a beggar or a sick person who needs food sitting on a street corner and you willingly give him a dollar with a great motivation, you can collect great virtue. That act is done for the sake of just one person. But if you come to a Dharma class with the motivation I just described, your purpose is to benefit all sentient beings. If the number of sentient beings is measureless, the virtue you collect with each step you take is also measureless.

You have to know what kind of virtue you can collect through your activities and, therefore, how valuable your activities are. You also have to remember what kind of activities you should be doing so that you don't waste your time. All of these points relate to your motivation.

Now you have learned the basic Mahayana attitude of Dharma practitioners. That is, you understand and know how to think about the equality that exists between yourself and all other beings. None of us wants to suffer or experience problems. Similarly, we all want to be happy. Therefore, we are all the same. As I said before, if you still keep the attitude that distinguishes between yourself and others even after using good reasons to realize this sameness, that is a useless and silly thing to do.

A Dharma practitioner also has to check whether his mind is getting better, more noble and kind. For example, see if your mind is better than it was a few months ago. If it is, then you are getting a good result from your efforts at learning, thinking, and practicing Dharma. If your mind is not changing, then you aren't getting any proper result and you should do more.

I have already described the activities that you should do to improve your mind.[74] They are also mentioned in this verse from the Panchen Lama's text *Honoring the Lamas*:

Please bless me to make meaningful my
    leisure and fortune,
By applying the skillful means of the four activities,
By integrating into meditation
    whatever I happen to encounter,
And by practicing the pledges and precepts
    of the Lojong instruction.

If you do these four kinds of activities, you will definitely get a good result, that is, your mind will definitely improve.

Practicing Lojong instruction makes the mind better and better, more and more gentle. It reduces the kind of mind that wants to harm other beings and increases the kind that wishes to help them. If you practice those four activities nicely and you begin to develop these kinds of positive attitudes, then your practice is going very well.

Whenever we do some good deed, such as going to a Dharma class, we can collect a huge amount of virtuous karma. That virtuous karma is like a mass of diamonds that we hold in our hands. After finishing that activity, we must put our virtue in a safe place to make sure we don't lose it. We have two great thieves that rob us of our virtue: one of them is anger, the other is wrong view. Therefore, we must dedicate our virtue before they are lost to those thieves. We can do this by thinking, "May these virtues turn into the causes for achieving a Buddha's state of perfect enlightenment. May they turn into the causes that enable beings who haven't yet achieved bodhichitta to quickly achieve it. May they increase and strengthen bodhichitta in those who have

---

[74]Verse 16. See pp. 113–116 above. The four activities being referred to are: collecting virtue, removing misdeeds, making *torma* offerings to harmful spirits, and directing Dharma protectors to carry out activities.

already generated it." Dedicating our virtue this way guarantees that it won't be lost until we achieve Buddhahood.

Buddha taught that if you have a mug of holy nectar and you want to keep it from disappearing, you have to pour it into the great ocean. If you mix it with the water of the ocean, it won't disappear until that great ocean disappears. Similarly, by dedicating your virtue as a cause for achieving Buddhahood in order to benefit all beings, you are making sure that you do not lose these virtues. The reason they won't go to waste or get damaged is that Buddha's virtue is measureless and benefits all beings.

As mentioned earlier, prayer and dedication are not necessarily different. In fact, every dedication is a form of prayer, although not all prayers are dedications. The wish expressed in the words "I want very much to achieve Buddhahood" or "May I achieve Buddhahood" is a form of prayer. "May I achieve Buddhahood through the power of these virtues" is both a dedication and a prayer. There are many dedication verses you can recite. For example,

By the power of these virtues,
May I quickly become my Lama-Buddha;
Each and every being without exception
May I lead to that supreme state.

Also, at the end of a Dharma class we usually recite this verse:

By the power of this virtue, may all beings
Complete the collections of merit and wisdom,
And may they achieve the two holy bodies
That arise from merit and wisdom.

"This virtue" means the virtue that you just collected during the class. The "two holy bodies" means a Buddha's wisdom body (*dharmakaya*) and form body (*rupakaya*). This is a dedication prayer that all beings should achieve that result by practicing the two collections of merit and wisdom.

4.

Be patient no matter which of the two you encounter.

According to Mahayana Dharma, you have to practice all the
time to subdue your mind. Although you may have a strong
wish to do so, most of the time you will give up the practice.
There are two main ways that this can happen. One comes
when you are very successful, whether in business or making a living. If you enjoy this success and happiness too
much, you won't think about Dharma. That is one dangerous way of losing your Lojong practice.

The other way is the opposite of the first, that is, when
nothing you do goes well and it seems that everything is always going wrong. If you are always failing and getting
more and more problems, you will become discouraged.
You run the risk of thinking, "Practicing Dharma doesn't
help me. Thinking about Dharma doesn't help me. My
situation is getting worse and worse. What can I do?" You
can also lose your practice this way.

If either of these two situations occurs, it is very important for you not to lose your general practice and attitude. As
I told you, if you are successful you have to understand that
this came about because of your virtue, which was its main
cause. The secondary causes might be your own skill and
knowledge, as well as help from other beings. If all these
conditions come together, you will be successful.

Whenever you are successful, you should think, "This is
due to the combination of the Three Jewels' blessing, other
beings' help, and my knowledge and skill. Through the
combination of all these factors, I am enjoying these good results. All of them have come about because of my good
karma. Their main source is my good karma." Therefore,
you need to have a strong belief in karma. All good results
from the beginning up to Buddhahood come from virtuous
karma. Having that belief when you meet with success will
make you want to do more and even better good deeds.

You also have to remember karma when you experience
bad situations and problems. Bad results come from bad

karma. Who collected it? You collected it yourself. When? You collected it not only in this life, but in countless previous lives as well. You have to try to remove the imprints of all that bad karma. The proper way to react to bad experiences is to think that you have to try to remove the seeds of the bad karma that caused them. If you think this way, you won't lose your practice at all. Therefore, you have to make sure that you don't lose your Mahayana attitude when you experience happiness or have problems and suffering.

5.

Protect the two even at the cost of your life.

For a beginner's mind, these instructions, attitudes, and practices are very difficult. Still, you should know about them and learn them even if you can't practice them properly and perfectly right away. You should keep the wish, "May I someday be able to do this practice properly and nicely."

Precept 4 said you shouldn't lose your practice either when you are very happy or when you are suffering and experiencing many problems. This fifth precept says there are two things you should keep with great determination: the Dharma's general pledges and especially the pledges of this Lojong instruction. You should keep them so strongly that you would never abandon them, even if you had to give up your life.

It's possible that you may encounter a situation that would cause you to give up your practice to gain your freedom. In such a situation it would be very difficult for a beginning practitioner to be able to keep his or her practice. Sometime you may be sitting on your cushion and think: "If I lose my life, I won't be here any longer. Therefore, it would be all right for me to give up this Lojong practice if it means I can stay alive." This is a very harmful attitude, especially for a Mahayana practitioner. Buddha said that if we give up our life for the sake of Dharma, only one life is finished. You have experienced countless lifetimes. All of those lives were lost without doing anything worthwhile; you couldn't help losing them and you didn't give them up for the benefit of other beings, as Buddha Shakyamuni did many times. If you had done this before, you wouldn't be the way you are right now; you would be much better off. So if you should have to give up this one life for the sake of Dharma, it would only be one life among the countless lives you've had since beginningless samsara up to now.

If we abandon this Mahayana attitude, practice, and path in order to save our life, it is a serious misdeed. Each bad deed produces four different types of result: a maturation result, two kinds of corresponding result, and a governing result.[75] Buddha said that if we abandon this Mahayana attitude to save our lives, we will not see, reach, or regain it for ten million lifetimes. That would definitely be an unbelievably bad result! Therefore, you should decide that it is easier to give up this life, when compared with the consequence of giving up the Mahayana attitude. If you learn about this point, it won't seem like such a difficult thing to do. Therefore, if the time should come when a great practitioner has to choose between giving up his life or his Dharma practice, he will be more than ready to give up his life.

In Tibet, many of my friends were practitioners and scholars who remained there because they were not able to escape during the Chinese takeover. Soon afterwards, the Communist Chinese soldiers captured and punished them, one by one, for many days. They were forced to go to meetings in which they were supposed to renounce their religion and their Lama, like His Holiness the Dalai Lama and Kyabje Trijang Rinpoche.

I had a Mongolian friend who was a Hlarampa Geshe and a great scholar. One day it was his turn to appear in a meeting. The Chinese told him, "Tell us here what is wrong with Kyabje Trijang Rinpoche."

---

[75]For a discussion of karmic results, see pp. 256–257 of *Liberation in Our Hands, Part Two.* See listing in bibliography.

He answered, "Kyabje Trijang Rinpoche is a real Buddha. A Buddha doesn't have any faults. Therefore, since there is nothing about him that is wrong, what can I say?"

The Chinese said, "No! Don't be like that. You must say something. You must tell us something!"

"No, I don't have anything bad to say," he repeated.

Then they continued to urge him very strongly. They didn't do this for just one day, but it went on for many days. They told him, "You think about this for a week or so. We'll see what you have to say next time."

Several weeks later, he was brought back to another meeting. But the same thing happened again. He said, "No, I don't have anything bad to say to you about Kyabje Trijang Rinpoche because he is a real Buddha, a real Vajradhara. He doesn't have any faults."

Then the Chinese arranged to have many people beat him publicly. He was badly injured, with blood covering his face and clothes. Still, his response was, "Go ahead and kill me. That will make it easier. I don't have anything bad to say." By doing this, he was able to keep his pledges. He was quite ready to give up his life. Many scholars in Tibet acted this way.

6.

Train in the three difficulties.

This precept includes three things that are difficult to do in order to maintain your practice. It is a crucial point that serves as a reminder for the kind of skill you need. The first is that you have to be able to recognize mental afflictions, wrong ideas, and bad thoughts when they arise in your mind. The second is to be able to apply the correct antidote to those bad thoughts right away. Third, you have to prevent mental afflictions from arising in your mind at all.

It is very difficult to recognize the mental afflictions or wrong ideas when they arise. Everyone knows that the three mental poisons are ignorance, hatred, and desire. In the monastery many monks have to live, work, study, and debate together. Of course, once in a while a monk will experience some problem and become angry with another person. Anger comes into the mind very quickly and is immediately evident to others.

In the monastery all of us know that it is wrong to become angry. So we feel ashamed and embarrassed when we get angry, and try and stop it immediately. Because we are always talking and thinking about the three poisons, it is also a little bit easier for us to realize when they have arisen in our mind. But a person who doesn't know or hasn't heard much about the mental afflictions has a very difficult time recognizing them as wrong, even when they arise very intensely. Such a person might think getting angry is the right thing to do. Just as every human being has certain rights, he also thinks he has a "right" to be angry or ignorant. Thinking this way increases the mental afflictions, making them grow stronger and stronger. This shows that the person does not understand the harmfulness or the results of the mental afflictions.

Many, many thoughts have arisen in your mind since you got up this morning. How many bad thoughts arose since then? How many good thoughts? Without receiving instructions on this subject, it is difficult to know how to think about it. Your mind has changed and experienced many different thoughts with each passing moment just since this morning.

If someone asked you, "Were you able to recognize what kinds of thoughts arose in your mind today? Were some of them bad and others good?" You probably can't even remember what most of your thoughts were. This means you weren't very careful about recognizing what kind of thoughts you had, and whether they were good or bad. But if you didn't recognize them when they came, then you also definitely did not apply any antidote when bad thoughts came. If you had applied an antidote, you would remember that you took some action against those bad thoughts.

When you have a good thought, you have to recognize it and cultivate it continually. At least you have to rejoice in that good thought. You should think, "That was good. I did a good job."

Whenever good or bad thoughts come to your mind, it's very important to recognize what kind they are. Although you shouldn't allow any of the mental afflictions to enter your mind, it is very difficult to stop them from doing so once something has caused them to arise. Because they can enter your mind in an instant, it is very difficult to be mindful about recognizing them. But if you know that they are bad, you can try to practice their antidotes. Otherwise, you will never try to do anything to remove the mental afflictions. This is the first difficult point.

Even if you recognize a particular mental affliction when it enters your mind, you must be able to apply the appropriate antidote. Each mental affliction has its own antidote, and you have to know how to apply it immediately. This is very difficult to do because your mind isn't used to applying antidotes. This is the second difficult point.

Even if you apply the appropriate antidote to mental afflictions, the most difficult thing to do is to completely stop the mental afflictions from arising and never allow them to arise again. The antidotes to the mental afflictions should not be applied on a temporary basis. This means that you have to apply them in such a way as to remove mental afflictions from their roots. It won't help if you just try to stop them temporarily or just reduce their strength. This is the third crucial point.

Therefore, if you really want to be a Dharma practitioner and really want to achieve some goal, like Buddhahood or nirvana, you have to keep these skills in mind all the time. You have to try to learn them very carefully and then put them into practice. If you do this, you will automatically become a real Mahayana practitioner, and a very good and noble person.

When you get up in the morning, the first thing you should do is to make a good motivation. Then, whenever a mental affliction enters your mind during the day, try to realize that it is harmful. After recognizing that mental afflictions have arisen, you have to apply their antidotes. For example, if you get angry, recognize this by thinking, "Anger has arisen in my mind." Then, practice patience. By doing that, you can stop your anger temporarily; but if you forget that practice, the anger will return again. Therefore, try to stop your anger completely, not allowing it to continue.

If you start having desire, you have to apply its antidote, which in this case means developing the two qualities of having few wants and being satisfied with what you have. The opposite of these two virtues is to have great desire and to lack satisfaction, which is described in the *Treasury of Higher Knowledge*:

> Lack of satisfaction is wanting more than
>   what you already have;
> Great desire is wanting what you don't have.[76]

These kinds of desire can't easily be stopped and so they force you to try to get things that are very difficult to acquire. Desires make you their slave by urging you to get things. Sometimes you may succeed in getting what you want, but most of the time you won't.

The first time you achieve a little success, you will enjoy it and be a little satisfied. You will think, "Now I got a little of what I want." Although you may relax and feel some satisfaction that day, the next day your mind will change. Your desire will urge you to feel that you need more and better of the same. This is what "lack of satisfaction" means. It makes you work more and harder to acquire more things.

After recognizing the mental afflictions, always apply their antidotes immediately. You have to develop the skill to reduce and terminate them. Whenever mental afflictions arise, practice applying the antidote right away. This is how you can make and keep yourself peaceful and relaxed. This is your actual daily practice—recognizing the mental afflictions when they come, practicing their antidotes, and trying to remove them from the root. The skill and knowledge of

---

[76]*Abhidharmakosha*, ch. 6, v. 6.

how to do these three difficult things is very important in order to subdue your mind.

By practicing this way you will collect a great amount of virtue. That virtue is very valuable, like having a lot of money or jewels. If you keep a treasure like that in your house, someone might come and take it, leaving you with nothing. Similarly, anger and wrong view are the worst of the mental afflictions in that they rob you of your virtue. Wrong view is unbelievably harmful; anger is almost as bad. Whenever either of them enters your mind, they will take away whatever virtue you have collected. They will burn it up just as easily as the fire from a single match can burn down an entire forest. Therefore, dedicate your virtue to the goal of achieving Buddhahood for the benefit of all beings. This will prevent it from being lost or wasted.

7.

Take up the three principal causes.

Usually people pray to be successful in their activities, to remove some bad situation, to find happiness, or to have a long life. Here the instruction describes the unique kind of prayer that a practitioner should make to achieve the three main causes that are needed in order to practice Dharma.

The first cause you need is to meet a good Lama in this life and in your future lives. If you meet a good Lama, you will definitely receive unerring instructions from him. Therefore, it is very important to pray to be able to meet such a Lama in this life and in all your future lives until you achieve Buddhahood.

It isn't enough just to be able to meet a good Lama. The second main cause is to have a suitable mind that wants to listen to, study, and practice Dharma. For example, Kyabje Trijang Rinpoche had several attendants that helped maintain his activities, including a treasurer, a cook, and so on. The cook in particular had to spend all his time working in the kitchen. When Kyabje Rinpoche gave teachings and initiations, the cook couldn't attend. So it isn't enough just to meet a good Lama.

A mind that is inclined to the Dharma wants very much to listen to, study, learn, and practice Dharma. This kind of mind is like a car in perfect condition that can easily take you wherever you want to go. The engine in a good car starts up the minute you turn the key. Similarly, your mind should also be very ready to do everything—to listen to Dharma, to study, learn, and practice.

Even if you are able to meet a good Lama and your mind is well disposed to Dharma, you still need to be able to acquire the basic necessities, such as food and clothing, without difficulty. This is the third cause. If you can't acquire material necessities easily, it will take too much of your time to get these things, which will become an obstacle to your practice.

During Buddha's lifetime people could see and hear him when he taught. But from their side, not every one of those people had all the material necessities, such as food and clothing. So they had to wander around begging for these things.

Therefore, you should make special prayers to achieve the three principal causes: "May I always meet with great Lamas, not only in this life but in all my future lives as well. May my mind always be inclined to listen to, study, and practice Dharma. May I always have all the material necessities for practicing Dharma." About this last aim, Shantideva also said,

> May the teaching remain long,
> Receiving support and honor.[77]

"Teaching" here refers to your knowledge of the Buddha's teaching. For that knowledge to remain undamaged in your mind and for it to increase nicely, you need to have the proper supporting causes of food, shelter, clothing, and the

---

[77]*Engaging in Bodhisattva Activities*, ch. 10, v. 57.

like. If you can acquire such necessities without difficulty, you can practice and improve your knowledge.

Since coming to this country, I have seen many times how difficult it can be for people to find the opportunity to practice Dharma. Therefore, I started making a special prayer: "Until they reach Buddhahood, may all beings in this and all their future lives be able to acquire all the good and necessary causes that will enable them to listen to Dharma, practice Dharma, and achieve the Dharma's goals."

There are many necessities besides food and clothing. You also need to have the freedom to practice. If you are missing any important factor, it can become a big obstacle. Therefore, it is very important that you pray to obtain these three main causes in all your future lives. If you do, you will definitely be able to do meaningful things all the time.

In the Dharma, your main attitude and motivation should be like arranging a horse race. Your actual Dharma activities are like the horses that race on the track. When you race, your horse should go in the direction of the finish line. This is controlled by the jockey who holds the reins. A prayer is like these reins in that it determines where your virtuous activities will take you. Otherwise, even if you have a very good horse, it can get confused if the jockey does not know how to use the reins properly. Although most horses run along the track in the right direction, sometimes one of them will get confused and start running back toward the starting gate.

Maybe some of you have never prayed for any of these three causes in your whole life. Even so, you should definitely pray for them every day, for example, just before you go to sleep. There are also many different verses and prayers that you can recite for each step and level of your practice. For example, the *Source of All Goodness*[78] contains a whole set of verses relating to all the stages of the path.

---

[78]See footnote 44 above.

8.

Practice to keep the three undamaged.

There are three things to cultivate to prevent your practice from degenerating and losing its power. The first is respect for the Lama who gives you instruction in the Lojong teachings. You should have respect and faith in the Dharma teaching that you are learning and in the person who gives you that teaching. If you don't have faith in the teaching or in the person who teaches it to you, you won't practice it nicely.

The second is to cultivate effort and enthusiasm for the Lojong practice. If you don't make effort to continue your practice, you will postpone it until tomorrow or next week. There is no end to "tomorrows" and "next weeks." In relation to this, one verse states:

Twenty years pass without thinking to practice;
Twenty more with "I'm going to, I'm going to."
Over ten pass, saying, "I've failed, I've failed!"
Such is the tale of a life spent in vain.[79]

If you aren't careful, it's very easy to let twenty years go by, as you think, "I will do it sometime, I will do it sometime." For the next twenty years, you will continue to think, "I still have time." But in the end you will have to say, "Now it's too late." This is the story of a practitioner who wasted his entire holy life. The definition of effort in this case is to have a willingness to do your Lojong practice happily.

If someone asks you, "What are you practicing?" You might answer, "I am practicing Lojong."

"What does Lojong mean?"

"It means Mind Training."

"What kind of Mind Training is it?"

---

[79]Pabongka Rinpoche identifies this verse as being from one of the spiritual songs of Je Gungtangpa Könchog Tenpey Drönme (1762–1823).

"Mind Training is the name of a daily practice that combines several elements—generating bodhichitta, Equalizing and Exchanging Self and Others, and doing the meditation called Giving and Taking, which means giving all your good things to other beings and trying to remove all their problems and suffering. Lojong practice is thinking this way and trying to maintain these attitudes all the time."

You can do the unbelievably great practice of Giving and Taking even when you are lying on your bed. By meditating this way, you can dedicate and give all your good things—knowledge, morality, wealth, health, everything—to beings who are suffering. At the same time, you can practice removing all their suffering. If someone comes to your room, they might think you're just resting. In reality, you might be doing a great Mahayana practice.

You should practice this way with great effort. Otherwise you won't practice at all. Sometimes I put good food in my dog Drölma's bowl. When she lacks effort, she won't eat. I have to urge her by saying "Please eat; be nice, be nice. Nice girl. Nice Drölma, please eat." Still, she won't eat. Sometimes when I am eating, she will come over and nudge me with her head, and then there's no need for me to say, "Nice."

Therefore, effort means to have a strong mind that is happy and willing to do something virtuous. Your practice will be as good as the strength of your effort. Effort is the mental factor that, by its own power, willingly exerts itself in relation to its object. Effort is a distinct mental factor that helps, urges, and leads your main mind or consciousness to do something. If you lack effort, your mind will remain at rest all the time. Therefore, the second point in this precept is to cultivate the effort that willingly practices the Lojong teachings.

In addition to these two, the third point is that you must use your recollection and alertness to check whether you are keeping all the precepts nicely or are missing some of the points. If you have forgotten anything, then you have to fix your practice.

Recollection and mental alertness are the two most important mental factors that you use when practicing. Recollection means to know and keep in mind what you are supposed to be practicing. Mental alertness is the quality that checks whether you are doing your practice perfectly or not. You have to use these two factors to try and keep all the precepts nicely and not allow them to become damaged.

Don't allow your wish to receive instructions and teachings from a good Lama to degenerate. Don't allow the effort you put into Lojong practice to decline. Don't allow your recollection and alertness to diminish. Keep them strongly in your mind.

9.

Never be parted from the three activities.

This precept literally means that you shouldn't let your body, speech, and mind remain idle; you have to try to keep them busy practicing virtue all the time. You might think, "That's a very bad idea. I would get sick or crazy if I did that."

In this country you often hear people say, "Relax, relax. Take it easy. Otherwise, you'll get sick or make yourself crazy." Everybody understands what this means and sometimes it can actually happen. A person can be so busy that he thinks about and tries to do too many things. If he can't finish them and isn't successful, he might even get so upset that he commits suicide. In that case, the advice to relax would be appropriate.

What this precept actually means is that you should never lose the basic attitude of this practice. Earlier, I mentioned that an elephant remains an elephant no matter what he is doing. Similarly, when you rest, you have to turn that activity into Dharma practice. When you wake up, wake up into the Dharma. When you eat, eat with a Dharma motivation. Turn everything you do into Dharma practice. If you do that, all your activities will be meaningful. You will always get the Dharma's flavor. Every single part of Buddha's teaching system has great meaning, but you have to know how to practice it.

Keeping your body busy means, for instance, getting up in the morning and cleaning your practice area at whatever time is suitable. Cleaning your room can be very virtuous if you do it with the right motivation. It also has great meaning for two reasons. The first is that we have to arrange our own paradise or Buddha field in order to achieve a Buddha's enlightenment. It is in that kind of completely clean and pure place that we will actually achieve Buddhahood. Therefore, cleaning your room and house every day with that motivation and understanding is a great way to collect virtue that actually helps to arrange your own paradise.

Second, you clean your room as a necessary preparation to invite the merit field of the Buddha, Dharma, and Sangha in order to practice the Seven-Limb Puja or any other regular devotional practice. If you don't, it is like saying to the holy beings of the merit field, "Please come and stay in this dirty room," which would be improper. Therefore, you have to clean your room before you invite the precious Three Jewels.

You can do other virtues by body as well, such as making prostrations. If there is a temple nearby, you can do circumambulations. Even sitting up straight during a teaching or as you meditate are virtues that can be done by the body.

10.

Train yourself to be impartial.

When you pray or practice compassion, it is improper for Bodhisattvas or Mahayana practitioners to focus exclusively on those they feel close to, such as relatives and friends, while excluding persons unknown to them, people they don't like, or enemies. You have to practice equally toward all beings. If you distinguish among beings and focus on some and not on others that is not true Lojong practice.

This is a most important point and one that is very difficult to practice. Since our mind has long associated with the three poisons of ignorance, hatred, and desire, it has become like a wild animal that is very difficult to tame. While we will automatically have compassion and loving-kindness toward our relatives and friends, it is very difficult for us to have these attitudes toward our enemies or persons we don't like and we always forget to practice in relation to people we don't know. This is why it is so difficult to have equanimity toward all beings when we are practicing Lojong.

11.

Most important is to practice toward all beings
from the depths of your heart.

The Lojong practice has many different key points, each emphasizing different aspects of our experience. Some points relate to developing compassion, some to developing loving-kindness or faith, and others to cultivating the wisdom that realizes emptiness. Therefore, every aspect of our lives can be used in the practice of Lojong and our practice should encompass all these different objects. The attitudes that you cultivate should also not be short-lived; you must be able to keep them in your mind very strongly and deeply.

12.

Constantly train in relation to special objects.

It is especially difficult for us to develop patience toward our enemies. Obviously, it is also more difficult for us to feel loving-kindness and compassion toward our enemies than toward our family and friends. Therefore, you have to make a point of practicing loving-kindness and compassion toward your enemies. When you practice you should deliberately single out such people and cultivate compassion toward them. Other special objects include your Lama, your father and mother, a roommate or someone you live with, because it is easy to collect very bad deeds or great virtue, depending on how you conduct yourself in relation to them.

How can you develop loving-kindness and compassion toward enemies? Whenever you think of an enemy, it immediately disturbs your mind and causes you to develop stronger anger, hatred, and aversion toward that person. Therefore, it is very difficult for you to practice patience and compassion toward them. Mahayana practitioners have to learn how to practice Lojong this way or their other practices will be ruined because they are not holding all beings equally.

Your main practice is to recognize the equality of yourself and others and to switch concern for yourself with concern for others. Through applying good reasons you will believe this and gain right view in relation to it. Therefore, Mahayana practitioners have to think, "I myself want happiness and don't want to experience suffering or problems. This enemy of mine is also the same. He wants happiness and doesn't want to suffer or have problems. There is no difference between us; we are equal. We all wish for the same thing in that sense. He doesn't like suffering any more than I do. Therefore, whatever I do for myself, I should do for him as well." Mahayana practitioners should use this kind of reasoning. No one can find fault with it.

You all know what it means to wage a negative political campaign. Mahayana practitioners shouldn't think that way, but instead find good reasons to always try to think positively and avoid thinking negatively. You have to try especially hard to develop this attitude, keeping it in your mind as firmly as possible. You have to make this awareness reach to the very depths of your mind.

13.

Do not depend on other conditions.

An earlier precept urged you to "take up the three principal causes." The first cause is to meet with a good Lama, the second is to have a mind that is well disposed to the Dharma, and the third is to have enough material necessities. This doesn't mean you should postpone practicing until you have all the necessities. You must be willing to practice all the time, whether or not you are having problems or feeling happy, and whether or not you have plenty of material necessities. You shouldn't lose your practice or allow the strength of your effort to decline. This is described in several lines of verse:

> With a full stomach and the sun's warmth,
> You seem to be a Dharma practitioner;
> But when hard times come, you become a
>   common person.

I don't know where these lines are from, but Kyabje Pabongka Rinpoche used to quote them all the time. I can still hear him reciting them and then laughing out loud. They mean that you shouldn't be someone who can sit nicely like a good practitioner if your stomach is full and your body feels warm, but who turns into an ordinary person—that is, someone who doesn't practice Dharma—whenever you have some problem. It shouldn't matter if your situation is good or bad; you must practice continually. This is very important.

Dharma practitioners can't remember instructions or put them into practice before hearing them. Once you have heard instructions, don't forget them and try to apply them when it is appropriate to do so. For example, it is pointless for a soldier to fire shots all day long at nothing, only to forget to fire when the enemy comes. Obviously, he will quickly get killed. Similarly, a practitioner needs to have the protection that enables him or her to strengthen Lojong practice whenever a problem arises.

14.

Practice now what is most important.

Is it difficult or easy to gain real bodhichitta? Of course it is very difficult. How important is it for us to gain it? It is crucial to achieve it because it is the main cause of gaining Mahayana knowledge and the main foundation on which that knowledge is built. It is the main highway that takes you to the city of Buddhahood. If you don't take this highway, you won't arrive there at all.

Why should we try to achieve it? Because bodhichitta is the main focus of the Lojong instruction and practiced for the purpose of achieving two goals—one's own welfare and the welfare of others. You cannot practice this instruction or achieve bodhichitta at all if your motivation is to have a long life and success. Bodhichitta is defined as a mind that is principally focused on two goals: to achieve Buddhahood and to help all beings. Therefore, you have to practice with the aim of achieving these two goals. You should not practice in order to secure this life's happiness. If you practice bodhichitta nicely, you will become happier and it will happen effortlessly.

Why is it much more important to pursue the happiness of future lives than this life's happiness? I am now sixty-seven years old.[80] If I live until I'm seventy and am only concerned with this life, I would be working hard to be happy for just three years, which is not very important. But we will have to continue wandering in samsara for eons and eons if we do not achieve Buddhahood. So, of course, the happiness that relates to that length of time is much more important.

We must also understand that the Dharma is far more important than worldly activities. All of these instructions are meant for Mahayana practitioners whose main aim is Dharma practice that transcends worldly happiness, such as achieving Buddhahood and nirvana.

Between teaching Dharma and practicing Dharma, our main aim should be to practice this particular Lojong instruction. The essence of Mind Training is to generate bodhichitta and to do all of our activities for the benefit of other beings in order to achieve Buddhahood. This essence is found in all the Sutrayana and Tantrayana teachings.

Before Lama Atisha came to Tibet, some people preferred the Tantric vehicle over the Sutra or Perfection vehi-

---

[80]This teaching was given in September 1988.

cle, while others preferred the Sutra vehicle over the Tantrayana. Each of these groups ignored the practices of the
other. The situation was very difficult, because both had lost
the main instruction of the Mahayana. Lama Atisha taught
that the essence of the Lojong teachings is also contained in
the Tantric vehicle.

Developing bodhichitta and cultivating the Lojong instructions should be your main practice. On top of that, you
can do whatever regular practice you may have. You have to
learn how to combine all of your practices so that they are
based on this Lojong. If you only do higher Tantric practices
without developing bodhichitta and applying the Lojong
teachings, those practices won't be effective at all. Similarly,
if you practice only the Lojong instructions without doing
Tantric practice, it will take an incredibly long time to
achieve Buddhahood. Therefore, the best approach is to
combine both elements. If you can base the higher practices
on bodhichitta and Lojong, your efforts will be extremely efficient.

15.

Do not do the mistaken activities.

Although you have to practice Dharma as much as you can
all the time, you shouldn't practice in a backward or mistaken way. Six types of wrong activities are described in this
instruction.

The first is *mistaken patience.* Mistaken patience means to
exert great effort in the wrong thing. If you cannot bear the
difficulties that come with practicing Dharma, you may easily give up doing your practice. For example, when it is a little hot in the temple during a teaching, many students can't
bear it so they jump up and open the windows right away.

You might take your cushion and go somewhere to
practice Dharma with other students. If it starts to rain,
you'll say, "Oh, we can't practice today," and leave immediately. If the sun is shining brightly, maybe you'll say "Oh,
it's too hot." If there is a cold wind blowing, "It's better to go

home." This is all because you can't endure such problems. But if you want to go to a stadium to watch a football or baseball game, sometimes you'll make sure to get there two hours early. It might be very cold and windy or very hot or even raining, but still you will stay there.

When driving along a highway in the summer, you often see men working very hard and using heavy machinery. Putting in that much effort and working so hard for worldly activities and not for the Dharma is mistaken patience. Therefore, you should be able to bear a little hardship for the sake of your Dharma practice.

The second wrong activity is *mistaken enjoyment*, which means that you shouldn't have wrong interests. For example, someone may come into a room and notice a group of people talking about the Dharma. But instead of approaching them, he will go to a different part of the room to look for something else to do. If he notices another group talking about business, he will eagerly go there and get involved in the conversation.

If you go to a Dharma teaching, you can listen to instructions. If you have a strong wish and try hard to learn the Dharma, you can gain more and more crucial points each time you listen to the teachings. By doing this you can experience more and more of the Dharma's sweet taste, and understand it more and more deeply. But if your effort is not heartfelt, you will quickly lose interest and become bored. On the other hand, you may prick up your ears whenever someone is talking about business or politics or war. Even if you tried, you can't stop yourself from going and joining the conversation. Taking a great interest in these kinds of subjects instead of the Dharma is mistaken enjoyment. Bodhisattvas and Mahayana practitioners shouldn't engage in this kind of activity.

The third wrong activity is *mistaken compassion*, or feeling compassion toward Dharma practitioners who lack material wealth, instead of feeling compassion toward those who are collecting very serious bad deeds.

In previous times, there was an Indian king who, while traveling in a forest, came across the great sage and monk

Drilbupa.[81] Drilbupa was sitting in a forest cave without any material necessities. When the king saw Drilbupa, he felt compassion for him and thought, "Poor monk! Living here with no house, no food, no clothes, and no mattress." Then he said to Drilbupa, "Don't stay here in poverty. Come to my palace. I will serve and feed you."

Drilbupa replied, "It is not my goal to live in a palace with good food and clothes. My aim is to achieve real peace and happiness." The rest of Drilbupa's story is incredibly beautiful, but this is enough to describe how the king's attitude toward him was mistaken compassion.

When Milarepa was meditating in caves, shepherds and many other people who went to visit him would react with great pity on seeing how poor his physical condition was. There were also gangs of rough people living in nearby barren areas. These gangs would fight one another and those who won would think of themselves as great heroes, although actually they were collecting huge amounts of bad deeds. Therefore, if anyone deserved to be pitied it was those people, not Milarepa, who was very close to achieving complete Buddhahood at that point. Feeling pity for Milarepa but not for those people who were collecting bad deeds is mistaken compassion.

The fourth wrong activity is *mistaken aspiration*. This is when people have no wish to practice Dharma properly or to achieve the goals, but instead want to achieve worldly happiness and wealth.

The fifth is *mistaken advice*. This happens when someone comes to you with the great hope of learning something that will benefit his future lives. But instead of teaching and leading him properly in the Dharma, you give advice on how to engage in business or how to argue a court case. This kind of instruction can actually harm a person terribly in future lives.

The sixth activity is *mistaken rejoicing*. The proper way to rejoice is to feel joy about someone's virtue and good fortune. If you see another person experiencing any kind of

---

[81]Skt.: *Ghantapada*; one of the eighty-four mahasiddhas.

happiness, such as wealth or good health, you should think, "This person is experiencing the good result of his virtue." Doing this will strengthen your belief in karma, which is a great benefit. It will reduce your bad activities and cause your good activities to increase. Therefore, by sincerely rejoicing at the good fortune of others we can collect virtue. On the other hand, if we react to others' success with jealousy, we will only collect bad deeds.

An example of mistaken rejoicing is when we feel happy that our enemies have gotten into trouble and are experiencing difficulties. That is obviously a bad deed and something we do very easily. Such an attitude only strengthens our hatred and causes us to collect bad karma.

During Geshe Potowa's time, there were two monks who did not get along. One of the two heard that his rival had committed an expulsory offense. There are four such offenses for monks: killing another human being, stealing, telling a great lie, and having sexual intercourse.

In the Vinaya system, there are eleven types of lie. The worst one is called a "great lie." For example, it may actually be true that you can see worldly gods coming to your house or demons passing through your yard, or that you have visions of Buddhas and they talk to you and you are able to ask them questions. Even so, monks are forbidden from telling others about these experiences. Even if you have achieved an Arhat's level, you are not allowed to tell others unless there is a special purpose. Of course, if you lie about such things or falsely claim to have perceived emptiness directly, that is a great lie. A monk who tells a great lie commits an expulsory offense and can no longer remain in the monastery. Buddha said that a monk who commits one of these offenses cannot remain with other monks and automatically requires that he be expelled.

When the monk I just referred to heard that his rival had committed such an offense, he knew that the other monk would be expelled from the monastery and so he rejoiced about that. When Geshe Potowa realized this, he told the monk, "By rejoicing about his expulsion you are collecting a greater misdeed than your rival did when he broke one of his root vows." Therefore, when you rejoice at another person's misdeeds, you yourself collect a huge amount of negative karma.

On the other hand, if you rejoice at someone who is practicing generosity, keeping morality, or cultivating patience, you can collect even greater virtue than the practitioner who is doing those activities. This is a very important attitude to keep in mind throughout your daily activities. When you encounter either of these situations, you have to correct your attitude nicely. This is the true meaning of Dharma practice.

16.

Do not practice sporadically.

Practicing sporadically means to try very hard sometimes and not at all at other times. You have to keep a nice balance and then slowly try to strengthen your effort.

There is a well-known expression that describes a kind of renunciation to avoid called "goose-bump renunciation." Many Tibetans got this kind of renunciation when they went to Kyabje Pabongka Rinpoche's teachings. When he gave a Lamrim teaching on the eight great commentaries,[82] sometimes it lasted more than three months and was attended by as many as fifteen thousand people.

Some of the monks who had been studying continuously in the monasteries gained genuine renunciation during these teachings. To gain actual renunciation you have to realize how unbelievably bad samsara's nature is and become disgusted with samsaric happiness and activities, viewing them as unreliable. You have to think that the best and only really meaningful activity is to practice Dharma and try to achieve nirvana or Buddhahood.

Some monks, however, would leave the monastery before completing their studies and go into retreat somewhere

---

[82]See footnote 13 above.

to practice meditation. But after three or four months, the power of their renunciation would become exhausted and they would come back to the monastery. That kind of renunciation is like the goose bumps you get when you are frightened or cold, that is, they don't last very long. Goose-bump renunciation comes suddenly, for example, when you hear a Lama give a Dharma teaching. You're ready to give away all your possessions and only practice Dharma. But it is very difficult to achieve nirvana and Buddhahood. You must be prepared to travel a very long way and practice with great effort. A person who has goose-bump renunciation won't keep that attitude very long. Although he may have a very strong desire to practice as much as he can for several days, weeks, or months, after that he will get tired and won't practice nicely ever again.

Sometimes you see rookies practicing unbelievably hard. You want to say to them, "Don't practice that hard. You'll get sick, you'll go crazy." After a while they get tired and do not even think about studying continually and practicing Dharma. This is what it means to practice sporadically. Practitioners should avoid being like that.

The Kadampa sage Gompa Rinchen Lama had a saying: "Set your sights far ahead, keep a strong mind, and remain inwardly free." If you are driving down a street, you have to look a little farther ahead to see what's coming to make sure the way is clear. Similarly, when you study you have to keep your attention focused far ahead; don't have the goose-bump attitude that appears suddenly and disappears just as quickly.

You have to think, "I will start here and not stop practicing until I achieve nirvana and Buddhahood." You should also have the firm determination, "I will practice until I finish." Finally, you shouldn't worry too much or be discouraged. Remain confident and think, "If I start now and practice continually, I will definitely achieve the result at some point in the future." Keep a balanced attitude that is neither too tense nor too relaxed, and be prepared to practice over a long period of time.

Make a schedule for all your daily activities. Start early in the morning with making a good motivation. From that point on, arrange a routine for yourself and keep it continually every day. Later, when you get used to this process, you can practice more extensively. You will never fail if you adopt such a system and doing it this way will help you make great progress. For example, if you try to walk from Washington D.C. to New Jersey, it will take a long time and require a lot of effort. But if you go by car, you can reach there much sooner. Similarly, if you practice regularly, follow a schedule, and gradually extend your practice, it will be very effective and you will make great progress.

There is a Tibetan fable about a louse and a flea. A louse usually moves around very slowly. But a flea can jump very quickly. As the story goes, a farmer arranged a race between a louse and a flea, saying to them, "Each of you strap one of these baskets onto your back and go collect pieces of firewood so that we can bake some bread and enjoy it. I will give a big loaf of bread to whomever comes back first, and a smaller loaf to the one who comes back later. Will you accept this challenge?" The louse and the flea agreed.

The flea thought, "The louse walks very slowly, but I can jump far; I'll definitely win the big loaf of bread!" Then they both went off into the woods to collect pieces of dry wood. Both of them filled their own basket and then made their way back. The louse started out very slowly. Although the flea jumped ahead pretty far, his basket fell off and so he had to collect the wood all over again. During this time the louse was able to slowly pull ahead. So in the end, the louse came in first and won the big loaf of bread.

Similarly, you shouldn't practice hard at one time and not practice at all at other times. The best way to practice is to start out slowly and then keep practicing steadily and continually.

17.

Train in a way that cuts through indecision.

Although you may have heard many different teachings and have a broad understanding of Dharma, your mind has to be committed one hundred percent to your daily Mind Training practice until you experience its result. Otherwise, when you hear about a different practice, you might think, "Hmm, maybe that one is better." Then you won't achieve any result at all. Therefore, you have to put all your faith and energy into your daily practice.

For example, when you are practicing to attain quiescence you have to meditate on the same object from the beginning until you achieve it. This is like starting a fire without matches or oil, but just by rubbing two sticks together. You have to rub together the same two sticks until the fire starts. If you rub the sticks for just a little while, and take another pair and rub those two together and then change sticks again, you won't be able to start a fire even after you've gone through a whole pile of sticks. You have to continue to use the same two sticks until the fire starts. Then you can cook your food. Therefore, this precept means you have to resolve not to give up practicing until you achieve the result.

There is an analogy for this precept that is taken from traditional Tibetan medicine. It is a form of treatment that involves making an incision in the patient's flesh, like surgeries that are done here in the West. When a doctor makes an incision, he has to know exactly how wide and deep to cut into the flesh so that he can get at the problem. Similarly, when practicing Dharma, you have to continue making strong effort from the depths of your mind until you gain the real meaning and result.

There is a Tibetan expression that says you should do something until you "reach rock and bone." If you cut into the body until you reach the bone, you don't need to cut any farther. You can correct whatever medical problem is found. When you dig into the ground, you dig until you reach the rock. Like this, you have to continue practicing until you reach your goal.

18.

Free yourself using investigation and analysis.

When you are trying to develop your Lojong practice, you have to use the mental factor of investigation to check any object you hear, see, or experience. You have to do this nicely and firmly, and not give up your effort until you gain the result.

Investigation[83] and analysis[84] are two mental states that you can use when you are focusing on an object during meditation. Investigation checks the object of your practice in a rougher manner. Sometimes it is enough to examine things in a rough way; sometimes it isn't. When you need more than a rough investigation you have to use analysis, which checks the quality or nature of an object in a finer, more detailed manner. Therefore, you have to practice whichever way is necessary in order for your understanding to reach bottom in relation to your meditation object.

Also, whenever mental afflictions arise in your mind, first you have to identify them. Because there may be several afflictions involved, you have to determine which of them is strongest. Once you do this, you should fight against the strongest of your mental afflictions. Later you can try to remove the weaker ones.

19.

Do not be conceited.

When you took the Bodhisattva vows, you promised, "I want very much to achieve Buddhahood in order to serve and help beings and to liberate all of them from samsara's

_____

[83]*rtog pa.*
[84]*dpyod pa.*

suffering." After taking a vow, you have to keep it nicely without breaking it. Once you take the vows, you have to practice doing activities that benefit sentient beings. For example, I give regular Dharma teachings and try to provide explanations that will improve your understanding and ability to practice. These are the kinds of activities to do after generating bodhichitta. However, this is also my duty, something that I must do. I shouldn't congratulate myself by saying to others, "I really did help you, didn't I!"

If someone saves another person's life, that other person will think, "He saved my life. How incredibly kind." He knows that you have helped him. If the individual who saved him goes to him every day and reminds him, "I saved your life, I saved your life," the one who received help will slowly lose the feeling of gratitude. He will think, "He saved my life, but this is unbelievable. Now he just keeps bothering me every day."

Therefore, you shouldn't be conceited. Instead, you should think of it as your duty to do things for others, because you took a vow to do so. On television you often hear people say, "I was just doing my job." This is a very good expression that nicely describes the meaning of this precept. Since you have taken Bodhisattva vows to help beings, you shouldn't boast or congratulate yourself or remind others of how you have helped them.

20.

Do not be resentful.

A Bodhisattva might feel resentment, for example, if someone stands up and scolds or criticizes him in the middle of a large group of people. But you shouldn't let yourself get upset or feel angry by what others may say about you. Instead, you should just forget about it.

21.

Do not be fickle.

This precept literally says "don't do things just for a *yü tsam*,"[85] which means that your mind shouldn't change every hour or so. A practitioner's mind should be very steady; it shouldn't shift in response to small causes. You shouldn't immediately become happy when some small good thing happens, or instantly get upset when some small bad thing happens. If you do that, you are behaving like the sky in spring.

In the springtime, you might say, "We should go outside today, the weather is very good." Then after you go out, it suddenly gets cloudy and starts to rain. So then you say, "Now it's raining, we have to go inside." When you get home, the sun starts to shine again, at which point you say, "We should have stayed out longer." A practitioner's mind shouldn't be like that, quickly changing over some small cause.

22.

Do not hope for gratitude.

If you do good things for the benefit of others, just do them. You shouldn't expect to hear, "Thank you so much. You were so unbelievably helpful." You shouldn't wait to hear that kind of response. From your side, just be willing to help.

———————————

[85]In ancient times when the Vinaya was first taught, there were no clocks. However, there were methods of measuring time from the smallest instants up to an eon. One way of measuring time was to count breaths. For example, six breaths is called one *chu sang*, sixty *chu sang* make one *chu tsö*, two *chu tsö* are equal to one *yü tsam*, and so on. One *yü tsam* is about forty-five minutes.

The *Seven Point Mind Training* says:

It transforms the rise of the five degenerations
Into the path that leads to enlightenment.

This instruction can transform the five degenerations into elements of the path that lead to enlightenment. These five are: degeneration of life span, of age, of mental afflictions, of views, and of sentient beings.

According to Buddhist cosmology, human beings have extremely long life spans at the beginning of a kalpa or eon. Later, their life spans become shorter because they collected more and more bad deeds. Buddha Shakyamuni appeared when the maximum life span of humans was about a hundred years. Compared with a human life span at the beginning of a kalpa, current human life spans have degenerated.

The Tibetan word for degeneration is *nyikma*.[86] In colloquial Tibetan, *nyikma* can mean the dregs left at the bottom of a cup of tea. Any liquid, such as water or oil, can have such impurities. Long ago, human life spans were fresh and long, without stains. Nowadays, they have degenerated and become impure because of our bad deeds. This is the first of the five degenerations.

Degeneration of mental afflictions means that in early times beings didn't have as many mental afflictions. As time went on, beings developed them more and more. Nowadays, mental afflictions are heavy in the minds of beings. Due to our mental afflictions, our conduct and activities have also become much worse.

Degeneration of views means that the wrong views of beings are deep and widespread.

Degeneration of sentient beings means that long ago beings were much more gentle and calm. Compared to them, beings have become very cruel. We are living in an age of degeneration in the sense that long ago beings were much more spiritually subdued. Nowadays, people argue

---

[86]*snyigs ma.*

and fight much more with one another. Lawsuits are getting bigger and more frequent.

The main point is that even though these five degenerations are flourishing, Mahayana practitioners who know this instruction can transform bad situations into good causes. They can turn them into causes for achieving Buddhahood.

How is that? If I ask you whether anger is good or bad, what will you say? Although anger is generally bad, you cannot practice patience if there is no anger. You also need to know about anger in order to practice patience. You need to know the essential nature of anger, as well as its bad qualities, its main function, and so forth. Knowing how bad anger really is helps you to gain patience. If these things didn't exist, you could not develop patience nicely. The same is true if you want to develop compassion and right view. You need to know everything about wrong views in order to gain right view. You need to know what the target is. If you don't know what the target is, you can't hit the bull's-eye.

How sharp and how long is a hare's horn? Since the horn of a hare doesn't even exist, you cannot gain any wisdom by contemplating that question. However, this instruction enables you to turn the bad situations of these degenerate times into good causes that will help you develop Bodhisattva activities.

I have taught the essence of this instruction—how to gain bodhichitta—in eleven categories or topics. About the source of the instruction, the *Seven Point Mind Training* states:

> This instruction, which is the
>   Essence of the Nectar of Immortality,
> Has come down in a lineage from
>   Suvarnadvipa Guru.

Through his study and practice the great Kadampa Lama Chekawa became an expert in this Lojong instruction.

Just as food has a good taste, he was able to find and enjoy the good taste of this entire Mahayana Lojong instruction. Afterwards, he composed the root text called the *Seven Point Mind Training*. Then he remarked, "Now that I have composed this root text with whatever knowledge I have, I am ready to die without any regrets. I have explained everything in this root text on Mind Training instruction."

This is the final point made, as the words of the root text state:

> Motivated by the great wish,
> I've ignored suffering and criticism
> To be able to receive instructions that
> Overcome belief in a self.
> Now I am ready to die without any regrets.

Right View

This concludes all of the Mind Training instructions except for the ones that have to do with right view. Bodhisattva activities are included in the six *paramitas* or perfections. Among them, the first four are: giving, morality, patience, and effort. Effort is practiced to develop the first three activities, as well as the last two. Concentration and wisdom, the fifth and sixth perfections, are related to the practice of right view.

There are many levels of instruction that relate to right view. In particular, there are two types of right view: worldly right view and transcendent right view. Worldly right view is practiced mostly by ordinary persons, or non-Aryas. The main element of worldly right view is the teaching of karma and its results. It is very important for ordinary persons to practice this teaching.

Karma is mainly divided into two types: good karma and bad karma. This instruction on karma also includes understanding the infallible relationship between good karma and its results, as well as the infallible relationship between bad karma and its results. If you develop a strong belief in karma, you have gained the worldly right view that is especially important for ordinary persons.

Why is the worldly right view so important? Because if you don't have a strong belief in karma, you will not try to collect good deeds and abandon bad ones. Therefore, the first important right view is the one that relates to karma. On top of that, the second important right view relates to the nature of the self or *atma*. The easy way to understand the meaning of "self" here is that it refers to an inherently existing person. The Tibetan term *dakdzin*, or grasping at a self, means the subject or mind that believes the self is real or self-existent. Some people translate *dakdzin* as egotism, but egotism is a mixture of pride and the belief that the self is real. Because the object of that mind, a self-existent person, does not exist, the mind that holds it as an inherently existing thing is mistaken in its view.

Therefore, our goal is to perceive that all persons are not inherently existent, because that is the actual nature of all persons. A person who lacks a self-existent nature still eats, goes to different places, does different things, learns, meditates, and so on. That agent does exist, but wrong view mistakenly regards that person as inherently existent, as an inherently existent agent, an inherently existent eater, an inherently existent doer, and so on.

There are many descriptions about right view in various Buddhist writings. Some of them are good, others are mistaken. During the early spread of Buddhism in Tibet, there were many mistaken descriptions about right view. If you check their explanations logically or meditate on what they described as the object's real nature, you do not find in them the authentic right view. Some of those explanations are like descriptions of the sharpness, length, or beauty of a hare's horn. That kind of investigation is meaningless, because the main object being referred to cannot be found—it is nonexistent.

One of Lord Tsongkapa's disciples wrote a commentary called *Mind Training Like the Rays of the Sun*,[87] which states

---

[87]*blo sbyong nyi ma'i 'od zer.*

that the right view must be explained according to the Madhyamaka-Prasangika school.

Mind Training means that Mahayana practitioners have to tame their minds in two ways: in relation to activities and in relation to right view. Both ways are included in the six perfections: giving, morality, patience, effort, concentration, and wisdom. Of these six, the fourth perfection, which is effort, must accompany all the other perfections. Without effort, you cannot practice any of them successfully.

The first three perfections—generosity, morality, and patience—relate to how we should perform our daily activities. The main point is that you must tame your wrong motivations when you do any activity. For example, without taming stinginess, you cannot practice the perfection of giving. Similarly, to practice morality you have to correct your bad motivations and bad deeds of body, speech, and mind. Without knowing what those are, you cannot observe morality properly. It is the same with patience. In connection with these three perfections, you must also develop effort. These four subjects make up the category of a Mahayana practitioner's activities. The Mind Training instruction about right view relates to the last two paramitas: concentration and wisdom.

These two categories, activities and right view, must be practiced together. They are described as being like the two wings of a young and healthy goose. With them, you can fly to a Buddha's paradise.

In Buddhist philosophy there are four schools about right view. These four schools are all authentic Buddhist systems that arose because of the different levels of understanding of Buddhist practitioners and scholars. If distinguished according to the different Buddhist "vehicles," they are known as the Listeners' or Shravaka vehicle, the Solitary Realizers' or Pratyekabuddha vehicle, and Bodhisattva vehicle. If distinguished according to philosophical schools, they are known as Vaibhashika, Sautrantika, Yogachara, and Madhyamaka. Within the Madhyamaka school, there are also two branches, the Svatantrika and Prasangika. The best school is the last one, the Madhyamaka-Prasangika school. It represents the Buddha's own view and that of such great teachers as Nagarjuna and Chandrakirti.

Lama Serlingpa was a Lineage Lama who was an expert in bodhichitta and in the instructions for a Mahayana practitioner's activities. Although he understood right view according to the Yogachara school, it is said that in the latter part of his life he revised his philosophical view, adopting that of the Madhyamaka-Prasangika school.

When Lamas give instruction in the Lamrim, they teach all the topics up through bodhichitta four times. They give the first explanation in detail, using both scriptural quotations and logical reasons. In the second explanation, they review the essence of each topic. The third explanation is more abbreviated than the second and mainly shows how to practice the instructions. In the final explanation, they give a brief summary of all the points. Lamas do not continue with this four-part system, however, after they have completed the instruction on how to generate bodhichitta. They teach these latter subjects in detail and only once, without reviewing any of the points.

This concludes the instructions on how to generate bodhichitta and how to keep the precepts relating to that instruction. In the context of the structure of the Lamrim teachings, a general explanation of the six paramitas follows the instructions on bodhichitta, with a detailed explanation of the last two paramitas. These two topics are called quiescence and insight.

I mentioned earlier that when Kyabje Pabongka Rinpoche taught the Lamrim extensively, the discourse started around nine o'clock in the morning. Usually after about three hours of teaching there was a break and everyone attending was served tea and bread. Many different patrons made these arrangements, including all the offerings. After the break, the teaching continued until around six-thirty in the evening. This was the schedule for the first two months or so. During the latter part of the teaching, when we reached the final two topics of quiescence and Madhyamaka philosophy, he would sometimes continue teaching until ten o'clock at night. Even when the teaching began at nine in the morning and ended at ten there was only one break. Still, everyone felt very fresh. It was unbelievable! Even though the main assembly hall at Sera Mey College was actually very large, during these teachings it was difficult for all fifteen thousand disciples to fit there. We all had to sit very close together. There was not even a seventh inning stretch.

Let me close by repeating what Kyabje Pabongka Rinpoche used to say at the end of his teachings:

"I kindly urge you to put into practice everything I have explained here."

May the merit of this work serve as a cause to firmly place all sentient beings in a state of complete enlightenment.

༄༅། །ཐེག་པ་ཆེན་པོའི་བློ་སྦྱོང་
དོན་བདུན་མའི་རྩ་བ་བཞུགས་སོ། །

ROOT TEXT
OF THE
MAHAYANA
SEVEN POINT MIND TRAINING

།ཕྱགས་རྗེ་ཆེན་པོ་ལ་ཕྱག་འཚལ་ལོ།

།ཆོས་ཁྱམས་བཅུན་པར་བསྟན་པའི་ཕྱིར་མཆོད་པ་པོའི་ཆེ་བ་བསྟན་པ།

།མན་ངག་བདུད་རྩིའི་སྙིང་པོ་འདི།

།གསེར་གྱིང་པ་ནས་བརྒྱུད་པ་ཡིན།

།གདམས་ངག་ལ་གུས་པ་བསྐྱེད་པའི་ཕྱིར་ཆོས་ཀྱི་ཆེ་བ་བསྟན་པ།

།རྡོ་རྗེ་ཉི་མ་སྣང་ཞིང་བཞིན།

།གཏུང་དོན་ལ་སོགས་ཞེས་པར་བྱ།

།སྐྱིགས་མ་ལྟ་པོ་བརྡོ་བ་འདི།

།བྱུང་ཚུབ་ལམ་དུ་བསྒྱུར་བ་ཡིན།

།གདམས་པ་དངོས་ཀྱིས་སྒྲིབ་མ་ཇེ་ལྡུར་བགྱི་བའི་རིམ་པ་ལ་དོན་ཚོན་བདུན་གྱི།

།དང་པོ་སྟོན་འགྲོ་རྟེན་གྱི་ཆོས་བསྟན་པ་ནི།

།དང་པོ་སྟོན་འགྲོ་དག་ལ་བསྒྲུབ།

། །གཉིས་པ་དངོས་གཞི་བྱང་ཚུབ་ཀྱི་སེམས་སྟོང་པ་ལ་དོན་དམ་བྱང་ཚུབ་ཀྱི་སེམས་སྟོང་ཚུལ་དང་། །ཀུན་རྫོབ་བྱང་ཚུབ་ཀྱི་སེམས་སྟོང་ཚུལ་གཉིས་ལས། དོན་དམ་བྱང་ཚུབ་ཀྱི་སེམས་སྟོང་ཚུལ་ཡིག་སྟེང་ ཕལ་ཆེར་དུ་སྟོན་དུ་གསུངས་ཀྱང་། །རང་ལུགས་འཛམ་མགོན་ཙོང་ཁ་པ་ཆེན་པོའི་བཞིན་སྲོལ་ལྟར་སྟོ སྟོང་ཉི་མའི་བོད་ཞེས། །སྐྲོ་བཟང་དགོངས་རྒྱ། །བདུད་རྩིའི་སྙིང་པོ། །ཀྱེ་ཚོང་རྟུ་ཚིག་སོགས་མང་ པོར་ལེག་ཏུ་གསུངས་པ་བཞིན་དགོས་པ་ཁྱད་པར་ཅན་གྱི་སྲུང་ལོག་ཏུ་འགོད་པར་བྱ་བས། །ངས་ན་ཀུན་ རྟོབ་བྱང་ཚུབ་ཀྱི་སེམས་སྟོང་བ་ནི།

།ཡེ་ལན་ཐམས་ཅད་གཅིག་ལ་བདག།

།གུན་ལ་བགད་རིན་ཆེ་བར་བསྒོམ།

།གཏོང་ལེན་གཉིས་པོ་སྤེལ་མར་སྦྱང་།

།ལེན་པའི་གོ་རིམ་རང་ནས་བརྩམ།

།དེ་གཉིས་རླུང་ལ་བསྐྱོན་པར་བྱ།

།ལུལ་གསུམ་དུག་གསུམ་དགེ་རྩ་གསུམ།

།རྗེས་ཀྱི་མན་ངག་མདོར་བསྟུས་པ།

།དེ་ལ་དན་པ་བསྐལ་བའི་ཕྱིར།

།སྒྱོད་ལས་གུན་ཏུ་ཚིག་གིས་སྦྱང་།

ཏོན་དམ་བྱང་ཆུབ་ཀྱི་སེམས་སྦྱོང་བ་ནི།

།བརྟན་པ་ཐོབ་ནས་གསང་བ་བསྟན།

།ཆོས་རྣམས་རྨི་ལམ་ལྟ་བུར་བསམ།

།མ་སྐྱེས་རིག་པའི་གཤིས་ལ་དཔྱད།

།གཉེན་པོ་ཉིད་ཀྱང་རང་སར་གྲོལ།

།ལམ་གྱི་ངོ་བོ་གུན་གཞིའི་རི་རང་ལ་བཞག

།ཐུན་མཚམས་སྒྱུ་མའི་སྐྱེས་བུར་བྱ།

།གསུམ་པ་རྒྱུན་དང་བྱུང་རྒྱབ་ཀྱི་ལམ་དུ་བསྒྱུར་བ་ནི།

།སྐྱོན་བཅུད་སྟེག་པས་གང་བའི་ཚེ།

།རྒྱུན་དང་བྱུང་རྒྱབ་ལམ་དུ་བསྒྱུར།

།འཕྲལ་ལ་གང་ཐུག་བསྒོམ་དུ་སྦྱར།

།སྐྱོར་བ་བཞི་ལྡན་ཐབས་ཀྱི་མཆོག

།བཞི་པ་ཚོགས་ཅིག་གི་ཉམས་ལེན་རིལ་ནས་བསྡུན་པ་ནི།

།མན་ངག་སྙིང་པོ་མདོར་བསྡུས་པ།

།སྒྲིབས་ལྟ་དག་དང་སྒྱུར་བར་བྱ།

།ཐེག་ཆེན་འཕོ་བའི་དམས་ངག་ནི།

།སྒྲིབས་ལྟ་ཉིད་ཡིན་སྒྱོང་ལམ་གཅིག

།ལྤ་པ་བློ་འབྱོངས་པའི་ཚད་བསྟན་པ་ནི།

།ཆོས་ཀུན་དགོངས་པ་གཅིག་ཏུ་འདུས།

།དཔང་པོ་གཉིས་ཀྱི་གཙོ་བོ་བཟུང་།

།ཡིད་བདེ་འབབ་ཞིག་རྒྱུན་དུ་བསྟེན།

།བྱུང་བའི་ཚད་ནི་ལོག་པ་ཡིན།

།འབྱོངས་རྟགས་ཆེན་པོ་ལྔ་ལྡན་ཡིན།

།ཨིངས་ཀྱང་ཐུབ་ན་འཕྲོངས་པ་ཨིན།

༏དྲུག་པ་བློ་སྦྱོང་གི་དམ་ཚིག་བསྩན་པ་ནི།

།སྱི་དོན་གསུམ་ལ་རྟག་ཏུ་བསླབ།

།འདུན་པ་བསྒྱུར་ལ་རང་སོར་བཞག།

།ཡན་ལག་ཉམས་པ་བརྗོད་མི་བྱ།

།གཞན་ཕྱོགས་གང་ཡང་མི་བསམ་མོ།

།ཉིན་མོངས་གང་ཆེ་སྙོན་ལ་སྦྱང་།

།འབྲས་བུ་རེ་བ་ཐམས་ཅད་སྤང་།

།དུག་ཅན་གྱི་ཟས་སྤང་།

།གཡུང་བཟང་པོ་མི་བསྟེན།

།ཁ༌ཕགས༌དན་མི་རྟོད།

།འཕྱང་མི་སྒྲུག

།གནད་ལ་མི་དབབ།

།མཛོ་ཁལ་གླང་ལ་མི་འགེལ།

།སྤྱོ་ལོག་མི་བྱ།

།མགྱོགས་ཀྱི་རྩེ་མི་གཏོད།

།ལྷ་བདུད་དུ་མི་དབབ།

།སྐྱིད་ཀྱི་ཡན་ལག་ཏུ་སྲུག་མི་འཚོལ།

ༀ་བདུན་པ་སྒྲོ་སྐྱོང་གི་བསླབ་བྱ་བསྟན་པ་ནི།

།རྐྱལ་འབྱོར་ཐམས་ཅད་གཅིག་གིས་བྱ།

།ཁྱོག་གཱོན་ཐམས་ཅད་གཅིག་གིས་བྱ།

།ཐོག་མཐའ་གཉིས་ལ་བྱ་བ་གཅིས།

།གཉིས་པོ་གང་བྱུང་བཟོད་པར་བྱ།

།གཉིས་པོ་སྟོག་དང་བསྟོས་ལ་བསྲུང་།

།དཀར་བ་གསུམ་ལ་བསླབ་པར་བྱ།

།རྒྱུ་ཡི་གཙོ་བོ་རྣམ་གསུམ་ལྡང་།

།ༀ་མས་པ་མེད་པ་རྣམ་གསུམ་བསྐྱེད།

།འབྲལ་མེད་གསུམ་དང་ལྡན་པར་བྱ།

།ཡུལ་ལ་ཕྱོགས་མེད་དག་ཏུ་སྦྱང་།

།ཁྱབ་དང་གཏིང་འབྱོངས་ཀུན་ལ་གཅེས།

།བགོལ་བ་རྣམས་ལ་རྟག་ཏུ་བསྒོམ།

།རྐྱེན་གཞན་དག་ལ་ལྟོས་མི་བྱ།

།ད་རེས་གཅོ་བོ་ཉམས་སུ་བླང་།

།གོ་ལྷག་མི་བྱ།

།རེས་འཇོག་མི་བྱ།

།དོལ་ཆོད་དུ་སྒྲུབ།

།རྟོག་དཔྱོད་གཉིས་ཀྱིས་ཐར་བར་བྱ།

          །བཏག་དཔྱད་ཅེས་པ་ལ་འདུག

།ལུས་ལ་བསྒོམ།

།ཁ་ལྷོང་མ་རྟོག།

།ལྱད་ཚམ་པ་མི་བྱ།

།ཟིར་ཆེ་མི་འདོད།

          །བྱང་ཆུབ་ཀྱི་སེམས་ལ་གདེང་ཐོབ་པའི་གསུང་གིས་མཐག་བསྟུབ།

།རང་གི་ཤེས་པ་མང་བའི་ཀྱུས།

།སྡུག་བསྔལ་གཏུམ་དང་ཁྱད་བསད་ནས།

།བདག་འཛིན་འདུལ་བའི་གདམས་ངག་ཞུས།

།དགེ་ཞི་ལྱང་མི་འགྱུད་དོ།

     །དེ་ལྟར་བློ་སྦྱོང་དོན་བདུན་མའི་རྩ་ཚིག་དང་འགྲེལ་པ་སོགས་བཀའ་གདམས་གསར་རྙིང་གི་
གསུང་གི་ཟིན་དུ་ཤིན་ཏུ་མང་བ་བཞུགས་ཀྱང་། །ཁྱལ་ཆེར་གཏུང་ཚིག་གི་གོ་རིམ། །ཚིག་སྒྲ་མང་ཉུང་

འདུ་མིན་ཤེན་ཏུ་མང་ཞིང་། །འགའ་ཞིག་ཁྱད་ཀྱི་སྣབས་ཀྱིས་བཅད་ལ་སྒྱུར་མ་བདེ་བ་ཡང་ཅེ་རེ་གས། །འགའ་ཞིག་ཡོངས་གྲགས་མིན་པའི་ཙུ་ཚིག་ཀྱང་སྨྲ་ཚོགས་སྲུང་བ་བཅས་ལ་བརྟེན། །རང་ལུགས་འཛམ་མགོན་ཚོང་ཁ་པ་ཆེན་པོའི་གསུང་རྒྱུན་ལྟར་གྱི་ནྲོ་སྒྲུང་ཉེ་མའི་འོད་ཟེར། །ཀྲོ་བཟང་དགོངས་རྒྱན། །བདུད་རྩིའི་སྙིང་པོ་རྣམས་ཀྱི་དགོངས་དོན་གྱུང་བསྐྱགས་པའི་ཙུ་ཚིག་ཅིག་བྱུང་ན་ཅི་མ་རུང་སྙམ་རིང་ནས་སེམས་སྒྱུར། ཞིང་ཕག་ལོར་ཆབ་མདོ་དགེ་ལྡན་བྱམས་པ་གྱིང་དུ་བྱང་རྒྱབ་ལས་རིམ་ཆེན་མོ་འཆད་སྐབས་གཅིག་ཏུ་སྐྱབ་པ་ལྱུར་ཤེན་ལས་རིམ་པ་ཕུན་ཚོགས་དཔལ་ལྱན་ནས་རྟེན་བཅས་ཇི་ལྱུར་བསྐྱལ་བ་བཞིན་ཙུ་འགྲེལ་མད་པོར་ཞིབ་བརྟག་གིས་ཙུ་ཚིག་ཕྱོགས་བསྐྱིགས་ཐོག །ས་བཅད་ཀྱིས་བརྒྱན་ཏེ་ཕྱོགས་གཅིག་ཏུ་པ་ཕོད་ཁའི་སྤྱལ་མེད་པས་ཐིས་པ་འགྲོ་དོན་འཕེལ་བར་གྱུར་ཅིག །

THE ROOT TEXT OF
THE MAHAYANA TEACHING ENTITLED
SEVEN POINT MIND TRAINING

I prostrate to great compassion.

> *The greatness of the originator, presented in order to demonstrate the authoritative source of the Dharma.*

This instruction, which is the
Essence of the Nectar of Immortality,
Has come down in a lineage from
Suvarnadvipa Guru.

> *The greatness of the Dharma, presented in order to generate respect for the instruction.*

Like a diamond, the sun, and a medicinal tree
Should the text's meaning be understood.
It transforms the rise of the five degenerations
Into the path that leads to enlightenment.

> *The method of leading the student by means of the actual instruction.*
> *Section one: The preliminary teachings that are the foundation for the instructions.*

Begin by training in the preliminary teachings.

> *Section two: The main instruction of training in the two forms of bodhichitta—ultimate bodhichitta and conventional bodhichitta.*

> *Most of the early editions present the practice of training in ultimate bodhichitta first. The view expressed in this edition is that there is an important reason for placing it later in the*

text. *In doing so, I am following the tradition established by the great Jamgön Lama Tsongkapa. This view is also reflected in numerous works, such as* Mind Training Like the Rays of the Sun, Ornament of Lobsang's View, Essence of the Nectar of Immortality, *and the edition of the root text compiled by Keutsang Jamyang Mönlam.*

Training oneself in conventional bodhichitta:

All blame rests with one.
Meditate on the great kindness of all beings.
Cultivate alternately the two of Giving and Taking.
Practice Taking gradually, starting with yourself.
Let these two practices ride on your breath.
There are three objects, three poisons, and
    three virtue-roots.
An abbreviated instruction for the period after meditation
Is to remind yourself of the practice by reciting words
    during all your activities.

Training in ultimate bodhichitta:

When you have gained mastery,
    practice the secret instruction.
View all things as being dreamlike.
Analyze the nature of unborn awareness.
The antidote itself is released right where it is.
Place the mind in the all-encompassing
    essence of the path.
Between meditation periods, view beings as illusory.

Section three: Transforming unfavorable circumstances into elements of the path to enlightenment.

When the world and its inhabitants are brimming with evil,
Transform bad circumstances into the path to
    enlightenment.
Immediately apply to your practice whatever is
    unexpectedly encountered.

The supreme form of spiritual training is accompanied by
    four actions.

*Section four: A summary presentation of what to practice over
one's entire lifetime.*

Briefly, the essence of the instruction
Is to devote yourself to the five strengths.
The Mahayana transference instruction
Is to practice the same five strengths and
To give special importance to your physical position.

*Section five: How to determine whether you have mastered
Mind Training.*

All Dharma teachings are based on one underlying
    thought.
Pay attention to the more important of the two witnesses.
Always keep a happy mind.
The measure of mastery is that self-cherishing has been
    turned back.
There are five great signs of having trained.
If you can practice even when distracted, you have
    gained mastery.

Section six: The pledges to be observed.

Always train in the three general principles.
Change your aspiration but remain natural.
Do not speak about the faults of others.
Do not be concerned with others' business.
Remove your worst mental affliction first.
Give up all hope of achieving results.
Avoid poisonous food.
Do not be patient [with your mental afflictions].
Do not engage in bitter quarreling.
Do not wait along a back alley.
Do not strike a vital point.
Do not displace a dzo's load onto an ox.

Do not practice wrongly as if doing worldly rituals.
Do not try to be the fastest.
Do not turn a god into a demon.
Do not seek others' misery as a way to be happy.

*Section seven: A presentation of the precepts to be observed by
practitioners of the Mind Training instructions.*

Do all yoga practices with one thought.
Respond with one antidote when overwhelmed by obstacles.
Two activities: one for the beginning and one for the end.
Be patient no matter which of the two you encounter.
Protect the two even at the cost of your life.
Train in the three difficulties.
Take up the three principal causes.
Practice to keep the three undamaged.
Never be parted from the three activities.
Train yourself to be impartial.
Most important is to practice toward all beings from the
　　depths of your heart.
Constantly train in relation to special objects.
Do not depend on other conditions.
Practice now what is most important.
Do not do the mistaken activities.
Do not practice sporadically.
Train in a way that cuts through indecision.
Free yourself using investigation and analysis.
Do not be conceited.
Do not be resentful.
Do not be fickle.
Do not hope for gratitude.

*The teachings are concluded with a verse expressing the satis-
faction that is gained by having attained bodhichitta:*

Motivated by the great wish,
I've ignored suffering and criticism
To be able to receive instructions

That overcome belief in a self.
Now I am ready to die without any regrets.

Among the writings of teachers from both the Old and New Kadampa traditions, there are a great many commentaries on the Seven Point Mind Training *instruction, as well as numerous versions of the root text. However, the order in which the instructions are presented varies significantly in these texts. Even the wording and body of instructions differ from edition to edition. Some editions of the root text did not correspond to the outlines for teaching the instructions as presented in different commentaries. The wording of other editions does not correspond to more popular versions in which some of the instructions have been preserved. Therefore, because of my long-standing wish to compile an edition of the root text that conforms with the views expressed in works such as* Mind Training Like the Rays of the Sun, Ornament of Lobsang's View, *and* Essence of the Nectar of Immortality, *which form part of our teaching tradition established by the great Jamgön Lama Tsongkapa; and in response to a request by Puntsok Palden, a devoted practitioner of the Lamrim teachings, which was accompanied by the traditional offerings, I, a monk recognized as a tulku who carries the name of Pabongka, compiled this edition of the root text, and after a careful study of numerous editions of the root text and many commentaries, added an outline of the topics. It was completed in the Wood Boar Year (1935) at the Gelukpa monastery known as Jampa Ling, which is located in the district of Chamdo, during the course of a Lamrim teaching I was giving there.*

May the welfare of all beings increase.

APPENDIX

EDITORS' NOTE: *As mentioned in the Introduction, the present volume was compiled from a series of teachings that Khen Rinpoche gave beginning one weekend in the late summer of 1981 at Milarepa Center in Barnet, Vermont. When he was requested to give this teaching on Mind Training, he was also asked to present it from a perspective of how to meditate on and practice it. To satisfy those requests, Rinpoche took time to explain some of the fundamentals of meditation during several of these teachings. Because of time constraints, he limited himself mainly to those points that would serve as a practical guide for the beginning practitioner who wanted to meditate on the steps for developing bodhichitta.*

Because explanations on how to meditate are not the main focus of the present volume, the editors have chosen to gather those instructions here in the Appendix. In addition, although this particular teaching series did not provide Khen Rinpoche with the opportunity to present all the instructions on how to achieve quiescence or shamatha, he did give a brief description of it along with some of its extraordinary benefits toward the end of his presentation. In order to supplement that presentation, the editors have incorporated material from other teachings given by Khen Rinpoche. At the same time, we wish to note that the portion of this section that is most relevant for meditating on bodhichitta is roughly what appears in the first half.

MEDITATION

MANY MEDITATION TEXTS QUOTE the following lines from *Engaging in Bodhisattva Activities*:

> The Knower of Truth declared that practicing
> with a distracted mind is meaningless.[88]

Other texts also say that if you try to recite, visualize, or meditate on something with a scattered mind, you would not gain any good result even if you practiced that way for eons. Similarly, Buddha said that it is meaningless to practice with a distracted mind, even if your body is in the meditation position. Of course, if you are not meditating properly, you are just wasting your time, which is what "meaningless" means. So, whether you are meditating for a long or a short period, you must do everything properly and perfectly. If you do, you can achieve concentration easily. The instruction for developing single-pointed concentration includes nine stages, six powers, and four ways of engaging the object. If you do everything nicely, you will be able to advance through the nine stages one by one and achieve their goals.

Meditation Posture

What is the proper way to sit during meditation? Meditation texts mention that we should sit in the position that has the seven qualities associated with the Eastern Buddha Vairochana:

1) The back should be very straight, leaning back just enough so that if a drop of water were to fall from the tip of

---

[88]*Engaging in Bodhisattva Activities*, ch. 5, v. 16.

your nose it would land on your navel; 2) the head should be tilted forward very slightly so that the larynx is pressed down just a little bit. Many people close their eyes while meditating, even though the great meditation texts don't say to do that. What they do say is that you should 3) direct your eyes toward the tip of your nose. This means that your gaze should not extend beyond that but should not focus closer in either. The gaze should be directed downward, but you should not focus on your nose.

The *Treasury of Higher Knowledge* discusses the functions of the five sense powers and the five sense consciousnesses. When a thunderstorm approaches, you can see lightning in the distance but you don't hear the sound of thunder until later. This means that the eye consciousness perceives outer objects more quickly than the ear consciousness and also perceives more of them. When you see something, your mind consciousness immediately follows your eye consciousness. Therefore, your mind can easily become distracted, which is why it is better not to be able to see outer objects. For that reason, it might be better for beginners to close their eyes during meditation. 4) The shoulders should remain level; 5) the mouth (lips, teeth, and tongue) should be closed in a relaxed position, the way it is when you aren't talking or doing anything in particular. The mouth should be closed but not clenched shut. If you are meditating for a short period, it doesn't matter; but if you plan to remain in meditation for an extended period of time, the tip of the tongue should touch the roof of the mouth. This helps to keep you from getting thirsty. These are very useful points and, with meditation experience, you can understand their significance. 6) If your body is flexible enough, you should sit in the vajra cross-legged posture.[89] If this is too difficult, sit comfortably in a cross-legged position. You should also sit on a cushion so that your back side is a bit higher than your front side. 7) The right hand rests face up on top of the

---

[89]*rdo rje dkyil dkrungs* (Skt: *vajraparyanka*) with the left foot resting on the right thigh and the right foot resting over the left leg on the left thigh.

left palm at the level of the navel, with the tips of the thumbs gently touching.

We have 72,000 different nerves in our body. Airs and unique substances that travel within those nerves affect the mind. If you keep the body straight, the nerves will be aligned and the airs will travel easily within them. The airs are like a horse, the mind like a rider. They function together. If the airs flow easily, you can gain knowledge more easily. This is the purpose of sitting in this way. If you enter the Tantric path in the future, these elements of meditation posture take on even greater significance.

Types of Meditation

There are many different types of meditation.[90] In general, meditation means one-pointed mind, which is the mind focused on its own object without thinking about or following other objects. Meditation does not necessarily mean to meditate on one simple object. If you are trying to gain quiescence, you can use one simple object, though it's not necessary to do so.[91] For example, you can meditate on the form of Avalokiteshvara or the image of the Wheel of Life. Each of these objects consists of many parts. In the case of the Wheel of Life, you shouldn't focus only on the central part, but rather try to visualize the entire image as a complete set.

There are also many meditation objects in which a whole set of points is your one meditation object. Your mind should not go beyond that to any other object. If you are meditating on the first point of the Sevenfold Instruction, which is to realize that all beings have been your mother,

---

[90] The two main types of meditation are placement meditation (*'jog sgom*) and analytical meditation (*dpyad sgom*). The main quality of analytical meditation is to repeatedly examine an object using many kinds of reasons and scriptural citations. In such meditation the main instrument is discriminating wisdom (*so sor rtogs pa'i shes rab*). The goal of placement meditation is to focus the mind on an object steadily and one-pointedly. The teachings being described here in which the five enemies and nine abidings are discussed, refer primarily to the practice of placement meditation.

[91] This means that while you do need to have one object, it is not necessary that it be a simple object.

you can meditate on all the different reasons mentioned already, but your mind should stay within that field and should not wander to other fields or objects. That whole set of reasons is one object of meditation.[92] Within that field there are many objects and your mind is focusing on many things, but this is not a case of mental scattering. All of those objects belong to one set; each set being one "object" of meditation.

Five Enemies of Meditation

First Enemy:
Laziness

ཉ ལེ་ལོ།

Briefly, there are five enemies of meditation. The first enemy is laziness. Laziness makes you postpone meditation: "Maybe not today; I'll start tomorrow, or the next day or the next." That is one type of laziness. Another type of laziness is when you lose confidence and think, "I just can't do it." The third type of laziness makes you give up meditating altogether—this is the worst one. Many people do this; they start something, do it for a little while, then give it up, never to return to it again. These are only a few of the many different kinds of laziness. Laziness doesn't just mean doing things slowly, like taking your time when you are drinking something.

In order to remove laziness you have to develop faith in meditation by learning about its object, purpose, and beneficial results. You have to do this by studying meditation. If you learn about the good qualities and beneficial results of meditation, you will definitely overcome laziness. Once you develop faith you will feel the need to try and therefore you will try.[93] For example, if a businessperson thinks of a plan

---

[92]This is an example of an object within analytical meditation.
[93]There are four antidotes to laziness: faith, aspiration, effort, and agility or *shinjang* (*shin sbyangs*). Here Rinpoche is making reference to aspiration and

and realizes that he can make a lot of money by following that plan, he will never give it up. If you develop that kind of determination, even if someone blocks you so that you can't go one way, you'll find another way to get there. You'll keep trying. Similarly, if you learn the results and good qualities of meditation, you will gain faith, aspiration, and effort, which automatically reduces and eliminates your laziness.

The ultimate antidote to laziness is agility (*shinjang*). *Shinjang* literally means extremely well trained. Because acrobats have trained their bodies, they can do a lot of extraordinary feats. Similarly, when your body and mind become used to meditation, your body won't feel tired or sore or uncomfortable; you won't get a backache or have to stretch your legs, because the power of meditation brings an extreme ease and relaxation of body and mind. You will feel very pleasant and happy, with no mental or physical problems. When you achieve that stage, you'll remember that happiness and ease and won't postpone meditation. At that point you will definitely meditate. So in all, there are four antidotes: faith, aspiration, effort, and agility. This agility is the main antidote to laziness because it produces extreme ease and well-being.

Second Enemy:
Forgetting the Instruction

༣ གདམས་ངག་བརྗེད་པ།

The second enemy of meditation is forgetting the meditation instructions. While the meditation instructions cover the meditation object, the mind that is meditating on it, and the explanation about how to practice, the specific meaning here of the second enemy is to lose your object during meditation. To "forget" means to lose the object that your mind is trying to hold. To remove this enemy you have to practice *drenpa*[94]

---

effort.
[94]*dran pa.*

or recollection. During meditation, recollection functions to regain the object you've lost.

If you forget your object, what tells you that you need to apply recollection? *She shin*[95] or mental alertness tells you. Mental alertness, therefore, is another factor that you must have. It is like a supervisor that immediately recognizes and then informs you that you have lost the object of meditation. When this happens you must immediately regain the object by placing your mind on it once again.

If you cannot control your mind during meditation, it will quickly go out and follow other objects. In order to control your mind, you have to practice bringing it back, as mentioned in Asanga's *Analysis of the Middle View and the Extreme Views*.[96] and other great meditation texts.

Meditation texts compare the mind to an elephant. There is a traditional line drawing depicting nine stages of meditation. In that drawing the elephant is a symbol for the mind, since that mind is like a crazy, wild creature that is very difficult to control. At the first stage, the elephant is shown as black in color, representing mental darkness. To tame and control that wild elephant, you have to use a hook and rope, which represent mental alertness and recollection, respectively.

Your object of meditation is like a very strong pillar. You have to tie one end of that rope around the elephant's neck and the other end to the pillar so that the elephant cannot escape. You then have to use mental alertness to check whether or not it is staying there nicely.

---

[95]*shes bzhin.* ·

[96]*Madhyantavibhaga*. The body of instructions for cultivating quiescence is based on several Indian Buddhist treatises including *Madhyantavibhaga, Mahayanasutralamkara,* and *Shravakabhumi.* There are two main formulations of this system: the first describes the five faults and the eight antidotes and the second describes a process of developing one-pointed concentration by advancing through nine stages. In conjunction with this process there are six powers and four kinds of attention or ways of engaging the object.

Third Enemy:
Mental Scattering and Mental Sinking

༣ བྱིང་བ་དང་རྒོད་པ།

The third enemy consists of two: mental sinking (*jingwa*)[97] and mental scattering (*göpa*),[98] which are the two main enemies of meditation. How can you tell if they have occurred during meditation? You realize it by using mental alertness. Rough mental sinking occurs during meditation when your ability to hold the meditation object clearly diminishes. An example of rough mental scattering is when your body sits in meditation but your mind goes off to the store or to the city, to work, to your office or wherever. That is not meditation. You should be able to recognize this immediately and then bring your mind back and place it on its object again.

For example, in a baseball game the catcher's main duty is to catch the ball thrown by the pitcher. At the same time, he has to keep an eye on first base to see if the man on first tries to steal second base. If the player runs, the catcher has to throw the ball immediately to second base. Likewise, during meditation your mind should stay on the object; it must hold the object of meditation. But meanwhile, you have to use mental alertness to check whether or not your mind is staying on the meditation object properly.

Is your mind going out to other objects? Is it sinking? If your mind sinks, you have mental sinking or dullness; your mind is not clear. Therefore, you have to restore your meditation. If your mind goes out due to mental scattering, you have to bring it back to the object of meditation.

Mental sinking and mental scattering can be easily discerned when you reach the third of the nine stages of meditation. Before that, they are more difficult to recognize. So before the third stage you have to use effort to control them. Each of these two major obstacles consists of two types,

---

[97] *bying ba.*
[98] *rgod pa.*

rough mental scattering and subtle mental scattering, as well as rough and subtle mental sinking. Although it's difficult to clearly distinguish between rough and subtle forms of sinking and scattering before you reach the third level, you still have to learn about the differences and try to identify them when practicing. If you don't, your meditation will most likely turn into subtle mental sinking because you haven't learned to distinguish subtle mental sinking from proper meditation. Even though your mind is staying on the object, if it associates with subtle mental sinking or subtle mental scattering, your meditation is still not perfect.

During meditation, the two main qualities that you are trying to develop are what we call in Tibetan *necha*[99] and *sel-cha*.[100] *Necha* means steadiness. When your mind is staying on the meditation object you have *necha*. *Selcha* means that the meditation object is appearing clearly to your mind. Your objective is to make these perfect. Since both are crucial, if you are missing either of these, you will not succeed.

In addition to the mind's steadiness and clarity of the object to the mind, you also need a third quality, *ngarcha* or *sel che ngar dang den pa*,[101] which is a clarity that has a sharp intensity. A very good example to illustrate this is a tightrope walker in the circus who holds a long stick. That tightrope walker is intensely focused on what he is doing. He has to picture what his position is, when he should lift his foot, how to lift it, and where to place it—all of these things must appear vividly in his mind. Not only that, they must appear precisely, steadily, clearly, and with great strength. If he loses the strength of the object's appearance in his mind, or his body's strength and steadiness, he will fall immediately. Just having steady attention on the object is not enough, nor is it enough to have the object appear clearly—both must be very strong. Your mind should have those two qualities and the clarity in particular should also have intensity or *ngarcha*.

---

[99] *gnas cha.*
[100] *gsal cha.*
[101] *gsal cha'i ngar dang ldan pa.*

If it does, that is perfect meditation. This is the kind of meditation that you have to try to attain.

Our minds, though, have associated with the mental afflictions of ignorance, hatred, desire, jealousy, doubt, and different wrong views for many, many eons. There is an expression in Tibetan, *kyang lang shorwa*, which in this case means something like "developing a bad habit." The mind's constant association with mental afflictions results in bad mental habits. For that reason, our mind is very difficult to control. Actually, though, the mind is neutral. Because it is neutral, it can associate with either bad or good thoughts. Take hatred and patience. We cannot be very patient, but we get angry easily because our mind has associated with anger for such a long time. The mind has that bad habit of getting angry. We cannot control or separate our mind from that anger. But we must believe that, though it is very difficult, not only is it possible to change our mind, we can definitely change it. When we have perfect patience, our mind will not associate with anger, which is very lucky for us.

Fourth Enemy:
Not Taking Action

༄ འདུམི་བྱེད་པ།

The fourth enemy of meditation is not taking action to restore the object of meditation when mental sinking or mental scattering have occurred. When you realize through mental alertness that sinking or scattering have occurred, you shouldn't allow those obstacles to continue. In the case of mental sinking, the mind's clarity toward the object has to be restored. If scattering occurs, you have to bring your mind back to the meditation object. Taking action as needed is the seventh of eight antidotes, and specifically the antidote to the fourth enemy.

The kind of action you should take depends on whether the obstacle is rough or subtle mental sinking, or rough or subtle mental scattering. Subtle mental sinking occurs when you have clarity and stability but your mind lacks intensity.

The mind cannot hold the meditation object with intensity. If you experience subtle mental sinking, you don't have to stop the period of meditation, but rather try to hold the object more strongly and more clearly. If even after applying effort your mind loses still more clarity, then you have to take other measures to refresh your mind, such as contemplating leisure and fortune or the holy qualities of the Three Jewels. When the mind is restored, you can then go back to the meditation object again. If not, you have to take more drastic measures such as going outside and getting some fresh air, taking a walk, splashing cold water on your face, or going to a high place and looking out into the distance.

Subtle mental scattering is when you start to become distracted even though you haven't lost the meditation object. This occurs when you are trying too hard to concentrate. Therefore, you should relax your mind's hold on the object. If that doesn't work, you will develop rough scattering. When that happens, don't stop meditating. Mental scattering is often caused by being overly happy. One antidote is to think about samsara's suffering nature, such as your own life's impermanence and samsara's suffering.

Breathing Meditation

If you still can't stop your mental scattering with these methods, you have to use a more forceful method. Breathing meditation is a way of placing the mind on the object very forcefully.

There are many types of breathing meditation. The practice to use here is described in the *Treasury of Higher Knowledge*, which explains the teachings followed by the Vaibhashika School system. If your level advances, there are other breathing meditations you can do.

In this practice, your object of meditation is your breath. As I said before, the breath is like a horse and the mind is like its rider; they function together. Breathe only through your nose, keeping the mouth closed. As you breathe, your mind is focused on the inside of your nose. Focus that the front end of a stream of your breath is inside your nostrils. Then slowly exhale and follow your breath as it goes out the nostrils to a distance of about one foot in front of you. The Vaibhashika School system describes four or five levels of this practice, but the beginner should only follow the breath out to the distance of one foot in front. During this practice, your mind should focus only on your breath and on nothing else. Your concentration should be so firm that if an alarm were to go off right next to your ear, you would remain undisturbed.

After exhaling, slowly inhale, watching the breath carefully as it comes in. When you exhale, don't continue too long. Start the next inhalation before you have completely run out of air. When you finish exhaling and inhaling once, that counts as one breath.

Continue to follow your breaths up to ten times. Exhale, inhale, one; exhale, inhale, two; and so on. You have to breathe out and in ten times without losing your concentration. If you lose your concentration, start counting again from one. When you can count ten breaths without losing your concentration, return to the meditation object you were practicing before.

Fifth Enemy: Taking Unnecessary Action

༥ འདུ་བྱེད་པ།

The fifth obstacle is to take action to maintain perfect meditation when no such effort is needed. The antidote to this obstacle is to remain in a state of equanimity. If your mind is free from scattering and sinking but you still feel the need to use mental alertness to examine whether either is present and then try to apply an antidote when it is not necessary, this is an obstacle to the mind's remaining still. To "remain in a state of equanimity" here means to relax the mind and resist applying mental alertness or any antidote when none is required.

THE NINE LEVELS OF
ACHIEVING QUIESCENCE

སེམས་གནས་དགུ

WE'VE ALREADY TALKED about the main points concerning meditation. Here I will just introduce you to the main features of the nine levels. The nine levels are achieved by means of six powers. The first is the power of listening. If you want to achieve quiescence, first you have to receive unerring instructions on how to practice.

First Level:
Placement

༡ སེམས་འཇོག་པ།

Of the nine stages, the first and second cannot really even be called meditation, because your mind does not stay on the object firmly or for very long. If someone asks you what you are doing and you say "I am meditating"—it's not true. The words you use and the meaning have to correspond perfectly. Therefore, in the first stage called placement, you are just setting the mind on the object. If you are doing that perfectly, then you have to keep your mind there for a little bit longer.

If you are going to build a house, first you have to gather together all the materials you need to build it and then you can start building and complete it very quickly and nicely without any difficulty. Without first properly arranging the necessary things, that is, if you are missing any of the building materials, it will take longer to accomplish. Sometimes people construct one side of a building and then just let it go. When you do it that way you won't be able to finish it nicely. Similarly, before starting meditation, the most important thing for you to do is listen to Dharma and study;

you need complete knowledge about that field of activity. Then once you start meditating, you'll be able to succeed at it. In the first stage you are just causing your mind to sit on the object. At this level, your mind is like a bee landing on a flower, just alighting, then leaving, then alighting again. You can't keep your mind on the object continually for any length of time.

Generally, if you don't meditate, but continue to think and talk in your usual way, it won't seem to you that your mind is very busy. But when you try to meditate, you become aware of the many things that are coming into your mind. Your body is on the cushion, but your mind seems very busy. Actually, it's not that your mind has gotten busier, but that since you are now examining your mind, you become aware of its activity. In this case "activity" refers to the many thoughts that are obstacles to your meditation. The fact that it now seems to you that you are having more thoughts than usual is actually a realization of how active your mind is, and a very good sign. Usually, when you aren't meditating, although many things do come to your mind, you aren't aware of your mind's activity. Because of this, many people wrongly conclude that their meditation is no good. "I have no control over my mind, I have no peace!" In fact, you are beginning to be able to recognize the obstacles.

Second Level:
Continuous Placement

༢ རྒྱུན་དུ་འཇོག་པ།

The second stage is called continuous placement or *gyundu jokpa*. At this point you are able to extend that perfect meditation a little bit longer. If you want your meditation period to be longer, you have to make sure that it is done perfectly. It is no good if you lengthen an imperfect meditation.

Agility is a good quality that comes from being accustomed to perfect meditation. However, you can also become habituated to meditating incorrectly—that is, thinking about other things—letting your mind follow other objects, letting it sink, or losing the object's clarity. If you don't correct those situations your mind will become used to imperfect meditation. This kind of habit is very harmful for your meditation. Instead of doing that, at the beginning it is better to meditate for very brief periods and to do each meditation perfectly. If you gradually lengthen those brief moments of perfect meditation, you will eventually develop a longer period of perfect meditation. This is a very important point to remember.

By keeping your mind on the object perfectly for a slightly longer period of time, you have reached the second level. The measure of having achieved this stage is to be able to keep your mind on that object without being distracted for the amount of time it takes to recite one round of the *Mani* mantra on your prayer beads. It is actually very difficult to keep the mind fresh and strong without sinking or scattering for that amount of time.

The power of listening gives you the knowledge that allows you to begin the practice of meditation. While you are meditating, along with the knowledge of what to do and what not to do gained through listening, actually applying that knowledge during meditation is the second power, known as the power of contemplation.

During the first two stages, the obstacles of mental sinking and scattering rush into the mind with great frequency. Because of that, the amount of time that the mind is actually fixed on the object is far shorter than the obstacles that rush in to distract it. At these two levels, you have to use a lot of effort to control your mind. During placement and continuous placement, you have to use the first of the four ways of engaging the object, known as forceful conveying.

ཕྱི

QUESTION: You spoke about how practicing perfect meditation for short periods of time is preferable to a long period of imperfect practice. Could you elaborate on this point?

KHEN RINPOCHE: Each twenty-four-hour day can be divided into four main periods for meditation practice. One period starts after sunrise and lasts until noon. Sunrise and noon are two times when you should break your practice.[102] Depending on the time of year, the morning period should be from about seven-thirty A.M. to eleven-thirty A.M. You can divide this time into eighteen short periods for practice. Between these short periods, you can rest and think about your meditation object, and then start to meditate again. If your practice is good, stop before you begin to feel tired and rest briefly. Then you can start meditating again. If your practice isn't clear, stop meditating and do something to refresh your mind. Try to refresh your mind while you are still sitting on your cushion, and then start to meditate again. If your practice still isn't good, if you feel tired or uncomfortable, you have to stop meditating and go outside and do something that will help. Sometimes it helps to walk in some pleasant surroundings and get some fresh air.

Then you can start a second main period of meditation in the afternoon around one o'clock and continue until around seven o'clock in the evening, just before the sun goes down. You can also divide this period into eighteen short sessions. This division is not exact. It is an instruction that is meant particularly for beginners. If your meditation is more advanced and you have reached the fourth or fifth of the nine levels, you can continue practicing for longer periods. You can judge for yourself what level you have reached while you are meditating.

QUESTION: What is the reason for not meditating at sunrise, sunset, noon, and midnight?

---

[102]The other two are nightfall and midnight.

KHEN RINPOCHE: This is mentioned in the Sutras and many other scriptures. It is related to astrology. During those times the sun, moon, and stars come out and the gods and demi-gods become very active. This activity influences our practice. The Kalachakra Tantra and related commentaries also give special reasons why those times are not good for meditation.

ཉྫ

Third Level:
Renewed Placement

༣ སླན་ཏེ་འཇོག་པ།

At the second level, you have been able to extend the period that your mind stays on the object. However, it won't remain there for very long. It will either become scattered or it will sink. When this happens, you have to restore the meditation by bringing the mind back to the object. This is the main activity of the third stage, called renewed placement. That activity is like putting a patch on a torn piece of cloth. The third stage is often referred to as patch-like meditation. The difference between the third and the first two levels is that in the first two levels the intervals of time that your mind is distracted are longer, because your alertness cannot immediately realize that scattering and sinking have occurred. At the third level, your mental alertness is quicker to catch the presence of obstacles, which allows you to bring your mind back to the object of meditation immediately. At this stage you are able to generate more powerful recollection. This means that as soon as your alertness realizes that your mind has gone out, you have to take action to bring it back. This action is taken by recollection. If that recollection is stronger, then you can return your mind to the meditation object more easily.

Fourth Level:
Close Placement

༤ ཉེ་བར་འཇོག་པ།

At the fourth level, called close placement, the power of your recollection is so strong that it becomes impossible to completely lose the meditation object, which is what distinguishes the fourth from the third level. There is a big difference between these two levels. Even though you won't lose the object of meditation completely, sinking and scattering still occur at this level; therefore, you have to exert effort to recognize them and apply the antidote to restore the meditation object. The third and fourth levels are practiced using the power of recollection. At the fourth level, the quality of your recollection has fully developed; it is like a full-grown adult.

What is meditation? Does it mean only to sit your physical body down and remain unmoving like a stone? What is the mind doing during meditation? Meditation is a form of single-pointed concentration. How do you develop meditation? Does it come about on its own? It comes about through the power of recollection. Without recollection it cannot come about at all; the mind will either become scattered or sink. The essence of meditation is the mental derivative of concentration or *samadhi*. This kind of mind is sustained by recollection. If recollection is lost, concentration collapses. Mental alertness is like a supervisor who notices whether an obstacle is coming or not. Mental alertness by itself does not have the power to do anything to stop the obstacle. It has to inform recollection, which does have the power to return the mind to the object.

Fifth Level:
Subduing

༥ དུལ་བར་བྱེད་པ།

The fifth level is called subduing, which means that the mind is becoming tamed. By what is the mind being tamed? The force of mental alertness is taming it. In the line drawing of the stages of quiescence, mental alertness is depicted as a hook that is used to restrain the wild elephant of the mind. When you achieve the fourth level, your mind's ability to stay on the object has improved. If you have focused the mind too strongly within, there is a danger that your mind will develop subtle sinking. Sinking refers to losing the freshness and clarity of your meditative mind. At the previous level you had to use the power of recollection. When you reach the fifth level, you have to use the fourth power, which is mental alertness. Strong mental alertness is needed so that you can detect subtle sinking.

Now, at this level, since your mind is staying on the object and clarity is fairly good, you may think that your meditation is perfect. While clarity is enough to block rough mental sinking, it is not enough to block subtle mental sinking. Subtle mental sinking is one of the worst obstacles to perfect meditation because it is extremely difficult to recognize. The difference between subtle and rough mental sinking is that in the case of rough mental sinking, the mind is still on the meditation object but the mind's clarity toward the object has decreased. With subtle mental sinking the clarity of the object is pretty good, but the mind's freshness or intensity toward the object has gone down. You have to increase the strength of your alertness and think about the good qualities of samadhi, which renews your mind. At the fourth level rough mental sinking still occurs, but not at the fifth level. Even though rough mental sinking no longer occurs at the fifth level, if you don't use recollection's power, then subtle mental sinking can still occur.

Sixth Level:
Pacification

༦ ཞི་བར་བྱེད་པ།

The sixth level is called pacification. To achieve perfect meditation, you must be free from these four obstacles: rough and subtle mental sinking and rough and subtle mental scattering. If you try too hard to revitalize your mind in order to overcome subtle mental sinking, your mind might then be inclined to subtle scattering, in which case you have to apply strong mental alertness to remove that fault. Subtle mental scattering occurs when, even though your mind is staying on the object, it feels as though you are getting ready to think about another object. This is like the flow of water beneath the surface of a frozen river. It is crucial to recognize this fault and stop it immediately. The power of mental alertness is used to develop the fifth and sixth levels—that is, subduing and pacification. After that, mental alertness is no longer the main power that is used during meditation.

Seventh Level:
Heightened Pacification

༧ ཉེ་བར་ཞི་བར་བྱེད་པ།

Since you have fully developed the powers of recollection and mental alertness by the time you have reached the seventh level, mental sinking and scattering won't occur much. However, you'll still have to maintain the fifth power, which is the power of effort in order to overcome subtle mental sinking and scattering when they occur. The seventh stage is called heightened pacification. At the fifth and sixth levels it is easier for the two subtle obstacles to come to mind and damage your meditation; but on the seventh level, they don't arise as frequently or as easily, and cannot damage the meditation too much. Still, those obstacles do occur at the seventh level, so you have to develop the power of effort to overcome them. From the third through the seventh levels, mental scattering and sinking break your concentration. During these levels the way in which the mind goes to the object is the second of four ways of engaging the object, called interrupted conveying.

Eighth Level:
Single-Pointedness

༈ རྩེ་གཅིག་ཏུ་བྱེད་པ།

At the eighth level, you only need to exert a small amount of effort at the beginning of the meditation period in order to prepare the antidote of recollection. This preparation is enough for you to prevent subtle obstacles from arising throughout the whole period. The power of the meditation's enemy has by this time almost disappeared. Therefore, at this level you don't need to apply mental alertness. Because your meditation at this level is unbroken by subtle scattering or sinking, the way the mind goes to the object is called un-interrupted conveying. This is the third of the four ways of engaging the meditation object. The seventh and eighth levels must be achieved using the power of effort.

Ninth Level:
Equipoise

༈ མཉམ་པར་འཇོག་པ།

Because of the effort exerted at the eighth level, your mind becomes accustomed to concentration, and you can maintain that concentration effortlessly, like someone who is thoroughly familiar with prayers and can recite them automatically. At the ninth level, you can immediately enter that state of one-pointed concentration completely without effort. This state is described as a one-pointedness of mind that is still part of the desire realm. While it has qualities that are similar to quiescence, the practitioner has not yet reached that goal, even though the practitioner can remain in meditation effortlessly. In order to achieve actual quiescence you have to develop that concentration further and gain the extraordinary ease that comes from the agility of body and agility of mind.[103] The ninth level is achieved through the sixth power, which is called "continued practice."

This system uses four meditation periods in a day if you do a retreat. Each of those periods can be divided into eighteen shorter sessions. Those eighteen sessions should be perfect. There is a special instruction for beginners that says if the meditation is going very well, you should stop. If it is going very badly, you should also stop. If you don't stop when it is very good, you will start to get tired and it will hurt your ability to extend a state of perfect meditation. If that happens, you won't be able to progress from the first to the second stage. Therefore, if the meditation is perfect, stop, relax, and then try again. If it is bad, you must also stop, check what's wrong, and make it perfect again.

Agility

Shinjang and the ease that comes from it are different. *Shinjang* in this case is like a cause and the ease that comes with it is a result. *Shinjang* literally means extremely well trained in concentration. After meditating for a long time, that activity brings extreme facility of mind. Just as your mind develops extreme facility, your body will also gain a similar facility. If you gain these two kinds of *shinjang*, you experience sensations of great physical ease and mental joy. Of the two kinds of *shinjang*, mental *shinjang* occurs first. But of the two sensations, the great ease that comes with physical *shinjang* occurs first.

---

[103]*Shinjang* is one of eleven virtuous mental states. Although you achieve some degree of this at earlier stages of your practice, you don't achieve this kind of *shinjang* until you have gone beyond the ninth level.

Agility of Mind

How does this happen? Our body is produced by samsara's causes. The four elements that make up the body are therefore samsaric. For that reason, the body's air element also has a samsaric quality, which is called *ne ngen len*[104] or "negative condition." Through the habit of concentration, that negative condition of the body's air element will almost completely disappear, producing a great sense of physical well-being. One sign of this is to have a sensation like a warm hand gently pressing on the top your head. As soon as this has occurred you immediately develop agility of mind or *sem shinjang*.

Generally, you can't control your mind and keep it from gravitating to worldly objects. At this point in your meditation, however, that negative quality of mind along with its air loses its power. This allows you to control your mind and easily direct it to whatever virtuous object you choose. This readiness is the main quality of mental agility or *sem shinjang*.

Agility of Body

Upon achieving that agility of mind, the body's air element develops a certain suitability. This air element is what brings you physical *shinjang*. That air fills your body throughout, freeing you of the negative condition of the body's air element. Because of this, you will no longer have any physical resistance to doing virtuous activities. For example, even though you might want to go to a Dharma class and tell yourself that you want to go, you might feel some physical resistance or disinclination. That negative physical quality is what you overcome here. When this happens, your body will do what you want it to and will feel as light as cotton.

---

[104]*gnas ngan len.*

This marks the achievement of agility of body or *lü shinjang*.[105]

That *lü shinjang* produces a sensation of extreme physical well-being, which is the first of two pleasures mentioned above. As you continue meditating, you gain a great joy that comes from mental *shinjang*. Because of that, the mind loses awareness of the body, as though the body has dissolved into the meditation object. This great joy is so intense that you can barely keep your mind on the meditation object. For example, if something very good happens to you, suddenly making you very happy, you can't sit still for very long. You feel the need to get up and do something. After a while this intense joy subsides a bit. As you become aware that this intense joy has gone down, you gain a one-pointed concentration, or *samadhi*, that can remain on the meditation object very strongly and you gain a kind of unwavering agility that promotes this firm concentration. When you reach this point you have achieved the state of quiescence or *shamatha*. This state of mind is no longer part of the desire realm but a preliminary stage of the first level in the form realm. This state of quiescence is crucial for the attainment of all the Buddhist paths.

If you want to practice meditation and you are going to spend two or three weeks meditating, for the first week try to meditate perfectly for very short periods. During the second week, extend those periods a bit without losing that perfection. The measure of having achieved *shamatha* is that your mind can remain on the object of meditation perfectly for four hours. Meditation texts mention that if your effort and your visualization and all the other necessary elements are done perfectly, you can achieve *shamatha* in six months. Many sages have achieved it in this way. As Je Rinpoche wrote in his *Brief Stages of the Path*:

---

[105]*lus shin sbyangs*.

Concentration is like a king that rules the mind.
When placed, it is as immovable as the
    Lord of Mountains;
When released, it engages any virtuous object.
It brings the great bliss of readiness of body and mind.
Realizing this, all great yogis defeat the enemy of
    distraction,
And continually develop the practice of concentration.

Quiescence or *shamatha* is often referred to as the king of concentration, or the king of meditation. In previous times there were many kings in India and the rest of the world, some of whom were very good kings. For example, many Bodhisattvas knowingly took birth as people who became kings. They ruled their countries, ministers, and subjects nicely. Shamatha is like that sort of king. Once you've gained quiescence, you will be able to complete all your practices very nicely and without difficulty, and be able to achieve your goals very easily.

Quiescence is also compared to the Lord of Mountains, Mt. Sumeru. When there's an earthquake or a volcano, small rocks, hills, or mountains might shake, but Mt. Sumeru is the most solid of mountains; it cannot easily be shaken. When you achieve quiescence, your mental concentration becomes like Mt. Sumeru; other thoughts or mental afflictions cannot disturb it. Because of that, you can very easily succeed in all of your practices. Once you achieve that firmness, your mind will automatically remain on whatever object you decide to focus on and will not move until you arise from that meditation. Whatever path or virtuous object you may want to focus on, you can easily visualize it and direct your mind to it without difficulty. Not only that, achieving shamatha makes your body and mind more suitable for meditation. You won't experience any problem with your body, mind, or with the object of meditation, and this will bring you extreme ease and happiness. Therefore, practicing to achieve shamatha is worthwhile and very meaningful.

About the Author

ठ̄ERMEY KHENSUR LOBSANG THARCHIN was born in Lhasa, Tibet in 1921. He entered the Mey College of Sera Monastery at an early age and proceeded through the rigorous twenty-five-year program of Buddhist monastic and philosophical studies. Upon successful completion of the public examination by the best scholars of the day, Rinpoche was awarded the highest degree of Hlarampa Geshe with honors. In 1954 he entered Gyu-me Tantric College, completed its course of study under strict monastic discipline, and shortly afterward attained a high-ranking administrative position.

In 1959 Rinpoche escaped to India along with His Holiness the Fourteenth Dalai Lama, Tenzin Gyatso, and tens of thousands of other Tibetans. Actively involved in Tibetan resettlement, he compiled a series of textbooks for the Tibetan curriculum and taught at several refugee schools in Darjeeling, Simla, and Mussoorie.

In 1972, Khen Rinpoche came the United States to participate in a project involving the translation of Buddhist scriptures. Upon its completion, he was invited to serve as the Abbot of Rashi Gempil Ling in New Jersey, a position that he continues to hold today. Rinpoche also founded the Mahayana Sutra and Tantra Center, with branches in Washington, D.C. and New York. Over the years he has offered a vast range of Buddhist teachings.

In 1991, Khen Rinpoche was asked by His Holiness the Dalai Lama to serve as Abbot of Sera Mey Monastery in South India. After a brief appointment there, he returned to the United States, where he continues to teach and direct a number of projects dedicated to the restoration of Sera Mey Monastery in India and to the flourishing of Mahayana Buddhist Dharma in the West.

BIBLIOGRAPHY

Canonical Works

Triskandhakanāmamahāyānasūtram In *Śikṣasamuccayaḥ*, Ch. 8 "Pāpaśodanam," pp. 94–95 (see listing below under Śāntideva). Tibetan translation: (*'Phags pa) Phung po gsum pa zhes bya ba theg pa chen po'i mdo* (also called *Byang chub sems dpa'i ltung ba bshags pa*). In *mDo mang* section of Kg., Vol. 22, (*za*), ff. 133b–164a (Toh. #284). English translation in *A Treasury of Mahāyāna Sūtras*, Ch. 15 "The Definitive Vinaya." University Park: Pennsylvania State University Press, 1983, pp. 265–267.

(*Mūlasarvāstivāda*) *Vinayavastu*. Buddhist Sanskrit Texts No. 16 (2 vols.). Darbanga, India: Mithila Institute, 1970. Tibetan translation: *'Dul ba gzhi*. In *'Dul ba* section of Kg., Vols. 1–4 (*ka–nga*) (Toh #1).

Indian Treatises

Asaṅga. *Śrāvakabhūmiḥ*. Tibetan Sanskrit Works Series Vol. XIV. Ed. Karunesha Shukla. Patna: K.P. Jayaswal Research Institute, 1973. Tibetan translation: (*rNal 'byor spyod pa'i sa las*) *Nyan thos kyi sa*. In *Sems tzam* section of Tg., Vol. 49 (*dzi*), 201ff. (Toh. #4036).

Atiśa (Dīpaṃkara Śrījñāna). *Byang chub lam gyi sgron ma* (Tibetan translation of *Bodhipathapradīpam*). In *dBu ma* section of Tg., Vol. 32 (*khi*), ff. 242a–245a (Toh. #3947). English translation in *A Lamp for the Path and Commentary*. Tr. Richard Sherburne. London: George Allen & Unwin Ltd., 1983.

Candragomī. *Śiṣyalekhaḥ*. Ed. by J. P. Minayeff. In Zapiski (notes) of the Imperial Russian Archaeological Society, Oriental Section, Vol. IV, pp. 29–52. St. Petersburg: Imperial Russian Archaeological Society, 1889. Tibetan translation: *Slob ma la springs pa'i spring yig*. In *sPring yig* section of Tg., Vol. 94 (*nge*), ff. 46b–53a (Toh. #4183).

Candrakīrti. *dBu ma la 'jug pa* (Tibetan translation of *Madhyamakāvatāraḥ*) In *dBu ma* section of Tg., Vol. 23 (*'a*), ff. 198a–216a (Toh. #3860).

Dharmakīrti. *Pramāṇavārttikam*. In *Pramāṇavārttika; The Kārikās with Manorathanandi's Vṛtti*. Varanasi: Bauddha Bharati, 1968. Tibetan translation: *Tsad ma rnam 'grel gyi tsig le'ur byas pa*. In *Tsad ma* section of Tg., Vol. 95 (*ce*), ff. 95b–151a (Toh. #4210).

Maitreya Nātha. *Abhisamayālaṃkāraḥ*. (Sanskrit and Tibetan texts) Ed. T. Stcherbatsky and E.E. Obermiller, Leningrad: Bibliotheca Buddhica, 1929. Tibetan translation: (*Shes rab kyi pha rol tu phyin pa'i man ngag gi bstan bcos*) *mNgon par rtogs pa'i rgyan zhes bya ba'i tsig le'ur byas pa*. In *Shes phyin* section of Tg., Vol. 1 (*ka*), ff. 1b–13a (Toh. #3786). English translation: *Abhisamaya Alaṃkāra*. Tr. Edward Conze. Rome: Serie Orientale Roma, 1954.

Nāgārjuna. *Ratnāvalī* (fragmentary text). In *Madhyamakaśāstra of Nāgārjuna*, Buddhist Sanskrit Texts No. 10. Darbanga, India: Mithila Institute, 1960. pp. 296–310. Tibetan translation: *rGyal po la gtam bya ba rin po che'i phreng ba*. In *sKyes rabs* section of Tg., Vol. 93 (*ge*), ff. 116a–135a (Toh. #4158). English translation in *The Precious Garland and the Song of the Four Mindfulnesses*. Tr. Jeffrey Hopkins and Lati Rinpoche with Anne Klein. New York: Harper and Row, 1975.

Śāntideva. *Bodhicaryāvatāraḥ*. (Sanskrit and Tibetan texts) Ed. Vidushekhara Bhattacharya. Calcutta: The Asiatic Society, 1960. Tibetan translation: *Byang chub sems dpa'i spyod pa la 'jug pa*. In *dBu ma* section of Tg., Vol. 26 (*la*), ff. 1–39a (Toh. #3871). English translation: *A Guide to the*

Bodhisattva's Way of Life. Tr. Stephen Batchelor. Dharamsala: Library of Tibetan Works and Archives, 1979.

_____. *Śikṣāsamuccayaḥ*. Buddhist Sanskrit Texts No. 11. Darbanga, India: Mithila Institute, 1960. Tibetan Translation: *bSlab pa kun las btus pa* In *dBu ma* section of Tg., Vol. 32 (*khi*), ff. 3a–396b (Toh. #3940). English translation: *Śikshā Samuccaya, A Compendium of Buddhist Doctrine*. Tr. Cecil Bendall and W.H.D. Rouse. Reprint edition Delhi: Motilal Banarsidass, 1971.

Vasubandhu. *Abhidharmakośakārikā*. Ed. G.V. Gokhale. Journal of the Royal Asiatic Society. Bombay, Vol. 22, 1946. Tibetan translation: *Chos mngon pa mdzod kyi tsig le'ur byas pa*. In *mNgon pa* section of Tg., Vol. 61 (*ku*), ff. 1–25a (Toh. #4089). English translation in *Abhidharmakośabhāṣyam* (4 vols.). Tr. Leo M. Pruden. Berkeley: Asian Humanities Press, 1988.

Tibetan Works

(Paṇ chen) Blo bzang chos kyi rgyal mtsan. *Bla ma mchod pa'i cho ga*. In Vol. 1 (*ka*) of the *Collected Works of Blo-bzaṅ chos-kyi rgyal-mtshan* (5 vols.). New Delhi: Mongolian Lama Guru Deva, 1973, pp. 777–797 (Toh. #5892).

mKhas grub rje (dGe legs dpal bzang). *dPal ldan bla ma dam pa rje brtzun tzong kha pa chen po nyid kyi rnam par thar pa mdo tzam zhig brjod pa'i sgo nas gsol ba 'debs pa'i tsigs su bcad pa* (*dPal ldan sa gsum ma*). In Vol. 9 (*ta*) of the *Collected Works of the Lord mkhas-grub Rje Dge-legs dpal bzaṅ-po* (12 vols.) (item #2 in *gSung 'bum thor bu*). New Delhi: Mongolian Lama Guru Deva, 1980, pp. 477–482 (Toh. #5500).

(sKyabs rje) Pha bong kha pa (Rin po che) Byams pa bstan 'dzin 'phrin las rgya mtso (sKyabs rje bDe chen snying po). *rNam grol lag bcangs su gtod pa'i man ngag zab mo tsang la ma nor ba mtsungs med chos kyi rgyal po'i thugs bcud byang chub lam gyi rim pa'i nyams khrid kyi zin bris gsung rab kun gyi bcud bsdus gdams ngag bdud rtzi'i snying po* (*rNam grol lag bcangs*). Vol. 11 (*da*) of *Collected Works*, 783 pp.

rGyal tsab dar ma rin chen. *Tsad ma rnam 'grel gyi tsig le'ur byas pa'i rnam bshad thar lam phyin ci ma log par gsal bar byed pa*. Vol. 6 (*cha*) of the *Collected Works of rGyal tsab dar ma rin chen*. (8 vols.). New Delhi: Mongolian Lama Guru Deva, 1980, 874 pp. (Toh. #5450).

(rJe) Tzong kha pa (Blo bzang grags pa'i dpal). *Byang chub lam gyi rim pa chen mo* (*Lam rim chen mo*). Vol. 13 (*pa*) of the *Collected Works of the Incomparable Lord Tsongkapa blo bzang grags pa* (18 vols.). New Delhi: Mongolian Lama Guru Deva, pp. 1978–1983 (Toh. #5392).

_____. *Byang chub lam gyi rim pa'i nyams len gyi rnam gzhag mdor bsdus te brjed byang du bya ba* (also known as *Lam rim bsdus don* and as *Nyams mgur*). In Vol. 2 (*kha*) of *Collected Works* (item #59, *bKa' 'bum thor bu*), pp. 308–313 (Toh. #5275). English translation in *Life & Teachings of Tsong Khapa*. Ed. Robert Thurman. Dharamsala, India: Library of Tibetan Works and Archives, 1982, pp. 59–66.

Reference Materials and Other English Language Works

Pabongka Rinpoche. *Liberation in Our Hands, Part One: The Preliminaries*. Trans. Sermey Khensur Lobsang Tharchin with Artemus B. Engle. Howell, New Jersey: Mahayana Sutra and Tantra Press, 1990.

_____. *Liberation in Our Hands, Part Two: The Fundamentals*. Trans. Sermey Khensur Lobsang Tharchin with Artemus B. Engle. Howell, New Jersey: Mahayana Sutra and Tantra Press, 1994.

Tharchin, Sermey Geshe Lobsang with Judith Chiarelli et. al. *King Udrayana and The Wheel of Life*. Howell, New Jersey: Mahayana Sutra and Tantra Press, 1984.

Tsongkapa, Je. *Preparing for Tantra, The Mountain of Blessings.* Trans. Sermey Khensur Lobsang Tharchin with Geshe Michael Roach; Howell, New Jersey: Mahayana Sutra and Tantra Press, 1995.